INTERTEXTUAL DYNAMICS WITHIN THE LITERARY GROUP – JOYCE, LEWIS, POUND AND ELIOT

Intertextual Dynamics within the Literary Group — Joyce, Lewis, Pound and Eliot

The Men of 1914

Dennis Brown
Principal Lecturer in English
Hatfield Polytechnic

St. Martin's Press   New York

First published in the United States of America in 1991

Printed in Great Britain

ISBN 0–312–05318–5

Library of Congress Cataloging-in-Publication Data
Brown, Dennis, 1940–
Intertextual dynamics within the literary group — Joyce, Lewis,
Pound, and Eliot: the men of 1914 / Dennis Brown.
    p. cm.
Includes index.
ISBN 0–312–05318–5
1. English literature—20th century—History and criticism.
2. Modernism (Literature)—Great Britain.   3. Joyce, James,
1882–1941—Criticism and interpretation.   4. Lewis, Wyndham,
1882–1957—Criticism and interpretation.   5. Pound, Ezra, 1885–1972–
Criticism and interpretation.   6. Eliot, T. S. (Thomas Stearns),
1888–1965—Criticism and interpretation.   7. Authorship—
Collaboration—History—20th century.   8. Influence (Literary,
artistic, etc.)   9. Psychoanalysis and literature.
10. Intertextuality.   I. Title.
PR478.M6B68   1990   90–42655
820.9'00912—dc20   CIP

For Sam, Darren and Andrew

Contents

Il n'y a pas dehors de texte

                    —Jacques Derrida

There are no texts. There are only ourselves

                    —Harold Bloom

A common theme . . . expressing itself in different ways through various mouths

                    —S. H. Foulkes and E. J. Anthony

Preface

In the Preface to my recent academic book *The Modernist Self*, I proposed, for a follow-up, to make my next venture a study of the interpsychic mechanisms whereby a Modernist discourse was constructed. This book is the result. It focuses on four key writers of the Modernist movement; however, it is more about intertextual influence than psychological mechanisms as such. I am grateful to my onetime postgraduate student Marilyn Miller-Pietroni (psychotherapist and editor of the *Journal of Social Work Practice*) for pointing me in the direction of group-psychoanalytic literature: my rather basic reading of this informs some of my interpretations of what the Men of 1914 were about. I am also grateful for the continuing interest of Hatfield Polytechnic lecturers and students in my work – and, in particular, for some brilliant suggestions by our part-time MA student Keith Miller in response to lectures based on my early work for the book. My colleague Jean Radford gave support and encouragement when I showed her early chapters and Eric Trudgill (of Hatfield) and Patrick Grant (of the University of Victoria) have again given advice and encouragement after reading my entire first draft. My one-time English teacher J. E. Lindsay and my ex-colleague Alexander Hutchisson both boosted my confidence at important moments during the writing, while my unknown Macmillan's reader offered some cogent advice about my original Introduction which I have followed in the main.

I am extremely grateful again to Margaret Carpenter who typed ongoing sections of the book, as they were written, with great speed and accuracy despite her heavy work-commitments. I wish, too, to thank Dorothy Koenigsberger who, as Humanities Research Coordinator, provided an ethos of scholarly effort and interdisciplinary discussion out of which this book was written and which contributed to whatever it has achieved, in finally incalculable ways. Alan Weir, of the Polytechnic, was also a valued inspiration through his interest in a year that was difficult for both of us. Most of all, I must thank my wife Sam for genuine and selfless enthusiasm for a project that could have divided rather than united us, but for her love – and Darren and Andrew (and Heidi) who tolerated, with good humour, the punctuation of their weekend leisure by my manic typing.

This book was initiated as a registered Research Project of the Hatfield Polytechnic Research and Consultancy Committee: I should like to acknowledge its continuing support for such ventures despite the politically-imposed dissipation of our academic efforts into nonsenses such as 'cash-generating' short courses. The writers whose texts form the subject of this book strove, in peacetime and World War, to create a literature which would be honest to both the possibilities and problems of twentieth-century life. The study of that literature is now under threat by both right-wing dogmatists (who artificially restrict the numbers of Humanities students) and left-wing populists (who prioritise social theory over creative art). I believe the works of Joyce, Lewis, Pound and Eliot are an implicit rebuke to both materialistic positions. The book is written partly in that conviction. My next book will turn to consider the spiritual crisis inherent in both the Modernist and Postmodernist situations under the title: *The Death of God and the New Life*.

DENNIS BROWN

Acknowledgements

The author and publishers would like to thank the following for permission to quote from the works of the author cited below:

Faber & Faber Ltd and Harcourt Brace Jovanovich Inc for extracts from *The Complete Poems and Plays of TS Eliot, 1969*; The Society of Authors and Penguin Books USA Inc for extracts from *Finnegans Wake*; Faber & Faber Ltd and New Directions Publishing Corporation for extracts from Ezra Pound: *The Cantos of Ezra Pound*. Copyright 1938, 1948 by Ezra Pound.

1
Introduction

Intertextual Dynamics is a book which focuses on textual manifestations of mutual influence within the core group of English literary Modernism. In some respects, then, it constitutes quite conventional academic criticism and adds to previous scholarship, for instance on the relationship between Ezra Pound and T. S. Eliot or the influence of *Ulysses* on *The Waste Land*.[1] My chief contribution, on this plane, is to argue for the stylistic influence of the early Vorticist prose of Wyndham Lewis on key texts of Joyce, Pound and Eliot and to reaffirm Lewis's important role within the Modernist venture. However, the close study of such intertextual influence has led me to a distinctly unconventional hypothesis which informs the overall discussion. The hypothesis is this: that the main literary texts of the Men of 1914 (as Lewis called them)[2] should, in important ways, be considered less in terms of individual stylistic development than as a series of moves within an overall intertextual group-game. The game, built up in terms of mutual appreciation and rivalry over some fifty years in all, is predicated on a common assumption – that each writer is involved in a concerted project to create new literature for the new age, our own. The book thus proceeds from the basis of normal literary scholarship to develop an innovative theoretical thesis with regard to the possible object of literary study.

The conventional research work here speaks for itself and is open to the usual kinds of refutation – in terms, say, of partiality, coincidence or overemphasis. I am more interested in the radical potentiality of the overall argument, since I do not know of any other criticism which has considered texts or writers in quite this way. The lack of a psychoanalytically-aware 'group perspective' on literature may be largely due to the fact that, historically, English literature has not been characterised by strong group-activity, certainly in terms of theoretical movements – the Lake School of poets notwithstanding. Hence we are used to considering authors as individuals, even individualists, who slowly develop out of early intellectual and stylistic influence to create distinctive works

1

in a process of literary self-determination. Such thinking is not, of course, confined to the realm of literary criticism; it seems to inform, for instance, academic publishing-ventures such as the Fontana 'Modern Masters' series, and can be evidenced in typical academic syllabuses for Philosophy or History of Ideas as well as Literature degrees. With respect to the Men of 1914, Joyce, Lewis, Pound and Eliot, such an approach is already encapsulated in some notable book-titles: for instance, *Joysprick, The Enemy, The Solitary Volcano* and *The Invisible Poet*.[3] Such emphasis, valid in many cases, becomes distortive where group-activity is virtually predominant. Books such as James Watson's *The Double Helix*[4] persuade me that this can be commonplace in science – especially at highly-collaborative laboratories like the Cavendish. At the same time, since the Second World War there has been a great deal of psychological investigation into the dynamics of work-groups which indicates the powerful bonding which can take place in group-situations. I shall argue that the Men of 1914, despite their strikingly individual personalities, were galvanised by Ezra Pound into a distinctive literary work-group, and that their varied texts demonstrate strong group-assumptions and mutual influence. The evidence will be provided throughout the book as a whole.

However, my overall theoretical hypothesis has not sprung, fully-armed as it were, out of old-style critical scholarship. The last twenty years or so have witnessed a dramatic, and sometimes disorientating, upsurge of theorisation within literary criticism and this book could not have been written outside that context – as some of my reference notes attest.[5] Nevertheless, the argument of *Intertextual Dynamics* is concerned more, in the end, with what seems to me at work in the texts addressed than with literary theory as such. In this sense, the book is essentially inductive and implicitly committed to the (ultimately) canonical idea that some texts matter a great deal more than others for the purpose of genuine enlightenment. In general, I have tried to let group-influence speak itself, through the texts, rather than impose an initial methodology on my material. The obvious methodology to have used was suggested by the studies of groups and group-work initiated by such psychologists as Wilfred Bion, and Foulkes and Anthony.[6] However, it soon became clear to me that the Modernist texts which were my primary interest tended to express, at creatively-*aware* levels, those group-dynamics which psycho-analysts interpreted from *unconscious* behavioural interchange. In particular, the four writers seemed almost over-insistently aware of the predominant assumption of their work-group: that they were all collectively involved in a project of literary renaissance – in psychoanalytical terms, the fantasy of birthing the group-Messiah[7] (although, as we shall see, there was disagreement as to the gender of the new 'text-child'). Specific texts such as *Enemy of the Stars*, *Ulysses*, *The Waste Land*, *The Cantos*, *The Childermass* and *Finnegans Wake* are essentially preoccupied with making the 'NEW',[8] and, in fact, their experimental discourse not only breaks wholly new aesthetic ground but implicitly challenges the assumptions of any methodology or theoretical discourse – whether critical or psychoanalytic – which would seek to interpret and control their meanings. So my aim is less to theorise the hermeneutic implications of the texts than to demonstrate how meanings, here, are built up in intergroup participation, influence and struggle. This will add a new dimension to the understanding of the nature of Modernism and also cast further light on that vogue notion, Postmodernism, whose meaning, by definition, depends on how we understand the modern.

Intertextual influence is, then, at the heart of the book. Irrespective of the larger argument, I seek to make a scholarly case for specific instances of the influence of texts upon each other. Some examples of such influence are the following: that of *Enemy of the Stars* and *Tarr* on aspects of *Ulysses*, *The Waste Land* and the *Cantos*; that of *Ulysses* on *The Waste Land* and the *Cantos*; that of *The Waste Land* on the *Cantos* and *Finnegans Wake*; that of Pound's 'Exile's Letter' on Eliot's 'Journey of the Magi'; and that of 'Work in Progress' on Lewis's *The Childermass*. At the same time, the book attempts to map a great deal of intertextual reference where actual stylistic influence is less at issue. This, quite naturally, occurs mostly in later texts when the 'mythology' of the group is well-developed: *The Apes of God*, *Finnegans Wake* and the later *Cantos* are particularly rich fields of such group-reference while 'Journey of the Magi', *Murder in the Cathedral* and, to an extent, *Four Quartets* seem to incorporate group-reference in a considerably-disguised form. A great variety of instances of group 'talk-back' will be collated throughout the book.

At the same time, the changing dynamics of the four writers 'groupography' (Joyce's term)[9] will be traced as the argument progresses chronologically. Some of the main stages of group-development are as follows: in 1914 Pound gathered the group together under his leadership, with Lewis as the most aggressively radical writer and aesthetician, whose example exercised powerful influence on the other three artists; by the early 1920s Joyce's *Ulysses* had begun to marginalise Lewis's contribution, radically influencing Eliot and Pound; by the mid-1920s Pound had left London and Paris behind him to live in Italy and he largely relinquished his leadership role, a role which Eliot slowly assumed, while Lewis took his revenge on Joyce by publicly attacking *Ulysses*; by the early 1930s only Joyce remained preoccupied with purely aesthetic renewal (in the form of 'Work in Progress' – material for the future *Finnegans Wake* – which Pound disowned as fruitless), while Lewis adapted his art to social satire and polemic, Eliot developed his as religious meditation and Pound restricted his to economic propaganda; from then on Eliot, as publisher and as editor of the *Criterion*, acted as group-trustee and chief interpreter, as the group broke up through differences and eventually deaths, with many later texts nevertheless recapitulating mutual group-dynamics and abounding in intertextual reference. Such developments will be charted in considerable detail, and with a great deal of textual evidence, as the book proceeds.

The reality of this notional group, it should be said, is not vitiated by any other influences or relationships affecting the individual members – any more than, say, the dynamics and morale of a soccer team are called into question by the pub, club or family-life of the constituent players. As will be shown, the various members all met each other at various times, but the validity of the group-notion by no means depends on such encounters. For the power of group-feeling was essentially provided by the fantasy fellowship and rivalry generated by Pound's primarily-mental construct, which associated them together as the four leading writers of their generation – and, indeed, the four men would communicate to each other far more in terms of their literary texts than their table-talk. The symmetry of the group – a fourway dynamic predicated upon two rival novelists and two rival poets – partly explains its mythic power to each individual, such that it virtually became a family-displacement for each of these individualistic 'exiles'.[10] Pound, as founder, encourager, provider and publishing entrepreneur, exercised an extraordinary leadership, as literary father and mother, which effectively bonded the group as an intellectual family. But, as is the way of groups, his final relinquishing of this role did not lead to the group's total dissolution, but to a replacement-bid – with Eliot, the doyen of English letters by this time (and a future Nobel Prize winner), as the natural successor. Thus, despite geographical distancing and the changes wrought by time, the group-mythology lived on while any of the men remained alive – the notion of a finally timeless shared adventure in which four artistic 'Magi' were attendant at the birth of the modern, and witnessed its crucifixion in the waste No Man's Land of the Great War. As literature, Modernism essentially consolidated itself around these two experiential poles of birth and death; and the Men of 1914 – far more formidable and authoritative as a group than the Garsington or Bloomsbury sets – would be the chief interpreters and mythologisers of these contrastive and momentous twentieth-century experiences. Without the Men of 1914, it might well be said, there would have been no meaningful English literary Modernism.

The initial foundations of my argument are somewhat elaborate and prodigal of reference notes. This seemed to me inevitable. The main study of intertextual dynamics (Chapters 3–6) was written first – and very fast[11] – as the momentum of discovery bore me along: I have decided to retain the slightly breathless pace and style as fitting to the intertextual struggle traced in those chapters. However, the tensions of influence I chronicle there could only have been founded in a context of mutual interest, expectation and trust, and the first main chapter (2) endeavours to describe that context, and the place of each writer within it, quite thoroughly – at a time before the main period of intertextual struggle began. Chapter 2 especially seeks to address itself to the transformative aspirations of the era 1900–14, and to the high prestige accorded to master-writers in that period – which all four artists strove to attain from their earliest literary ventures. In effect, through Pound's organisation, the Men of 1914 virtually 'canonised' each other, as prophets of the New, and from the standpoint of the 1990s, when poets and novelists have far less prestige (and hubris),[12] this group-morale needs to be historically placed in some detail. This I have attempted to do, as well as to give an account of the early writing of Joyce, Lewis, Pound and Eliot, before Pound organised them as a group.

The progression of the book is essentially (and inevitably) chronological.[13] At the end of each chapter I describe, in biographical terms, the relations between the writers at evolving stages. However, the momentum of the argument is generated by progres-

sive challenges and responses of specific texts as the group-game
proceeds. Hence the third chapter centres on Lewis's early prose-
Vorticist challenge and the textual responses of the other three
writers; Chapter 4 is dominated by the phenomenon of *Ulysses* and
its effect upon Eliot, Pound and Lewis in turn; Chapter 5 is initiated
by Joyce's next radical move, in 'Work in Progress', and discusses
the reactions and new stylistic directions of the other three men;
while Chapter 6 is again built up around Joyce's last contribution,
with the publication of the completed *Finnegans Wake*, and the late
developments of Eliot, Lewis and Pound. As we might expect, the
most dynamic period of textual interchange was in the first decade
or so of the group's formation, say 1914–24. The beginning of
'Work in Progress', most particularly, marked the start of a parting
of the ways; yet, as we shall see, the presence of intertextual
allusion continues in the works of the four men until Pound's last
cantos in the late 1950s. The book traces, then, the history of a
literary 'family' and their influence one upon the other, in intertextual terms. And, at certain points, I also hint at a family secret
which perhaps adds a touch of literary *scandale* to an already
contentious argument. A separate book would be needed to trace
the overall influence of the Men of 1914 upon the work of Samuel
Beckett. However, I seek to evidence at certain points, *en passant*,
that with respect to intertextual influence on the great texts he
wrote in the 1950s and 1960s, Beckett is revealed not as the heir to
Joyce, the legendary Master, but to Wyndham Lewis – Joyce's
acknowledged prose rival.

My book is inevitably indebted to the biographies of each '1914'
writer[14] and is written out of the context of some forty years of
critical discussion about the modern movement.[15] However, while
some critics have made much of the shared intellectual climate of
the time, or specific forms of influence (for example Pound's editing
of *The Waste Land*), no one has so far treated the four key writers
of the period as a group, in terms of intertextual groupwork, and
Lewis has rarely been given his due as Modernist at all. The book,
which in a sense follows on from my earlier study *The Modernist
Self*,[16] seeks both to focus on intertextual influence at the heart of
Modernist literature and to reinstate Lewis as Modernist. In this,
as I have already suggested, I appear to have written the first study
of any group of writers in English which is aware of psychoanalytic
group-theory and reads texts as a species of group-sharing and
conflict. The justification for such a project must lie in the whole

of the evidence and argument that follows. However, I can imagine that some readers may already be reacting with radical scepticism to my claims. To spare such a reader the labour of first reading my founding chapter, I suggest s/he turns first to the two sections 'Shem's Choice' and 'Riverrun' (pp. 125–32 and 158–65), in particular, to see if the battery of coded allusions quoted there, from one of the most apparently individualistic texts ever written, may persuade him or her that there is an argument to be made.

2

To Announce a New Age

James Joyce, Wyndham Lewis, Ezra Pound and T. S. Eliot were all children of the 1880s. Joyce was born on 2 February 1882 in a south Dublin suburb; Lewis on 18 November of the same year, on board a yacht docked at Amherst, Nova Scotia; Pound on 30 October 1885 in Hailey, Idaho, a tiny frontier town; Eliot on 26 September 1888 in St Louis, Missouri.[1] Only six years, then, separated the ages of the four individuals who, more than any other writers in English, conspired to create literary Modernism and transform the 'decadent' aestheticism of their birth-decade into the prophetic experimentalism of the 1920s. Each aspired to artistic greatness at quite an early age. In his self-portrait, Joyce shows his persona, Stephen, as fascinated by words from infancy and an assiduous composer of poems during adolescence; at Rugby School, Lewis became known as a 'frightful artist'[2] and proceeded straight to the Slade School of Art; Pound also embarked early on his ambition to know more about poetry than 'any man living'[3] and, in *Hilda's Book*, wrote teenage lyrics to the future poetess H. D.; and Eliot, whose mother wrote poems (one of which, *Savonarola*, Eliot would later arrange for publication), brought out eight issues of his own magazine, *The Fireside*, when eleven years old, and contributed early work to the *Smith Academy Record* when seventeen.

Each of the Men of 1914, in pursuance of ultimately aesthetic aims, embarked on courses of Higher Education – Joyce at University College Dublin (later at the Sorbonne), Lewis at the Slade, Pound at the University of Pennsylvania (then at Hamilton College), and Eliot at Harvard and later at Oxford. Each of them, too, tended to find friends (and rivals) among other creative artists during their early years: Joyce with Oliver St John Gogarty, Lewis with Spencer Gore, Pound with William Carlos Williams and H. D., and Eliot with Conrad Aiken. And each of them achieved a degree of aesthetic reputation at their respective institutions – Joyce by corresponding with Ibsen, Lewis as the 'best draughtsman at the Slade since Augustus John',[4] Pound as knowledgeable enthusiast for Provençale lyrics and Eliot as intellectual *poète maudit*, who impressed Bertrand Russell by comparing Heraclitus to Villon in a philosophy seminar. On completion of their courses of study, each set about building an artistic career – Joyce as poet and story-writer, Lewis as story-writer and painter, and Pound and Eliot as poets and critics. All of them had produced significant work by the time Pound began to organise them as a creative work-group in 1914.

Even before they became grouped together, all of the Men of 1914 were both self-consciously and unconsciously men of the new century – a peer-group Robert Wohl has characterised (in international terms) as 'the generation of 1914'.[5] As Wohl suggests, they were the first such group to think of themselves in specifically generational terms, as distinct from 'the old men' – a division made decisive when war came – and, on the aesthetic front, it was this generation which brushed aside *fin de siècle* weariness and replaced it with rampant artistic ferment. Lewis would later record how Ford Madox Ford found the BLAST group a 'haughty and proud generation' and admitted that 'we were a youth racket'.[6] He continues: 'Europe was full of titanic stirrings and snortings – a new art coming to flower to celebrate or to announce a "new age"'. And, indeed, if Conrad, Yeats and Ford himself (most notably) had negotiated an uneasy transition from nineties' aestheticism to Edwardian impressionism, it was Joyce, Lewis, Pound and Eliot who would constitute the new revolutionary movement which heralded the twentieth century's countdown to the double-millennium. And as Ford helped to launch 'les jeunes' in his *English Review* so did A. R. Orage in *The New Age* – a periodical whose title encapsulated the aspirations of the young generation. It was precisely the sense of a new age which informed the pages of BLAST 1 and 2 in 1914 and 1915. If Vorticism was never quite Futurism, it was the sense of a galvanic future that gave to both movements their inspiration. Poets needed 'a new technique, a new convention, to turn ourselves loose in', T. E. Hulme asserted.[7] The Men of 1914 set out with a similar challenge in the name of the future. 'Our . . . Risorgimento . . . will make the Italian Renaissance look like a tempest in a teapot',[8] Pound declared. Eliot, with his friend Conrad Aiken, looked forward to 'the immense, the wonderful future' which they felt was 'theirs to create'.[9] In BLAST 1 Lewis asserted: 'WE ONLY WANT THE

WORLD TO LIVE, and to feel its crude energy flowing through us'.[10] And Joyce was to write of his early prose that it was 'the first step towards the spiritual liberation in my country'.[11]

These men's sense of the future had political, social and moral dimensions, yet their chosen arena of challenge was specifically aesthetic. From a Postmodernist viewpoint, their sense of art's importance must appear highly inflated. How could they seriously believe that the world would be changed through the writing of poetry or fictional prose? In this, they were partly the heirs of such nineteenth-century literary prophets as Coleridge, Carlyle, Ruskin, Dickens and Morris. It was still assumed that the words of a great man of letters must have the power to bring enlightenment and liberation. Who read such words, or how the readers might, in fact, have an effect upon the great economic, political and social mechanisms of the age seems rarely to have bothered the 'generation of 1914' before the war. What mattered was to find new literary forms of expression to convey the sense of a new 'modern' reality. Artists, Pound insisted, were 'antennae', 'litmus papers', 'barometers', 'thermometers', 'steam-gauges' or 'seismographs'[12] – they showed the contemporary world in its true reality and so could act as a guide to the future. Not until much later would Pound begin to realise that few people, except some other writers, were noting what the instruments registered – let alone trying to apply the readings to the state of the world. It was Auden's generation which came to acknowledge that 'poetry makes nothing happen'; it was Joyce's which believed that the writer could reforge the 'conscience' of the 'race'.[13]

In this exalted idea of the importance of literature, neo-Paterian aestheticism became joined up with the institutional growth of 'English Literature' itself. All four of the Men of 1914 grew up with the grand notion of Art, and a belief in the inherent value of the Aesthetic, at the centre of their thinking. The legacy of the 1880s and 1890s is important here – not only in terms of aesthetic creation but also in terms of artistic appreciation. Works of art history, musicology and literary criticism were important constituents in their education. Pound's first decisively Modernist poem, for instance, would evoke Venus through the pages of the art historian Reinach, while in the twenties he would allow himself a diversion from the developing *Cantos* to write a *Treatise on Harmony*.[14] Lewis studied the history of art and conscientiously sketched from the masters in the National Gallery, the Louvre and the Prado. Eliot upheld the tradition of art from the 'Magdalenian'[15] cave painters onwards. And Joyce's first fully-drawn hero is specifically an 'Artist' and comes equipped with a theory of art elaborated to bring together radiance, wholeness and harmony.[16] By the turn of the century, the idea of the Aesthetic as an autonomous, potent and inherently significant realm was fully established in the minds of the young intelligentsia. And the rise of literary studies (somewhat complicated by the Germanic love of philology) focused the written text as key locus of the aesthetic experience, and a major site of cultural values.[17] Joyce, Pound and Eliot all read literature as an academic subject at university – and Pound briefly taught literature at that level. Hence they were educated in the contemporary version of the literary canon, and when they came to write, themselves, they inevitably aspired to key positions in the developing canon of twentieth-century literature. Lewis, as mentioned, was trained as an artist, but his extended European sojourns, after the Slade, are as much a tale of literary education as of iconographic apprenticeship, and his immersion in such writers as Dickens, Flaubert and Dostoevsky demonstrates a desire to ground himself in the most recently-canonical texts as a springboard for his own earliest literary efforts. As Pound in his early London days learnt from sculpture and painting, while he wrote, so Lewis in his continental wanderings learnt from literature, as he sketched. For all four men the primacy of great art was unquestionable and fired their own early efforts. In this they were very much men of their time.

The prestige of institutionalised literature was approaching its height during this era. In the educational sphere it was beginning to replace religion as a source of precedents and values and it was increasingly held to be the gateway to an understanding of the culture at large – thus establishing for itself in English academic life a role similar to that of philosophy in France. As the natural sciences were held to register the truth of the physical universe so the arts, and literature in particular, were believed to register the truth of the realm of emotion, experience and morality. The academic orthodoxy began to construe literature in the terms that Carlyle ('The Poet as Hero'), Arnold (*Essays in Criticism* and *Culture and Anarchy*) and Conrad (Preface to *The Nigger of the Narcissus*)[18] had already established – as a specialism of humane intelligence. Thus writers of the 'generation of 1914' were educated to believe that literature was a vital intellectual pursuit, on a par with scientific investigation – and even more relevant to the development of genuine civilisation. Joyce's élitist arrogance, Lewis's disputatious scorn, Pound's indignant polemic and Eliot's 'pontifical' generalisations only make sense in the context of this intellectual ethos. They regarded themselves as specialist experimenters, as scientists were in the realm of nature, and they frequently used scientific analogies to expound the writer's function. Thus Eliot would use the example of a 'catalytic chamber' to describe the workings of the poetic mind, and came to liken Joyce's 'discovery' of the 'mythical method' to the findings of Einstein.[19] Eliot had studied 'Religion, Art and Science in their Historical Development' with George Santayana, just as Joyce had (briefly) taken *'physiques, chimiques et naturelles'* at the Sorbonne, while Pound became obsessed with medical metaphors and 'Agassiz' fish' and Lewis learnt enough of the philosophy of science to argue with Einstein, Whitehead and Alexander in *Time and Western Man*. The Men of 1914 were, on the whole, highly appreciative of scientific method and discovery and sought to emulate scientific professionalism in their own sphere. In this they overestimated society's tolerance for a specialism which could not be justified in terms of visible material improvement. Einstein, Bohr and Heisenberg have not normally been accused of obfuscating élitism, despite the arcane nature of their theories: Joyce, Pound and Eliot have frequently been so impugned, even among literary critics, while Lewis's fictions and cogent polemics have been largely ignored. The aesthetic pretentions of these men belong to an era less commercial and material than our own, and more tolerant of complex expertise in matters of the experiential and moral realm. An awareness of the passing of such social prestige, in the interwar years especially, may help to explain the strong emotional fidelity of the group to each other, despite the growing intellectual differences which will be chronicled below. In important senses, these writers and their peers constituted the last of the socially-sanctioned 'Great Authors'.

The enormous self-confidence of these writers in their specialist role is clearly voiced in Lewis's proclamations in *BLAST* 1: 'Intrinsic beauty is in the Interpreter and Seer, not in the object or content'; 'It may be said that great artists in England are always revolutionary' (7); 'We are Primitive Mercenaries in the Modern World' (30); 'WE the moderns . . . through the incessant struggle in the complex city, have . . . to spend much energy. . . . The knowledge of our ivilisation embraces the world, we have mastered the elements'

(158). It is unlikely that even the most conceited writer would make such claims in the 1990s – and if he did, he would be confined to 'Pseud's Corner' rather than invited to discuss culture with the Prime Minister at 10 Downing Street, as Lewis was.[20] Yet Lewis's claims were not exceptional for their time; they merely assert, in triumphal tones, what the 'generation of 1914' had learnt to expect from writers and painters – that they were, indeed, 'antennae of the race',[21] as Pound was to put it, and that what they registered had precisely the social and political relevance that Asquith probed for when he gave Lewis lunch. Joyce's first novel ends with a personal declaration just as hubristic as *BLAST*'s manifestos; and a similar sense of prophetic mission will underlie all the poetry and criticism of Eliot and Pound. Nor, perhaps, were such claims wholly false. Had the Liberal Prime Minister read, with due attention, Lewis's *Enemy of the Stars* (also in *BLAST* 1, 20 June 1914), he might have been more prepared for the 'guns of August': for the play depicts rampant masculine aggression, in a No Man's Land of broken machinery, and ends with a murder followed by suicide. Be that as it may, the Men of 1914 came to their earliest creative ventures with a highly exalted notion of the relevance and function of art. And as they felt their role to be highly valuable, so they would expect, from the start, that readers would take trouble to comprehend what they were saying – however difficult or arcane – and take it seriously. There were problems in this expectation from their early work onwards. If Yeats could admire Joyce's youthful epiphanies, no publisher was keen to print *Dubliners*, as the stories stood. Similarly, Conrad Aiken met only bafflement when he tried to interest London editors in Eliot's 'Prufrock' poems in 1912, while Lewis's *Enemy* was so original and Expressionistically grotesque that only a venture like *BLAST* could have printed it. Before 1914 only Pound had founded a literary reputation – and that was largely because his early poems were consciously archaic. Thus, from the beginning, the specialist claims of this generation of writers were always in danger of marginalising their efforts within society at large. They set out in the spirit of artistic experimentation in order to bring expression and transform-ation to the social issues of their times; but the specialist nature of their experiments threatened to cut them off from the wider public right from the beginning.

Yet the very experimentalism of such writers was, I suggest, partly based on an underlying anxiety about the adequacy of the traditional arts to express the realities of the contemporary world. This was especially so in the case of literature, which in the post-Gutenberg era had established a virtual hegemony of discourse, based on the authority of sequential, continuous and coherent textuality. That hegemony of expressive method was increasingly under threat in the modern era as new media of communication developed. The inventions of the electric telegraph, wireless, movies and gramophone, and the use of wire-photos and tabloid presentation of disparate news-items in newspapers, had begun to challenge the authority of sequential textuality as major mode of communication.[22] Writers and painters were generally excited by such revolutionary developments in registering the contemporary world, but the most *avant-garde* seem also to have been conscious, at some fundamental level, that the new media of communication demanded a corresponding modification of artistic conventions. *BLAST*, for instance, implicitly acknowledged the revolution in communications by adopting headline formats, including iconographic devices and employing extreme typographic techniques. The significance of this experimentation to such key later-Modernist texts as *Ulysses*, *The Waste Land* and the *Cantos* is evident. In particular, *BLAST* helped inaugurate the modern practice of employing radical juxtaposition instead of rhetorical transition as a means of textual development. Yet *BLAST* merely found a journalistic mode of expression to represent what was evident in many of the new generation of writers from the start of their careers – a tendency to express the contemporary world in terms of discrete and discontinuous fragments. Joyce's brief 'epiphanies', Eliot's Symbolist fragments held together by mood, Pound's development of the image as a mode of 'superimposition', as well as Lewis's disparate 'headlines' all convey reality as inherently fragmentary. As 'antennae of the race' (rather than as 'unacknowledged legislators of the world',[23] for instance), early twentieth-century artists were prone to present modern experience in terms of felt discontinuities rather than as coherence embodying universal law. And because of this the developing works of Modernism would appear to the conventional reader as wantonly irrational and chaotic.

Clearly for writers such as Joyce, Lewis, Pound and Eliot this fragmentary tendency was merely the result of attempting to bear true witness to the realities of the new age. As Eliot was later to put it, poets must be 'difficult' because contemporary society was so complex.[24] This 'difficulty' was as much a matter of juxtaposition as allusion in the mature works, for in literature, most particularly, radical collage upsets precisely the conventions of the old hegemony which had penetrated nearly every aspect of rational Western culture. So the early work of the Men of 1914 was already revolutionary in its implications. Joyce's 'epiphany', for example, constituted a kind of prose snapshot – autonomous and not logically related to other such snapshots – where reality appears illuminated and transfigured. Such heightened presentations of discontinuous experience seemed to Joyce to capture the essence of modern awareness: hence Stephen's rather ludicrous sense of self-importance as ruminated in *Ulysses* – 'Remember your epiphanies on green oval leaves, deeply deep, copies to be sent to all the great libraries of the world, including Alexandria' (p. 46). This relativistic mode of rendering the real is similar to the way the early Eliot brings together the most disparate images in the mind of J. Alfred Prufrock, or attributes them to the unidentified persona at the end of 'Preludes'. 'Presentation',[25] from the beginning of these writers' careers, tended to come in the form of fragmentation and collage. Pound's imagistic method of around 1912 is similar: the likening of a sleeping woman to a 'wet leaf' or of a Metro platform to a 'black bough'[26] is similarly adventitious – and in the last case no verb is provided to ease the transition between disparate realms. Such imagistic superpositioning becomes an Expressionistic *tour de force* in Lewis's *Enemy of the Stars* (see below, pp. 60–7). Thus, in each case, the early work of these writers renders the 'New Age' as chaotically relativistic – its strange fragments only arbitrarily brought together through collage methods. The early Eliot wrote: 'The worlds revolve like ancient women / Gathering fuel in vacant lots'. The sentiment and shock-technique here encapsulates a whole generation's way of seeing and rendering experience. So, even before the Men of 1914 were construed as a specific literary group, their perceptions and techniques had much in common. And this meant that when Pound began to organise them as the literary *avant garde* there was a natural consonance between them, out of which the intertextual dynamics of the major texts could develop.

THE MIND OF EUROPE

The phrase 'the mind of Europe' occurs in Eliot's 1917 essay 'Tradition and the Individual Talent'. Although the purpose of the essay is to campaign for a notion of tradition which Eliot found lacking in English literary life, it is clear that the Men of 1914, at least, established their early careers within a very conscious ethos of European civilisation and thought. As has been mentioned, they all undertook higher education and in many ways they remained perpetual students ever afterwards. Pound was a university specialist in Romance languages and literature, Eliot wrote a PhD dissertation in philosophy, Joyce developed a virtually neo-scholastic theory of aesthetics, and Lewis would write several non-fictional works on European thought – *Time and Western Man* being merely the most brilliant. All four men, too, were brought up in the great age of historical studies and all developed elaborate ideas about the meaning of historical process which would centrally inform such mature works as the *Cantos*, *Finnegans Wake*, *Four Quartets* and *Self Condemned*. As 'antennae of the race', they thought of themselves as points of mediation between past and present thought – cerebral transmitters in communication with the central nervous system of society. If this was only partly the case, it can nevertheless be claimed that in the aesthetic realm, at least, they were indeed key representatives of European intelligence in their time. Joyce, Pound and Eliot, in particular, wrote as Eliot recommended with 'the whole of the literature of Europe' in mind, and Lewis, most spectacularly at first, wrote with 'his own generation in his bones'.[27] The dynamics of creative rivalry which would develop between them became concerned precisely with the relationship between tradition and innovation in writing the 'New Age'. In short, the main writings of the Men of 1914 would debate exactly what 'the mind of Europe' constituted within the first half of the twentieth century.

The concept of Europeanness is fundamental here. For all Pound's Yankee bravado, for instance, it was the almost spiritual ideal of Europe which called to him and determined where he would choose to live his adult life. Similarly, it was Europe in general, and England in particular, which lured Eliot away from his American family and background. Joyce, too, notoriously left the Ireland of his youth for a changeable Continental life – a decision proudly vaunted in the 'signing' of *Ulysses*: 'Trieste –

Zurich – Paris, 1914–1921'. Finally, though Lewis had his own transatlantic connections, he was educated in England, loved travelling in Spain and France, and found his Second World War sojourn in Canada a devastating experience of cultural deprivation.[28] All four men, then, were committed to the idea of Europe and founded their literary careers in terms of a specifically European tradition of literature. Joyce's 'dialogue' with Ibsen, Lewis's with Dostoevsky, Pound's with Browning and Yeats, and Eliot's with Laforgue were all conscious engagements with recent expressions of the European mind, just as their mutual admiration for (in particular) Dante (variously influencing several mature texts)[29] demonstrates their rooting in the specifically Christian aspect of European tradition. For three of them, quite evidently, this made the Great War all the more traumatic when it came, since the mind of Europe appeared to be in the process of violent disintegration from within just as the literary group were in the process of getting organised. Later works such as 'Hugh Selwyn Mauberley', *The Waste Land* and the 'Hell' cantos would become key testimonials to the breakdown of European mind, while Lewis's *The Childermass* would satirise the mental ghostland which remained afterwards and even *Finnegans Wake* (for all Joyce's professed indifference to geo-political struggle) might be read as a version of interwar European intellect reduced to the wild imaginings of a drunken Irish dream. Much of the task of mature Modernism would be to salvage what was left of the 'mind of Europe' and attempt new literary structures where it could be set into relation with the 'monuments' of the past. Nineteen-seventeen was a year of fearful uncertainty and despair:[30] the date of Eliot's celebrated essay seems far more relevant than it has been seen to be. And after the war's conclusion, the Mandarin babbling of European tongues in texts like *Ulysses*, *The Waste Land*, the *Cantos* and *Finnegans Wake* sounds like the frantic stridency of a shattered brain trying to reconnect its myriad neural murmurings.

However, if the mature work of these men was inevitably concerned to reassert connections with European tradition, the dynamic of the world they grew up in was essentially futuristic. The rash of new artistic movements just before the Great War – Cubism, Futurism, Expressionism, etc. – is the most obvious sign that the 'mind of Europe' was bent upon innovation, and all four men would be – in one way or another[31] – implicated in English Vorticism, with Lewis and Pound right at the centre. But if the

arts were caught up in innovatory ferment, the ultimate dynamic
of change was surely located in the realm of scientific technology.
This is implicit in the enthusiasm of both Futurism and Vorticism
for modern machinery. It was science and technology, fuelled
by mature Capitalism, which created a society constantly, and
increasingly, given over to change. The scientific mind of Europe
and the technological organs within European society, were in
rapid metamorphosis and the aesthetic sensibility whirled along
with them. Henry Adams's perceptive comments about the Paris
International Exhibition are pertinent here:[32] the spirit of the
dynamo had replaced that of the Virgin who had inspired the
building of Notre Dame. Yet Adams could have made more of a
reality beyond the dialectic of idealism and materialism – simply
that the Virgin had conceived one Christ-child for all time, whereas
the dynamo not only breeds, as it were, constantly newer dynamos
but also generates new technological mutations *ad infinitum*. Building upon the Industrial Revolution, the turn of the century
witnessed the consolidation of perpetual revolution in its technological form. The Men of 1914 came to adulthood in a world where
scientific technology was creating changes that were momentous,
rapid, continuous and of immense prestige. So the artistic 'tradition
of the new'[33] was based not only on scientific notions of evolution
but also on technological precedents of constant transformation –
which would become a prime motivator of the modern economy.
The Modernist 'experiments', 'discoveries' and aesthetic 'methods'
were essentially based on the model of scientific technology.

One aspect of this ethos was the proliferation of new academic
specialisms and disciplines. In an expanding intellectual universe,
disparate subjects of enquiry broke away from their original
matrices and developed new specialisms of their own. Particularly
relevant to the four writers would be the development of ethnology
(later anthropology), archaeology, psychology (and particularly
psychoanalysis), linguistics, sociology and the new physics. At the
time, such newly-discovered territories of the intellect tended to
come stamped with the names of individual intellectual explorers –
Frazer and Lévy-Bruhl, Schliemann and Arthur Evans, William
James and Freud, Grimm, Durkheim and Einstein. The new
intellectual interests would capture the imaginations of the Men
of 1914 in a variety of ways. Hugh Kenner's admirable book *The
Pound Era* suggests all kinds of ideational interconnections, while
Paul Johnson's polemical *History of the Modern World* sets the

writing of the period firmly within a general context of intellectual relativism.[34] It might be briefly noted here that Joyce (despite disclaimers) became a major fictionalist of psychoanalytic quirks, and was praised for this by C. G. Jung,[35] Lewis developed into an eloquent opponent of both Bergson's and Einstein's theories of time,[36] Eliot would make the greatest single poem of the century distinctly Frazerian, and Pound became a noted heretic in such fields as languages, anthropology, Renaissance history and economics.[37] At the turn of the century, the climate of awareness was eclectic, progressive and inherently exciting. And major young writers, far from retiring into ivory tower aestheticism, actively undertook wide-ranging intellectual *bricolage* in order to relate their works to the expanding empire of European thought. As Eliot's creative work was always, in a sense, a species of philosophy or theology, so Lewis's would tend to mediate between 'space-philosophy' and politics, Pound's would set language-theory within agnostic history and Joyce's would structure, through neo-scholastic schema, a dazzling array of ideological discourses. All were aware that 'knowledge grows from more to more', but they did not, like Tennyson, express reservations about this; they simply tried to influence the direction of its growth. For Pound, the significant writer was someone who 'invents something': all of the group were in the business of intellectual and artistic discovery, and in this they were creatures of the progressive ideology of their day.

Yet despite the instituted ethos of research and discovery, this was still the age of the great individual thinker – perhaps the last such time. The work of the Men of 1914 was heavily influenced by specific personalities. Five major thinkers were particularly important for members of the group in their developing careers; they are Sir James Frazer, Friedrich Nietzsche, Henri Bergson, Sigmund Freud and Albert Einstein. This is not just a matter of individual influence (whether direct or diffused) – for example, that of Frazer on Eliot and Pound or of Nietzsche and Bergson upon Lewis; and indeed, as Harold Bloom has shown,[38] influence itself can operate negatively as well as positively (mature Lewis always attacked Bergson). Rather, it is a question of perceived intellectual energy operating in new areas of awareness which caught the imagination of the future group-members in different ways and helped determine the way they wrote. Thus Frazer's *The Golden Bough* inspired in the two poets a lifelong preoccupation with primitive ritual (which perhaps seeped into *Finnegans Wake* too). Lewis's reading of Nietzsche fired in him a passion for authenticity (equated with artistic energy) and Apollonian clarity, and a hatred of bad faith and uniformity which (borrowing from Bergson's theory of comedy, while denouncing his connoisseurship of flux) helped set up his own satiric method which (I shall argue) would have a powerful influence on Eliot, Pound and even Joyce. Bergson's influence upon Eliot (for all that Eliot quarrelled with him on philosophical points)[39] is evident not only in early poems like 'Rhapsody on a Windy Night' but in the meditations on subjective time in the late *Four Quartets*; and the same influence, if mediated through other writers, seems evident in Joyce's stream-of-consciousness method. Joyce argued about Freud, as he refused analysis with Jung, yet his renderings of the consciousness of Stephen, Bloom and Molly in *Ulysses* are also notably Freudian – as, indeed, are the symbolic dreamscapes in *The Waste Land* and the dream-babble of *Finnegans Wake*. Finally, the space-time relativities of *The Waste Land* surely owe a debt to the intellectual climate that Einstein, above all, had created,[40] while Lewis would accuse *Ulysses* of embodying the 'time–philosophy' that he attributed to Bergson and Einstein alike – a charge which in *Finnegans Wake* Joyce would overtly refute (see below pp. 127–8), at the same time supplying enough complex relativism to make it liable to stick. The mature work of the Men of 1914, then, evidences a preoccupation with fertility ritual, the Dionysiac and Apollonian orders, subjective time and flux, the unconscious and dreamwork, and relativistic space-time which were the legacy of Frazer, Nietzsche, Bergson, Freud and Einstein – many of whose ideas they were aware of at an early age. In such ways did the writing group absorb the new knowledge in order to express the contemporary 'mind of Europe'.

The early manifestos, articles and letters of these writers clearly indicate that they conceived of literature as an essentially intellectual manifestation, rather than a means of general enjoyment. Joyce's letter to Ibsen, for instance, is couched in terms suitable between two philosophers, or even scientists: 'your lofty impersonal power . . . your wilful resolution to wrest the secret from life . . . your absolute indifference to public canons . . . higher enlightenment lies – onward'.[41] Such a view of the function and qualities of an author would surely have been incomprehensible to, say, Restoration dramatists, or the picaresque novelists, or even more contemporary writers such as Dickens or Swinburne. But

Pound's description of his poetic method in 1908 would equally have amazed earlier generations of writers: 'I record symptoms as I see 'em. I advise no remedy. I don't even draw the disease usually. Temperature 102⅔, pulse 78, tongue coated etc., eyes yellow, etc.'[42] If this is a description difficult to relate to the poems Pound had actually written at that time, there is no doubt that this 'symptomatic' ideal was what he aspired to, and in essential ways had achieved by 'Hugh Selwyn Mauberley' (1920). Poetry was to have a major intellectual function in expressing actual social and cultural conditions in the contemporary world – to provide 'data' to equip the current 'mind of Europe'. In *BLAST* 1 Lewis apostrophised the intellectual function of writing in terms of a more dynamic model: 'Blast sets out to be an avenue for all those vivid and violent ideas that could reach the Public in no other way';[43] but in his statement on satiric method (not published until 1917) his cold impersonality is similar to Pound's ideal: 'Moran, Bestre and Brobdingnag are essays in a new human mathematic. But they are each simple shapes, little monuments of logic. I should like to compile a book of forty of these propositions, one deriving from and depending on the other'.[44] It was also some time after his earliest creative work that Eliot came to formulate his model of the poet's function and mind in 'Tradition and the Individual Talent'. The model was quite a shocking one in the contemporary Georgian climate of aesthetic ideals:

> I . . . invite you to consider . . . the action which takes place when a bit of finely filiated platinum is introduced into a chamber containing oxygen and sulphur dioxide. . . . The mind of the poet is the shred of platinum. . . . The poet's mind is in fact a receptacle for seizing and storing up numberless feelings, phrases, images, which remain there until all the particles which can unite to form a new compound are present. . . . The emotion of art is impersonal. And the poet cannot reach this impersonality without surrendering himself wholly to the work to be done. And he is not likely to know what is to be done unless he lives in what is not merely the present, but the present moment of the past, unless he is conscious, not of what is dead, but of what is already living.[45]

Thus do 'loftly impersonal power', the recording of 'symptoms' and 'little monuments of logic' come together in a literary function where past and present coexist and express the contemporary 'mind of Europe'.

TITANIC STIRRINGS

The European 'stirrings and snortings' which Lewis was later to memorialise in *Blasting and Bombardiering* had their somewhat millenarian origins at the end of the previous century. These were scarcely evident in *fin de siècle* literature (especially in England) but they were present in painting (the Impressionist project) and in post-Wagnerian music. However, the most compellingly futuristic of the arts was the one most closely linked with technology – the new architecture, which had indeed found a 'new medium of expression' for its practitioners to 'turn [them]selves loose in'. For the possibilities created by advances in steel frames, concrete, tougher glass, and electrical machinery to power lifts, afforded architects the means to transcend in bulk, tensile efficiency and above all height, any building hitherto created on earth. Here the European intellect was inspired by American pioneering energy: Paxton's Crystal Palace and Eiffel's Tower became superseded by Sullivan's brownstones and Lloyd Wright's protofunctionalist elegance. Above all, the rising skyline of New York would fill the imaginations of future giants of design like Le Corbusier. The combination of technological invention and architectural vision was able to give public expression to the inchoate social and political aspirations of the turn of the century. The vertical thrust and prophetic possibility of the skyscraper – whether metal tower or stoneclad – was the millennial emblem of the era. If the consequences of this in terms of implicit social engineering now seem totalitarian, architecture, at the time, was the epitome of artistic aspiration on the move. It is not surprising, then, that the future *Finnegans Wake*, apogee of literary Modernist ambition, should virtually commence with an evocation of futuristic city-building: 'a waalworth of a skyerscape of most eyeful hoyth entowerly, erigenating from next to nothing'.[46]

The other visual arts clearly caught something of the revolutionary spirit of architecture – Léger's cityscapes and Delaunay's obsession with the Eiffel Tower, for instance, are clearly inspired by building developments. At the same time, painting was itself responding to technological developments in two-dimensional iconographic representation. As Nikolaus Pevsner's classic *Pioneers of Modern Design*[47] attests to the futuristic dynamism of an architecture informed by technological development, so Aaron Scharf's *Art and Photography*[48] charts the way in which painting responded to the challenge of photography as it developed in the mid-nineteenth century. Outbid in the Realism stakes, even by sepia-tinted prints which nevertheless seemed to capture the moment itself (and at the very time when fiction, and then drama, were elaborating realistic techniques, unrivalled as yet by the development of motion pictures), painting branched out into Impressionism, Symbolism, Fauvism, Expressionism, etc., in order to preserve its historical significance. Arguably, such (defensive) diversionary tactics produced a richer and more humane version of Modernism than did architecture – impelled towards functionalism by technological progress. Certainly the new types of painting were more various and gave rise to yet newer and more diverse movements. In 1907 Picasso finished painting 'Les Desmoiselles d'Avignon', and shortly, in close collaboration with Braque, he had established the basis of 'Analytical' Cubism. This would be the subject of much propaganda and theorisation by such as the poet Apollinaire. Meanwhile painters like Mondrian, Kandinsky, Klee, Malevich and Ernst were beginning to extend the possibilities of art in new, and largely conflicting, directions. At the same time, Marinetti was organising Italian painters under the banner of Futurism – a movement he tried, enthusiastically, to export to England. He had some success: but the main effect of his efforts would be to stimulate the growth of an oppositional movement – the Vorticism of Wyndham Lewis, Gaudier-Brzeska and Ezra Pound.

In music, the ferment of experimentation was somewhat less strident yet still evident. As in literature, the sense of new possibility was at times almost drowned out by a profound nostalgia for dying conventions. In Bruckner and late Mahler, for instance, the break-up of harmony is signalled as heartrending sonority. More forward-looking, if essentially transitional, was the musical Impressionism of such French composers as Debussy and Ravel; while Erik Satie was a genuine Parisian original whose striking inventions achieved social culmination in the collage-orchestration of *Parade* (with Picasso, Cocteau and Diaghilev as collaborators in the production). In Vienna, Schoenberg was pioneering his way toward Serialism, the Utopian creation of a new kind of musical scale; and in Russia the young Stravinsky was experimenting with *ostinato* rhythms based more on folk music than on the great classical tradition – an attempt to renew music from its popular base which was similar to the project of America's Charles Ives. However, the most vigorous proclamations of new musical possibilities tended to emanate from Futurist Italy – though more in the form of ardent theory than actual composition. Here, for instance, is Luigi Russolo in his most fervent strain:

> Let us cross a great modern capital with our ears more alert than our eyes, and we will get enjoyment from distinguishing the eddying of water, air and gas in metal pipes, the grumbling of noises that breathe and pulse with indisputable animality, the palpitation of valves, the coming and going of pistons, the howl of mechanical saws, the jolting of a tram on its rails, the cracking of whips, the flapping of curtains and flags. We enjoy creating mental orchestrations of the crashing down of metal shop blinds, slamming doors, the hubbub and shuffling of crowds, the variety of din, from stations, railways, iron foundries, spinning mills, printing works, electric power stations and underground railways. . . .
> WE WANT TO ATTUNE AND REGULATE THIS TREMENDOUS VARIETY OF NOISES HARMONICALLY AND RHYTHMICALLY.[49]

In literature, the chief impulse for change came from France. In the previous century, the prose of Zola, Flaubert and the Goncourts and the poetry of the Symbolists (especially Baudelaire, Rimbaud, Laforgue and Mallarmé) had been committed to novel modes of representation. Such writers, with their dedication to technical specialism, had considerable influence on the generation of English authors prior to the Men of 1914. James, Conrad and Ford in prose, and Yeats, Symons and Ford in verse, negotiated a transition between High Realism and 'Impressionism'[50] or Symbolism which would provide a place to start from for the next generation. However, despite some technical innovations, these writers scarcely generated a futuristic spirit: Conrad, for instance, was almost congenitally pessimistic about the possibility of beneficent progress and Yeats was, at heart, a Romantic reactionary, for all his involvement in the Irish 'literary renaissance'. In some ways, Shaw's comedic version of Ibsenism was the most forward-looking literary art at the turn of the century. However, Ford in the *English*

Review (1908–10) sponsored new writers, such as Lawrence, Lewis and Pound, and called in his editorials for more exacting literary techniques to convey contemporary social life. Pound felt that Ford's commitment to concise, concrete poetry had been worth two years of his own experimentation and Lewis would publish part of *The Saddest Story*[51] in *BLAST* 1.

But the most dynamic ideas about literature in England before the 1914 group emanated from the circle of T. E. Hulme, toward which both Pound and Lewis eventually gravitated. Hulme took considerable interest in continental ideas, and he and his henchman F. S. Flint were the first to translate Bergson's 'Essay in Metaphysics' into English (in 1912). From Bergson, in particular, Hulme took the idea of the image as liberation from 'dead' language: '*Creative* effort means *new* images. . . . The accidental discovery of effect, not conscious intellectual endeavour for it'; 'the creative artist, the innovator, leaves the level where things are crystallised out into . . . definite shapes, and, diving down into the inner flux, comes back with a new shape which he endeavours to fix'; images constituted, for him, 'the very essence of an intuitive language'; and he wrote:

> To this piling-up and juxtaposition of distinct images in different lines, one can find a fanciful analogy in music. A great revolution in music when, for the melody that is one-dimensional music, was substituted harmony which moves in two. Two visual images form what one may call a visual chord. They unite to suggest an image which is different to both.[52]

Such ideas concerning the revolutionary potential of the image were the staple of Hulme's intellectual soirées at which Pound became a participant. Pound rapidly assimilated the group's interest in *vers libre* and haiku, as well as the doctrine of the image and Hulme's excited sense that a radical poetic change was in the offing. Like Hulme, he was fascinated by developments in the other arts, especially painting and sculpture; where he differed was in preferring practice to theory and in organisational genius. Rapidly Pound appropriated 'Imagism', as he called it, organised like-minded friends such as H. D. and Richard Aldington to collaborate in writing Imagist poems, propagandised for it in *Poetry* (Chicago) and eventually put together for the first Imagist anthology, *Des Imagistes* (1914).

By this time Pound was also acquainted with Percy Wyndham Lewis,[53] whose energy and talent were even more volcanic than his own. Lewis was primarily a painter at the time, and had already established himself as a brilliant experimentalist. He knew even more than Pound about painting developments going on in Paris, had attended Marinetti's 1913 London lecture, and having rebelled against Roger Fry's 'Omega Workshop' created the 'Rebel Art Centre'. But he also had literary aspirations, and while in France had sketched out some stories about Breton life,[54] one of which, 'The Pole', Ford put into his *English Review* – after a legendary first encounter with Lewis.[55] In Ford's account, Lewis had highly revolutionary notions about literature, as well as art, from early on: 'You and Mr. Conrad and Mr. James and all those old fellows are done. . . . Exploded! . . . *Fichus!* . . . *Vieux jeux!* . . . No good! . . . Finished!'[56] However, Lewis's radical zeal showed more in his painting than his early writing. His *Kermesse* of 1912, for instance, was 'a whirling design of slightly cubist forms expressed in terms of cool but strong colour contrasts'.[57] Lewis followed this up with brilliant proto-Vorticist designs for *Timon of Athens*, some 'abstract hieroglyphics' for Frida Strindberg's nightclub, the 'Cave of the Golden Calf', and 'The Laughing Woman' and 'Creation'. In painting, Lewis was as revolutionary and talented as anyone on the Continent at that time, and his achievement in art was far greater than the Imagists' modest breakthrough in literature. He and Kate Lechmere set up the Rebel Art Centre in 1914, and shortly before the publication of *BLAST* 1 in the same year, he galvanised Epstein, Hulme, Gaudier and Edward Wadsworth to help disrupt Marinetti's Futurist lecture in the Doré Galleries. In Lewis, England had found a 'Titan' to stir and snort as effectively as any artist in Europe. And, in combination with Pound, he was about to launch the magazine which would bring together the four most revolutionary talents in modern English Literature. Further, until the publication of *Ulysses*, I will argue, it was Lewis's imaginative force which most galvanised, and most influenced, the efforts of the other three – Pound, Eliot and even James Joyce.

DUBLINERS AND BRETONS

James Joyce's *Dubliners* was first published in 1914, some ten years after most of the stories had been written; *Chamber Music*, a short collection of lyrics, was published in 1907. The stories in *Dubliners*, sometimes worked up from earlier 'Epiphanies', are quite representative of the prose brilliance by which Joyce's work would come to be known, and their final publication was the direct result of Ezra Pound's early interventions on Joyce's behalf.[58] Until he began *Ulysses*, Joyce tended to think of himself as poet, fiction writer and dramatist. However, his lyrical gift (which Pound acknowledged by including 'I Hear an Army' in the first Imagist anthology) was specialised and fundamentally archaic – as much so as Pound's earliest poems. It is doubtful whether Joyce could ever have modified his poetic gifts to write specifically Modernist poems and Pound pointedly[59] encouraged him to write prose, invoking the names of Stendhal and Flaubert to indicate his place in the fictional Pantheon. Further, Pound's reaction to Joyce's play *Exiles* (one fruit of Joyce's admiration for Ibsen) was not very encouraging – especially in regard to its stageability in wartime England. In acting on Joyce's behalf, and using his publishing contacts for first *Dubliners* and then *Portrait of the Artist*, Pound not only got Joyce's prose into print, he succeeded in helping channel Joyce's often-distracted[60] energy into its future literary direction. Within the space of three years, Pound would have helped transform a Bohemian belletrist of varied talents and interests into the major prose novelist in English of the twentieth century. In more senses than one Pound was, as Joyce dubbed him, a 'wonder worker'.[61]

As we have noted, Joyce had already established himself as one of the coming men in Irish literature while still at Trinity College. Ibsen had thanked him for his review, Yeats admired his early epiphanies, A. E. had assessed his potentialities and helped introduce him to Arthur Symons, whose assistance led to the publication of *Chamber Music*. But by leaving the British Isles to eke out a living in Trieste, Joyce had cut himself off from his immediate literary base and publishing contacts – a strategic error Pound would repeat when he ensconced himself in Rapallo in 1924. Though Yeats and Symons remained sympathetic, Joyce was bogged down and frustrated until he achieved publication. The insistent realism of some of his stories remained a stumbling block to seeing his book appear,[62] even when Grant Richards appeared interested in bringing out *Dubliners*. For Joyce, this was one more instance of parochialism and a vindication of his choice of Europe over both Irish and English petty moralism. It needed an expatriate American with contacts, energy, devotion to literature and quite selfless generosity to generate enough interest for Joyce's prose career to achieve lift-off. In the process, Pound would stress Joyce's contribution to the new experimentalist ferment in literature – a role that Joyce would eventually develop far beyond his mentor's intention or approval.[63]

Pound's prescience about Joyce's potentiality was extraordinary, since Joyce's early prose is only a little more forward-looking than his lyrics. Wyndham Lewis would later accuse *Ulysses* of being *passé*, static and dead[64] – a highly unfair charge, yet one in many ways applicable to *Dubliners*. If the notion of 'epiphany' had proto-Experimentalist possibilities, Joyce's conscious theme in the stories was paralysis[65] and the moments of Symbolist illumination in *Dubliners* are all constrained by a Naturalist rationale which constantly denies the possibility of transcendence or change. The predicaments of Eveline (who cannot leave Dublin even when a possible chance arises), Little Chandler (whose poetic 'infant hope' is drowned out by the yelling of his infant son) or Gabriel Conroy (whose modest contribution to 'the living' is subsumed, by symbolic snow, into the dominance of 'the dead') proclaim the inherent message of the collection. Despite Joyce's personal rebellion from Dublin, his early writing suggests no alternative to urban paralysis: there is no real future for Dubliners (or himself as Dublin writer-in-exile) to be futuristic about. Both the content and form of the collection construct contemporary Irish reality as achieved stasis, where the weight of established conventions effectively stifles any liberating forces. *Dubliners* conveys a deadly urban suffocation through a perfected, but scarcely progressive, combination of late nineteenth century Realism and Symbolism. Joyce was abreast of, say, Chekhov; but, like the Russian writer, he was so far a chronicler of decay rather than experimentalist architect of any sort of future. There is little sense of actual artistic renewal in his characteristic precision of style:

No one wanted him; he was outcast from life's feast. He turned his eyes to the grey gleaming river, winding along towards Dublin. Beyond the river he saw a goods train winding out of Kingsbridge Station, like a worm with a fiery head winding

through the darkness, obstinately and laboriously. It passed
slowly out of sight; but still he heard in his ears the laborious
drone of the engine reiterating the syllables of her name.

('A Painful Case', pp. 432–3)

Just so, one feels, does Joyce's relentless piling up of details, the
'laborious' repetitiveness of his rhythms, build up the whole. This
is not to 'MAKE IT NEW' for a 'New Age' but a bid for literary
attention by conveying stasis through an accomplished consolidation of established stylistic means.

The overall matter of the stories is wholly appropriate for such
stylistic consolidation and constriction. Dublin is not presented as
a Modernist city in a ferment of constant reconstruction (for all the
evidence of a railway station here, or a speaking-tube there): it is, by
contrast, Paris which is characterised as full of 'gaiety, movement,
excitement' ('A Little Cloud', p. 402). The world of Dublin is given
as fixed, repetitive, mean: 'poor stunted houses' ('A Little Cloud',
p. 400); 'the lamps of the street . . . feeble lanterns' ('Araby', p. 369);
'the lonely road which leads from the Parkgate to Chapelizod' ('A
Painful Case', p. 429); 'along some tortuous passages and up a
dark staircase . . . to a secluded room' ('A Mother', p. 454). Dublin
is rendered as dingy, static urban uniformity. And by an inherently
Naturalistic causality the habits of the Dubliners are equally
paralysed, miserable and uniform: 'familiar objects she had dusted
once a week for so many years' ('Eveline', p. 374); 'sitting night
after night alone in that room' ('A Painful Case', p. 432); 'The moist
blue eyes blinked at the fire and the moist mouth fell open at
times, munching once or twice mechanically when it closed' ('Ivy
Day in the Committee Room', p. 433); 'She had been through the
Academy and gave a pupils' concert every year in the upper room
of the Antient Concert Rooms' ('The Dead', p. 477). Religion,
politics, business-hours, drinking bouts, family customs are all
implicated in a repetitive urban rhythm as alienating and inauthen-
tic as mature Eliot would render city-life by far more radical means.
Dubliners conveys urban life as limbo without any contrastive vision
of genuine paradise – or even authentic hell.

If there is a sense of transition in the volume, it surely concerns
the preference for atmosphere over plot, and a corresponding
emphasis on inner feelings over actions. Very little happens in
these stories – certainly in terms of 'well-made' plotting. An
essential implication of the 'paralysis', then, is not only the active

influence of urban environment but also the passive inauthenticity of virtually all the characters described. If this is Joyce's revenge on the Dublin he rejected, it is enacted in negative existential terms as The City of Total Bad Faith. The hope of Eveline, the dream of the boy in 'Araby', the ambition of Little Chandler and the sense of self-worth in Gabriel Conroy are all chimera subsumed into overall self-deception and moral failure. Granted the Naturalistic implication that Dublin renders its inhabitants thus fundamentally paralysed, it is in the end difficult to see how, or even why, the characters might change, or in what sense the stories could promote 'spiritual liberation'[66] rather than yet more desperate paralysis. Whatever his positive ambitions, in theory, Joyce's practice here is a strange combination of satire and sympathy. In so bleakly portrayed a world, moral censorship ('the conscience of my race'[67]?) becomes undermined by sorrow and pity. And Joyce's own ambivalence (however malevolent his motive of vengeance)[68] is evidenced in his concern to register inner feeling – formally indicated by his frequent use of free indirect speech. Here Joyce's heart overrules his head and renders his writing a species of what he exposes: 'If she went, tomorrow she would be on the sea with Frank. . . . Could she draw back after all he had done for her? . . . All the seas of the world tumbled about her heart. He was drawing her into them: he would drown her' ('Eveline', p. 377); 'It was useless, useless! He was a prisoner for life' ('A Little Cloud', p. 409); 'Why had he withheld life from her? Why had he sentenced her to death? He felt his moral nature falling to pieces' ('A Painful Case', p. 432). The emotional force of Joyce's empathy, here, makes his liberational project as out-of-place as the volumes of Nietzsche on Mr Duffy's bookshelf (p. 428). *Dubliners*, as artistic venture, returns to Joyce's hometown to mock and stays to pray. Joyce, too, is thus far still a Gabriel Conroy, preoccupied by stasis. In such symbolist release as the stories offer from the stifling Naturalism, the poetry is still in the pity.

That poetry is most expressed in the occasional 'epiphanic' moments, when the chains of the real suddenly seem to dissolve and a way out of Joyce's own stylistic paralysis seems to shine in terms of some possible future. As in the later epiphanies in *A Portrait*, such heightening of both subject and style is frequently associated with sexual idealisation, as in the following examples from the third story and the last:

These noises converged in a single sensation of life for me: I imagined that I bore my chalice safely through a throng of foes. Her name sprang to my lips at moments in strange prayers and praises which I myself did not understand. My eyes were often full of tears (I could not tell why) and at times a flood from my heart seemed to pour itself out into my bosom. . . . my body was like a harp and her words and gestures were like fingers running upon the wires. ('Araby', p. 370)

He stood still in the gloom of the hall, trying to catch the air that the voice was singing and gazing at his wife. There was grace and mystery in her attitude as if she were a symbol of something. He asked himself what is a woman standing on the stairs in the shadow, listening to distant music, a symbol of. If he were a painter he would paint her in that attitude. Her blue felt hat would show off the bronze of her hair against the darkness and the dark panels of her skirt would show off the light ones. *Distant Music* he would call the picture if he were a painter. ('The Dead', pp. 503–4)

Such moments lighten the mood of the overall grim realism, and suggest a higher realm of experience which the characters might aspire to if they only had more courage and energy. Yet the images of the harp and portrait seem distinctly mid-Victorian, and the rhythm and texture of the writing is merely a variant of an overall monovocal consistency which contrasts most strongly with the virtuoso polyvocality of Joyce's maturity. In *Dubliners* Joyce still seems at least one step behind his master, Ibsen, whose last play was called *When We Dead Awaken*. There is still a long journey beyond the volume's final words, 'all the dead', through 'Welcome, O life' and 'Yes I said yes', to Joyce's final experimentalist summation in *Finnegans Wake*.

As Joyce founded his prose career on brief portraits of Dubliners, so Lewis founded his on deft sketches of Bretons.[69] Yet the methods are rather different: Joyce's is detached, even-grained, patient and sympathetic; Lewis's is personalised, uneven, energetic and caricatural. Both represent founding positions within the current conventions – Joyce as aestheticist story-writer, Lewis as satiric *raconteur*. Yet though Lewis's technique looks ragged compared to Joyce's, it is his prose that possesses an energy and element of risk-taking which suggests an experimentalist future. From the start, Lewis displays a sudden perceptive brilliance which stands out from the narrative as nothing does yet in Joyce: 'I expect when the French laws become a little more consistent there will be added to the *crime passionnel* a *crime commercial*, with the same attenuating circumstances attached' ('Some Innkeepers and Bestre', p. 227); 'he treated all of us rather coldly, bowed stiffly and walked back to the cart with the air of a man who has just received a bullet wound in a duel, and refusing the assistance of his friends, walks to his carriage' ('Les Saltimbanques', p. 243); 'But as Roland is the sun of this system round which all revolve, they also are affected to each other. The lesser members of this household are doubly servient and satellite, circling in turn round that member that possesses most of the Roland fire, and most negative moral magnitude' ('A Breton Innkeeper', p. 272); 'Charlaran completely recovered from his relapse, and in a burst of energy that lasted two afternoons built a summer-house at the bottom of the garden' ('Unlucky for Pringle', p. 309). Not only is there wit and deft observation in such prose there is also rhythmic energy and a concentration on the vitality of human behaviour. If Joyce's theme is paralysis then Lewis's is galvanic energy, however constrained into social conditioning and eccentricities of habit.

Lewis's imagination, from the first, is captured by Bohemian eccentrics (whether 'Poles' or peasants).[70] His key figures here, as later, are wastrels, rebels or 'artists' who assert the dangerous energy of the rogue male. Where Joyce's characters are constrained by the familial chains of petit-bourgeois patriarchy, Lewis's grotesques typically refuse familial constrictions, either as sponging bachelors indulging 'self-assertion' (p. 213) and 'independence of spirit' (p. 214) or as tyrannical husbands whose wives are chosen to bolster their self-esteem through a ritual humiliation in the sex war. Brobdingnag is a spectacular type of the latter ('He has been married twice, and in the first ardour of youth beat Julie's predecessor to death', p. 292); Père François of the former ('Eventually he sprang up, struggling and stamping about the room, and made believe to fling an antagonist out of the door. He came back and sat down again, looking at me for a long time silently, with an air of most insolent triumph', p. 282). It is, in particular, Lewis's focus on masculinist assertion which makes his eccentrics somehow 'barometric' representatives of a powerful underlying aggression in society at large. In this world the sex-war is conducted almost entirely at the expense of women, whose most effective form of revenge on the tyrannical males is to cook badly. So although Lewis chooses the Breton countryside as setting, and eccentrics as characters, his tales resonate with the implications of contemporary European gendering.[71] With an almost anthropological gaze, expressed through a loose and generalising narrative style, he exposes the mechanics of patriarchy through a varied study of wastrelism. His assertive, often obsessive, scoundrels typically reject their gender-role in the patriarchal order – pursuing their own idiosyncracies, ignoring the claims of procreation, and living off women rather than labouring to support them and a family. In many respects, Lewis's male characters are precisely what Joyce's would like to be if they could stir themselves out of their Dublin conditioning.

However, the existential self-assertion of Lewis's figures has a distinctly sinister appearance. They tend to assert themselves in ways that are truculently combative rather than creative of any-thing. First published between 1909 and 1911 (and later collected in *The Wild Body*), the stories demonstrate a prescience as to the underlying energy of the 'New Age' which *Dubliners* entirely lacks. Where early Joyce presents contemporary society as irretrievably bogged down in Victorian suburban stuffiness, the young Lewis portrays a seething energy at work in the world, whose quality is essentially negative and whose typical image is ruthless warfare: 'some anarchist outrages are the work of very violent and extreme snobs, who lie in wait for some potentate, and shoot him, that in the moment of death the august eyes shall become more expressive and show more interest in him than they have ever shown in anybody before' (p. 216); 'Bestre conducts long and bitter cam-paigns with some neighbour . . . like a war in which two armies should take up successive strategical positions' (p. 229); 'these score of substitutes for war' (p. 253); 'he turned on me to enjoy his victory, and triumphed over me with as much ruthless exultation as though I had been his hereditary foe' (p. 278); 'Brobdingnag's mind is stunned and invaded by a torpor, at the sight of such overwhelming hate and daring, complicated with such unspeakable ingenuity as his rival has given proof of', p. 295. Lewis, who had met Kropotkin and would simulate Marinetti's aggressiveness, is already the prose laureate of Death Wish. The inherent interper-sonal aggression which in *Heartbreak House*, *Women in Love* and *Parade's End* will be 'written back' into Edwardian society from the

standpoint of the Great War, is already distributed throughout the
French countryside in the form of Lewis's bellicose grotesques.
Lewis was also aware of the psychosomatic aspects of such
aggression: 'Bestre is perfectly unconscious of this weird dumb-
passive method of his, and, quite on the contrary, considers himself
on the verge of a death struggle at any moment when in the
presence of one of his enemies', p. 231; 'He is thereby purged
completely for the time of all the suggestions, all the excretions of
violent thought, emotion, black anger, bilious dreams, deposed in
small quantities each day, inevitably, beneath the suave surface of
his existence', p. 293; 'to outrage, in his intangible fashion, some
unfortunate man, who refrains from striking for fear of the criminal
penalties of such an act, and who takes the blow back into his own
bosom, as it were, and is stifled by his own oath', pp. 229–30. If
artists are 'antennae of the race' Lewis was one of the truest, for
the early stories (like the future *Enemy of the Stars*)[72] implicitly
foreshadow the coming holocaust in which he, himself, would be
a participant. It is fitting that when he came to put the stories
together later, in revised form, the unifying figure should be an
ex-soldier, Kerr-Orr.

However, Lewis's stylistic power could not yet match his
prophetic insight – the two would come together in *Enemy*. These
are off-the-cuff pieces, reminiscent of Defoe or *The Spectator* in their
personal anecdotage and casual generalisations. Nevertheless the
basis of a modern satiric theory underlies the vision[73] and Lewis's
psychological canniness is expressed, at times, through proto-
Vorticist brilliance of imagery. Lewis had attended Bergson's
lectures in Paris and Bergson's view of comedy as the spectacle of
a mechanisation of human vitality is similar to techniques and ideas
that Lewis was exploring. In his early, and slightly inconsequential,
essay 'Our Human Body' (1910) Lewis identifies our physicality as
central to our being, looks for the fuller 'expressiveness of the
body' (p. 255), stresses the importance of the male's physical
aggressiveness ('war is the equivalent in man's life to marriage
in woman's, p. 254) and sketches out, far earlier than Lawrence,
the English division of 'body from soul' (p. 255). It is physico-
psychic manifestations (and transactions) which most fascinate him
in the early stories published in *The English Review* and *The Tramp*.
Like Joyce's early tales these are short on plot – but they are far
less interested in 'finish' than *Dubliners*. What they depend on
is lively narrative, filtered through the medium of a curious,

generalising antagonist-raconteur, and the Vitalistic self-expressive-
ness of the anti-heroic protagonists whose behavioural singulari-
ties are the centre of interest – the German in 'The Pole' who beats
up his mistress, then dances 'violently' with her (a foretaste of
Kreisler in *Tarr*), Bestre who by 'tremendous effort of concentration
destroys a nosy painter's wife by a single, devastating glance,
the 'showman' who makes frantic rushes at the little boy who jeers
at him ('Les Saltimbanques'), the 'rolling' walking-rhythm of
Roland in 'A Breton Innkeeper' or the aggressive singing of
Père François ('in which he thirsted for my blood', p. 278). The
aggressive-defensive nature of interpersonal transactions is the
theme here, as the satiric focus is all on the physical manifestations
whereby the protagonist expresses essentially psychological drives.
Here Lewis's sharp and ruthless painter's eye combines with his
satirical intention to achieve powerful effect.

   Lewis had yet to become the achieved artist in words. Yet the
very casualness of the writing enables him to combine quasi-
philosophical speculation, personal anecdote, incisive psychological insight and proto-Imagistic observation in a single brief sketch.
His constructed personality becomes a feature in the stories in a
way that never features in Joyce's fiction – even when his persona
is at the centre of interest, as in *Portrait*. 'Lewis' comes over as
interesting and stimulating even when his *dicta* seem *outré* or his
point of view seems to sponsor outrageous personalities. If aesthetic
values seem missing here (and Lewis's early productions are not
liable to be considered in critical analyses of the Short Story),
intelligent readers will always respond to Lewis's insights. They
are disturbing, thought-provoking and uncannily prophetic. They
also, at times, reach under the surface anecdotage to find and
foreground a stylistic brilliance which will soon become his
hallmark: 'in his rigid and absorbed manner, with his smiling
mask, he looked as though a camera's recording and unlidded eye
were in front of him' (p. 217); 'She paled, rendered quite speechless
. . . her glassy look shivered to atoms – hurried on and home, and
was laid up for several days' (p. 230); 'this lugubrious personage
had woken to the sudden violence of an automatic figure set in
motion' (p. 239); 'he grew more and more violent, after getting up
and whirling round without reason, like a dervish, with his
ruined umbrellas shaken at arm's length' (p. 283). There is an
expressionistic energy and incisiveness here on which Lewis could
found the wild verbal Vorticism of *Enemy of the Stars*, and *BLAST*

in general. It is the voice of intelligence manipulating the possibilities of contemporary discourse to find the stylistics of the future.
Granted that with *Ulysses* and *Finnegans Wake* Joyce would thoroughly outbid Lewis as Key Modernist, it should be remembered
that in the early fiction Joyce was content to perfect a prose
consolidation while Lewis, already the visual pioneer, stretched
his imagination and stylistic technique to break a way towards the
fiction of the future.

PERSONAE AND PRUFROCK

Pound's first book of poems, *A Lume Spento*, was published at his
own expense in 1908; the best of the poems in it were republished,
alongside newer pieces, in *Personae* (1910).[74] As mentioned above,
these were essentially archaic in spirit and technique, and showed
the varied influences of Browning, the 'nineties poets and the
Provençal troubadours. For the man who would reiterate 'MAKE
IT NEW' as his watchword, and whose name has become synony-
mous with Modernism, the poems are surprisingly Romantic –
evoking the spiritual within nature and praising the beauty of
womanhood from the standpoint of the balladeering vagrant.
However, Pound was at the very beginning of his career and came
to his own writing with a close acquaintance of the Romance
tradition in Mediaeval France. He always had a powerful, futuristic
energy and he landed up in England partly to see how 'Yeats did
it', as a springboard for his own future work. However, Yeats was
self-confessedly one of 'the last Romantics', and it would be the
theory of Hulme, and the very practical criticism of Ford,[75] as well
as his own experimentation, which would lead towards 'Hugh
Selwyn Mauberley' and the *Cantos*. Yet Pound's identification of
Yeats as the major contemporary poet in English was unerring in
the era of Kipling, Housman and Hardy – an act of critical genius
that would be repeated when he identified the importance of such
men as Lewis, Joyce and Eliot. It is now well-known that Pound
influenced the later Yeats at least as much as he learned from him.
Yet Pound revered literary apostolic succession, and psychologically resolved his 'anxiety of influence' by marrying the daughter
of his poetic hero's ex-mistress.[76] In the short term, he wooed a
muse of forgotten beauty, and the precedent of the Irish poet, in
particular, helped justify this.

'The Tree' and 'Cino' represent the essence of early Pound: the first expresses nature mysticism through mythology and archaisms such as ''Twas' and 'nathless'; the second conjures up a Provençal persona to balance the 'White Goddess'[77] with sun-worship and deploys Browningesque colloquialisms like 'Bah!' and ''Pollo Phoibee'. Pound shortly recognised the provisional nature of his early work in remarkably self-aware terms:

> In the 'search for oneself', in the search for 'sincere self-expression', one gropes, one finds some seeming verity. One says 'I am' this, that, or the other, and with the words scarcely uttered one ceases to be that thing. I began this search for the real in a book called *Personae*, casting off, as it were, complete masks of the self in each poem. I continued in a long series of translations, which were but more elaborate masks.[78]

The 'masks' which the young Pound used could be quite various. If 'Cino' is Pound's Song of the Open Road, 'Sestina: Altaforte' is a rumbustious praise of battle which has an ominous ending redolent of the aggressive impulses in Europe[79] which Lewis had also expressed:

> Hell grant soon we hear again the swords clash!
> Hell blot black for always the thought 'Peace!'
>
> (p. 21)

By contrast, 'Ballad of the Goodly Fere' hymns masculine *camaraderie* in essentially peace-loving company – the disciples of Jesus – while 'Na Audiart' simulates orthodox Provençale adoration of the feminine.

Pound's translations represent, in a sense, a way for the poet to begin updating his poetic technique while still expressing antique postures and emotions. 'The Seafarer' for instance combines alliterative mimicry and some archaisms with neatly understated concreteness:

> Disease or oldness or sword-hate
> Beats out the breath from doom-gripped body. . . .
> Tomb hideth trouble. The blade is layed low.
>
> (pp. 37–8)

Understatement (usually through visual concreteness) was at the heart of the Imagism that Pound was learning from Hulme and developing in his own poems. And he would use it to great effect in translations like 'Exiles's Letter' – a poem that would later haunt Eliot (see below pp. 133–5). While the interest remains antiquarian, the language is very much as Ford would have it – concise, specific, to the point, and the more moving for that:

> What is the use of talking, and there is no end of talking,
> There is no end of things in the heart.
> I call in the boy,
> Have him sit on his knees here
>   To seal this,
> And send it a thousand miles, thinking.
>
> (p. 72)

The measure of what Pound was trying to achieve in shunning abstraction to achieve concrete simplicity can be gauged by comparing the last word, above, with Wordsworth's phrase 'in vacant or in pensive mood'. The success of such translations lies in Pound's finding concise colloquial expression for the delicate emotions inscribed in the originals, so that the poems appear startlingly contemporary at times: 'I won't say it wasn't hard going, / Over roads twisted like sheep's guts', or 'I went up to the court for examination. . . . / And got no promotion' (pp. 71–2).

It was Imagism which made possible such felicities, but Imagism proper, of course, would be committed to a quite Utopian ideal of the image: 'an intellectual and emotional complex in an instant of time'.[80] In poems like 'In a Station of the Metro' or 'Alba' this, arguably, occurs yet these are haiku-like double-image constructs of a quite limited kind. It would be the application of the 'ideogrammic method', the montage-collation of varied 'luminous details',[81] which would enable Pound to effect sustained poetic writing in the later 'Hugh Selwyn Mauberley' and *Cantos*. Meanwhile, at the time that he first met Lewis, Pound was still searching for poetic directions. As he noted later: 'Nineteen twelve was a bad year, we all ran about like puppies with ten tin cans tied to our tails. The tin cans of Swinburnian rhyming, of Browningisms, even in Mr Ford's case of Kiplingisms, as resonant pendant, magniloquent, Milton, sonorous'.[82] Pound must have been very aware that painters like Lewis had developed new techniques for a new vision that even the forward-looking Imagists could not begin to rival. In reviewing Lewis's 'Timon' drawings (shown at the second Postimpressionist show in 1912) Pound recognised in them the new 'Zeitgeist' and bracketed Lewis with Matisse, Cézanne, Picasso, Gauguin and Kandinsky.[83] First introduced as opposing 'bulldogs',[84] Pound must have been aware of Lewis's ascendancy in his visual medium. Pound could claim to be the most progressive poetic practitioner in London, but poetry was well behind painting in the race to make Art new. Furthermore, Lewis's pose of energised abrasiveness outbid Pound's somewhat aestheticist stance. Pound, I believe, introjected much of Lewis's dynamism. Pound's biographer, Noel Stock, has entitled his chapter on Pound between 1913 and 1915 'Ernest Fenollosa',[85] but his own account (as Tytell's more recent one)[86] provides evidence that it would more fittingly have been headed 'Wyndham Lewis'. Fenollosa was a dead Orientalist who bequeathed Pound a backlog of half-truths about Japanese and Chinese poetry which Pound would mine for the rest of his life. Wyndham Lewis was an egregiously alive quasi-Futurist who was revolutionising painting and publishing some strikingly energised prose-pieces. Perhaps Pound's chief 'persona' for the next few years was himself as Lewisian poet. Only Lewis's proximity can explain that strange aberration in the behaviour of 'kind-hearted' Ezra[87] – the challenge to Lascelles Abercrombie to fight a duel!

Despite the oddity of 'Sestina Altaforte', Pound's earliest vein is slightly antiquarian and gently 'feminine' in emotion. Lewis – who sensed Pound's archaic sensitivity early on – had already developed a futuristic and self-consciously 'masculine' style. The impact of Lewis on Pound's poetry (as well as his public pose) is, I believe, even more important than Hulme's theory of the image. As if by sympathetic magnetism, Lewis drew out the assertive aggression in Pound and, even before *BLAST* 1, helped a new poetic persona to develop – masculinist, volcanic, satiric. Hence the abrasive, cocksure voice that coexists uneasily with the lyrical Imagism in the later *Lustra*, in poems which were written from about 1912 onwards. The Imagist voice seems more truly Poundian: 'The apparition of these faces' (p. 53); 'See, they return; ah, see the tentative / Movements' (p. 39); 'Three spirits came to me / And drew me apart' (p. 46); 'I long for thy narrow breasts, / Thou restless, ungathered' (p. 54). Yet the other voice, if slightly over-strident, expresses the brash confidence of a newly-discovered part of the self – the Lewis, as it were, that had been always lurking within Pound: 'The mauve and greenish souls of the little Millwins/Were seen lying along the upper seats/Like so many unused boas' (p. 47); 'O generation of the thoroughly smug/and thoroughly uncomfortable' (p. 42); 'This thing that hath a code and not a core' (p. 35): 'Go out and defy opinion,/. . . Be against all sorts of mortmain' (p. 45).

The Lewis within Pound had hitherto only appeared, at times, as the robustness of Browning. Pound now declared a 'pact' with Walt Whitman,[88] which was his way of negotiating Lewis's anarchic influence by modernising Whitmanesque assertion into newly-formed Poundian 'yawp'. This would shortly appear in *BLAST* as an attempt, in verse, to approximate the volcanic prose-energy of Lewis's extraordinary 'head-lines' and Expressionist play *Enemy of the Stars*:

> Go! rejuvenate things!
> Rejuvenate even "The Spectator".
> Go! and make cat calls!
> ('Salutation the Second', p. 43)

Even pale imitation is a sincere form of flattery. The poems eventually collected in *Lustra* (1916) represent Pound's varied experimentation for, at least, the previous four years. The Imagist successes represent Pound's development of the theories of Hulme and Flint in terms of his own lyrical gift. But the vehement satiric voice represents, I believe, the first instance of radical influence between two men who will later define their efforts, in group terms, as the art of the Men of 1914: and the influence is all one way – the spirit of Lewis has entered Pound's consciousness and poetic voice, and will never again entirely leave it. It was Lewis's approximation to Futurism – in painting, conversation and early prose – which would, above all, underlie Pound's future commitment to 'MAKE IT NEW'.

During the years of Pound's early struggle for 'sincere self-expression' T. S. Eliot had also made a start at a poetic career. In 1914 Pound was to write enthusiastically to Harriet Monroe: 'He is the only American I know who has . . . trained *and* modernised himself *on his own*'.[89] This was virtually true· of all the Men of 1914 Eliot alone had founded his own distinctly Modernist place in literature by 1912 – an equivalent achievement to Lewis's contri-

bution to painting, and in a far less conducive climate:[90] but it
would be Pound's critical acumen which brought that achievement
to the notice of the literary world. Eliot's solitary victory was, itself,
the result of striking intertextual introjection. Prompted by Symons'
The Symbolist Movement in Literature,[91] Eliot had invested in three
volumes of Laforgue, and other modern French writers, and
developed a haunting, ironic voice out of the resultant struggle
with Symbolist influence. The transition between Eliot's earliest,
traditional lyrics and his knowing, proto-Modernist 'observations'
can be seen in 'Poems Written in Early Youth',[92] some almost as
much *bricoleur* translations as original productions. Yet Eliot was
only twenty-two when he began poems such as 'Preludes', 'Rhapsody on a Windy Night', 'Portrait of a Lady' and 'The Love Song
of J. Alfred Prufrock', early classics of poetic Modernism in English.
When Conrad Aiken, on a trip to London, showed them to Harold
Monro, of the Poetry Bookshop (and no committed antiquarian),
he declared them 'insane'.[93] Whether or not Monro would have
appreciated the fact, it was precisely those poetic features which
occasioned the remark that qualified Eliot for primacy as the
effectual father of the poetic New, irrespective of Hulme's theories
of the image. Pound, who through actual publication in London
had so far achieved this reputation, was acute enough, and
generous enough, both to recognise this and to ensure that others
would. By 1912, when 'Prufrock' was completed, Eliot had already
established a poetic style and subject-matter fitting to the 'New
Age'.

'Preludes' and 'Prufrock' most spectacularly demonstrate Eliot's
futuristic possibilities, yet 'Portrait of a Lady' and 'Rhapsody on a
Windy Night' are themselves clear pointers to a Modernist future.
'Portrait' represents the Victorian dramatic monologue recollected,
as it were, through soliloquy. The immediate voicing of a live
situation – as in Browning's 'Fra Lippo Lippi' or Tennyson's 'St.
Simeon Stylites' – is transformed into a dramatic scenario recalled
and edited by the persona: 'Among the smoke and fog of a
December afternoon / You have the scene arrange itself – as it will
seem to do –'. The real tension here, then, is less between the
defensive character and the 'lady' than between self-parts of the
dramatic speaker. He is characteristically a self-questioner ('Are
these ideas right or wrong?') and so manifests both the relativism
and the psychoanalytic preoccupations of the new century. The
poem, continued always as personal utterance, speaks out of

contrastive seasons, in sectional sequence, but this is less relevant than the overall sense of a self reviewing its partial (and guilty?) commitment to another self, reconsidered in the sort of temporal limbo which will characterise the world of Prufrock. The abrupt transitions mark the poem as a gateway to the coming literature: from the false-plangent 'life, what *cauchemar*!' to the reactive 'dull tom-tom'; from 'journey's end' to 'the sporting page'; from 'serving tea to friends' to 'Cry like a parrot, chatter like an ape', or the more reflective 'should I have the right to smile?' The poem breaks down rationalist progression to suggest that the new poetry must be constructed as a species of *collage*. Yet so far the reflective context holds all in place – as it will do in Eliot's poetry until *The Waste Land*. The voice – both dramatic and ironic – anticipates a whole range of other such voices, from Leopold Bloom, through Lewis's Satters in *The Childermass*, the self-conscious persona of 'Four Quartets' and Pound's last 'Drafts and Fragments' to Beckett's attenuated speakers in *The Unnamable* or *Not I*. At one stroke, Eliot has hit the characteristic tone of the new century: 'Not knowing what to feel or if I understand. . . .'

'Rhapsody on a Windy Night' offers an updated realism combined with a version of Expressionism. The Bergsonian influence[94] has helped elicit images which can be as striking as those in Lewis's later *Enemy of the Stars*: 'broken spring in a factory yard, / Rust that clings to the form that the strength has left / Hard and curled and ready to snap'. There is a protosurrealist vision, throughout, expressed as 'lunar incantations' which evidence the now-celebrated Eliotic music: 'That cross and cross across her brain'. The street-lamp articulates time – 'twelve o'clock' through to 'Four o'clock' – in an insistent litany which looks forward to the hour-schema of *Ulysses* and the clocks of Mrs Dalloway's London, as well as the 'unredeemed time' of Eliot's 'Burnt Norton'. Woman, here, is as central and as problematic as she will be in many texts of the coming era:

> 'You see the border of her dress
> Is torn and stained with sand,
> And you see the corner of her eye
> Twists like a crooked pin'.

Beyond the Victorian opposition of Magdalene and Madonna,[95] the feminine here suffuses the poem as woman and moon together;

like the future Molly Bloom: 'She is alone / With all the old nocturnal
smells'. So, too, is the protagonist who finally mounts to his
desolate room – a tormented outsider for whom the night has been
a lonely confusion of sensation, memory and desire.

Wyndham Lewis published the first poems by Eliot in England.
BLAST 2 includes 'Rhapsody' and 'Preludes' and the lines, from
the latter, which most struck Lewis,[96] show that his radical notion
of the new art could include transmutations of the Romantic:

> I am moved by fancies that are curled
> Around these images, and cling:
> The notion of some infinitely gentle
> Infinitely suffering thing.

Yet the emotion here is clearly mediated through neo-Laforguean
sophistication and it is the overall stylistic context which makes
the dramatic *cri de coeur* stand out as remarkable. For 'Preludes',
as a whole, demonstrates the modern sociological imagination in
deftly imagistic[97] discourse. It begins with deliberately impersonal
evocation: 'The winter evening settles down / With smell of steaks
in passageways'. Section I continues to evoke a rain-shower, dead
leaves, newspapers, blinds, chimney-pots and a 'lonely cab-horse'.
Section II evokes a kind of collective consciousness which embraces
beer-smells, muddy feet, coffee-stands and shades in rented rooms.
In III, consciousness is further elaborated as a feminine 'you' whose
situation seems to foreshadow the typist's in 'The Fire Sermon'
(*The Waste Land*), where spirituality is ironically reduced to 'sordid
images' and hair-curling techniques and clasping one's own dirty
feet are constituted as primary modes of modern being. Section IV
evokes the alienated presence of some supernatural being who
sounds very much like Christ, painfully attenuated throughout the
insistently urban environment. This last section moves on to evoke
a comforting presence in the lines admired by Lewis and concludes
with the image of old women scavenging in a kind of demolished
limbo – premonitory for a man who would become Air Raid
Warden in the 'blitzed' London of the 1940s.[98] The whole poem
presents a startlingly contemporary picture of city life in any
postindustrial country and raises insistent and culturally-relevant
issues which neither the represented society nor the poet is in a
position to answer. In this, too, it is a specifically futuristic creation:
for Modernist literature will be characterised less by new answers

than by questions which remain to vex the reader.

'The Love Song of J. Alfred Prufrock' remains the most striking and revolutionary of Eliot's poems until *The Waste Land*. It creates a specifically Modernist consciousness,[99] within a contemporary urban environment, and expresses both through a fluid, imagistic *vers libre* which includes early collage technique. In contrast both to the nineties aestheticism which preceded it and the Georgian robustness which followed its writing, the verse sounds from the beginning like the voice of the future:

> Let us go then, you and I,
> When the evening is spread out against the sky
> Like a patient etherised upon a table, . . .

The poem is remarkable for its combination of licence and overall control. Rhyme is used freely, but not in terms of any formal scheme, and the rhythm (while often reminiscent of blank verse) is as naturally cadenced as any Imagist could wish, line-lengths varying between long and short according to subjective require-ment. This discourse is determined not by notions of the con-sciously 'poetic' but by the rhetorical procedures inherent in contemporary educated discussion: 'Streets that follow like a tedious argument / of insidious intent'; 'as if a magic lantern threw the nerves in patterns on a screen'. Hence the updated diction – 'overwhelming question', 'hundred indecisions', 'formulated phrase', 'digress', 'malingers', 'politic, cautious and meticulous', 'almost ridiculous' – which is particularly striking if we compare it with the diction of early Yeats. When Pound was beginning to shun abstraction, Eliot undermined its deadly authoritativeness by subtle irony. At the same time, the 'Love Song' is packed with striking images: the cat-like fog, the eyes that pin Prufrock 'wriggling on the wall', the braceleted arms, the smoking pipes of lonely men, the universe squeezed into a ball, the mermaids 'combing the white hair of the waves blown back'. The voices of the women 'talking of Michelangelo' are collaged freely into the inconclusive train of thought and typographically distantiated to arrest the reader. Other transitions within the poem – from lonely men to the crab-claws, or from *Hamlet* to the latest fashion in trouser-bottoms – operate more in terms of juxtaposition than rhetorical transition, and look forward to the main technique of *The Waste Land*. The verse technique here replicates some of the methods of early Cubism and Futurism and as truly indicates the forward movement in the arts.

Eliot, in short, has found here a Modernist method for expressing the same urban alienation and wry introspection which Joyce gives in *Dubliners* by essentially traditional means. A comparison of the interiorised epiphanies quoted above (p. 31) and any part of 'Prufrock' manifests the difference between past and future modes of literary representation – and it is likely that Joyce partly had Eliot's early verse in mind when he devised the early poetic stream-of-consciousness in *Ulysses*.[100] Both writers were intensely preoccupied with the effects of urban conditioning and with finding expression for that frustrated introspection which was to become the hallmark of Modernist consciousness. But where *Dubliners* is haunted (and entranced) by the past, Prufrock's world is full of immanent possibilities that suggest a world on the verge of sudden new revelations: 'to lead you to an overwhelming question', 'there will be time, there will be time', 'how should I begin?', 'I am Lazarus . . . / Come back to tell you all', 'Shall I part my hair behind?' Prufrock's world is one of up-to-the-minute (and changing) fashion, of social encounters which might change everything, of possible transcendental revelation, of infinite existential potentiality. Prufrock appears paralysed precisely by this sense of infinite choice within a diverse social world somehow on the brink of momentous transformation. Written from an early twentieth-century America, whose future world greatness was already almost fact, the poem precisely captures the moment of early Modernism with immanent change apparent everywhere: 'time to murder and create, / And time for all the works and days of hands / That lift and drop a question on your plate'. The writing of the poem, itself, indicates that Eliot's choice is to 'create'; the paralysed anguish of his anti-hero also suggests an awareness that 'murder' may also be on the historical agenda. Two years before the outbreak of World War, the tension is partly in the waiting, where decision can still lead to revision and both can so far be reversed. Perhaps it is not paradoxical, but the twentieth-century norm, that the youngest of the Men of 1914 has first indicated, here, a decisively futurist potential for Modernist literature.

THE MEN OF 1914

BLAST was first published on 29 June 1914. Lewis edited it with the enthusiastic collaboration of Pound, who coined the term 'Vorticism' to describe what the participants were trying to do. At Pound's suggestion, James Joyce was officially 'blessed' in the first number (much of which was given over to strident 'Blasts' and 'Blessings') and it was Pound who solicited the poems of Eliot which Lewis published in the second and final number (1915). In a sense, then, *BLAST* constituted the visible expression of the grouping together of the four most revolutionary writers in English Modernism, and its radical characteristics fittingly expressed the dynamic potentialities of such a confluence of genius. For by its sheer bulk, its garish puce colour and its typographic Expressionism, *BLAST* made a futuristic statement unparalleled hitherto in England. There had, of course, been precedents: Roger Fry's Post-Impressionist Exhibition which caused his Bloomsbury colleague, Virginia Woolf, to pronounce (long after the fact) that in 'or about December 1910 human nature changed'; and Marinetti's incursions into artistic London backed up by disciples like Christopher Nevinson. Lewis learned from both Cubism and Futurism, but in the field of painting he was abreast of both, and by 1914 he had aggressively broken with both Fry and Marinetti. In *BLAST* he was decisively allying himself with Pound and the newest English visual artists and providing leadership for a Modernist movement which aimed to renew Western culture from scratch. In this he was most ably assisted by the sculptor Gaudier-Brzeska, whose talent and intelligence were formidable (but who would shortly die in the trenches), and by Pound whose enthusiasm for the New was unbounded, but whose sensibility and verse Lewis felt to be inherently antiquarian.[101]

Lewis had first been introduced to Pound, through intermediaries, at the Vienna Café in 1909 or 1910. In Canto LXXX Pound recalled: 'So it is to Mr Binyon that I owe, initially, / Mr Lewis, Mr P. Wyndham Lewis. His bull-dog, me / as it were against old Sturge M's bull-dog'.[102] Sturge Moore (brother of the philosopher G. E. Moore) had brought Lewis to the meeting, as Laurence Binyon had brought Pound, and Lewis too would remember the first meeting as a tense one – if not a matter of 'bull-dogs' exactly. However, his account in *Blasting and Bombardiering* stresses the later development of their friendship more generously than is usual in Lewis's anecdotes:

> I should say it was with a complete passivity on my side, tinctured with a certain mild surliness, that acquaintance with Ezra Pound was gradually effected. But once it was in being, not in spite of quite, but with no assistance from, myself, I enjoyed that acquaintanceship immoderately. This theatrical fellow, as he first seemed to me, I found to be 'one of the best'. I still regard him as one of the best, even one of the best poets.[103]

Both men had mutual friends and patrons in the form of Ford Madox Ford and A. R. Orage, for instance, and by the time of *BLAST* they were quite closely associated, for all Lewis's native suspiciousness of others. They had much in common, including their modes of self-presentation in a philistine world: 'Pound contrived to look 'every inch a poet', while I have never seen anybody so obviously a 'genius' as Wyndham Lewis', as Douglas Goldring wrote: 'in clothes, hairdressing and manner [they] made no secret of their calling'.[104] And if Lewis was always to doubt Pound's revolutionary credentials, he discussed the strategy of *BLAST* with him in detail. Perhaps he also somehow sensed that this 'cowboy songster'[105] had been enormously influenced by his own vitality and talent, and that the difference between the 'exquisiteness' of *Cathay* (which Lewis would rate higher than 'all the Cambridge aesthetes could muster between them')[106] and the assertive verse 'yawps' in *BLAST* 1 was essentially accounted for by his own impact on Pound. At any rate, they forged a strong working relationship over the composition of *BLAST* and it was towards this artistic field of magnetism that Pound drew Joyce and Eliot as he came into contact with them.

Pound's 'discovery' of James Joyce is now legendary.[107] Despite his acquaintance with men like Yeats and Symons, Joyce's literary career seemed completely bogged down until Pound's intervention. *Dubliners* was still not published and it looked as if it might well never be. All Joyce had to show for ten years and more of effort was the publication of a few stories in Irish magazines and a very slim volume of poems. Joyce was currently trying to convert his autobiographical novel *Stephen Hero* into what became *A Portrait of the Artist as a Young Man*, but granted the almost complete lack of

interest in his work by the literary world, in both Ireland and
England, there was little incentive to keep him at it. However, the
doyen of Anglo-Irish letters, Yeats, did Joyce one life-long service
in mentioning his name to Pound. Pound's first letter to Joyce in
December 1913 is tentative, and ends: 'I imagine we have hate or
two in common – but thats [sic] a very problematical bond on
introduction'.[108] However, the bond, building up for some time
through an exchange of letters as Pound found outlets for Joyce's
writing, was to be one of the strongest emotional ties in modern
literature, despite Pound's later rejection of 'Work in Progress',
and the most moving tribute in *Finnegans Wake* would be addressed
to the old 'wonder worker'[109] (see below, p. 165). In the meantime,
Joyce was blessed in *BLAST* 1, had a poem in *Des Imagistes* (1914)
and was put into contact with Harriet Shaw Weaver and others
through Pound's good offices. But the confidence Pound's intervention gave to Joyce had already helped him persuade Grant
Richards finally to publish *Dubliners*.[110] It came out, in fact, just
five days before *BLAST* 1 and in July Pound gave it a very
favourable review in the *Egoist*. At the same time Pound arranged
that *Portrait* (still not yet completed) should be published serially
in the *Egoist*: Joyce sent chapters to Pound, as they were completed,
and they were duly published in a magazine that was already
establishing itself as the key forum for new writing along with
BLAST.

It was in September 1914 that Pound met up with Eliot, the
fourth of the Men of 1914. The details of the first meeting are
not recorded, but the effect on Eliot's career thereafter was as
momentous as Pound's impact on Joyce's career. At the time, Eliot
had written no poems since 'Prufrock' and he was settling into
Oxford to write his doctoral dissertation on F. H. Bradley. After
meeting Pound, Eliot sent 'Prufrock' and 'Portrait' to him and
Pound told him: 'This is as good as anything I've ever seen. Come
around and have a talk about them'.[111] After this, as Peter Ackroyd
notes in his biography:

Even while Eliot was at Oxford, they kept up a continuous
correspondence. Pound was sending him poems and manifestoes
[sic] to which Eliot responded in his cautious and meticulous
style – pointing out platitudes, warning against excessive general-
ization and suggesting the need for concreteness in statements.

Pound was meanwhile distributing Eliot's poetry to anyone who cared to look at it.[112]

The first results of Pound's intervention were the publication of 'Prufrock' in *Poetry* (Chicago) and 'Preludes' and 'Rhapsody' in *BLAST* 2 in the next year. In that same year Pound created the *Catholic Anthology* largely, as he said, to get Eliot into print; five of Eliot's poems were published in it. In 1915, then, through Pound's good offices, Eliot's literary career was founded. For the moment, his only problem on this front was that inspiration had deserted him and he found it hard to write. The atypical 'Bostonian poems' of 1915 were as much written to keep Pound happy, and his name in print, as they were to express anything that Eliot really wanted to say.

Between 1914 and 1915, then, the new literary group had effectively come into being. Lewis was later to describe it in terms that give all credit to Pound:

> It was scarcely our fault that we were a youth racket. It was Ezra who in the first place organized us willy nilly into that. For he was never satisfied until everything was *organized*. And it was he who made us into a youth racket – that was his method of organization. He had a streak of Baden Powell in him, had Ezra. . . . He never got us under canvas it is true – we were not the most promising material for Ezra's boyscoutery. But he did succeed in giving a handful of disparate and unassimilable people the appearance of a *Bewegung*.[113]

Lewis's wonderfully entertaining descriptions of 'First Meeting' Joyce, Pound and Eliot in *Blasting and Bombardiering*[114] are required reading for any study of the Men of 1914; but the short chapter 'The period of *Ulysses, Blast, The Wasteland*' is even more important in understanding the group-dynamic which was built up, despite the fact that the four men never actually met all together.[115] Although Lewis's role as editor of *BLAST* was important, he is certainly right in seeing Pound as the organisational wizard. For it was Pound who invented the idea that, as the literary *avant garde* (in his view), they should think of themselves as a distinctive group, and he persuaded the others to think of themselves in these terms. He was active not only in promoting the work of each member to the literary world but also in recommending the work

of each to the other members – introducing the writing of Joyce
and Eliot to Lewis, Eliot's and Lewis's work to Joyce, and to such
an extent involving Eliot in the art of Joyce and Lewis, that when
Pound eventually left England for good Eliot, at the *Criterion*, took
over his promotional role for the other two – and, indeed, for
Pound himself.[116] Pound's dynamic role and sense of group-loyalty
is evident not only in his letters to Joyce, Lewis and Eliot but also
in those to others:

> I want a place where I and T. S. Eliot can appear once a month
> (or once an "issue") and where Joyce can appear when he likes,
> and where Wyndham Lewis can appear if he comes back from
> the war.
> (To Margaret Anderson, January 1917)

> I am not yet in the position of a Van Dyke or a Tennyson; but
> still, I have got Joyce, and Lewis, and Eliot and a few other
> comforting people into print.
> (To Marianne Moore, December 1918)

> Despite *The Egoist's* having been necessary to print Joyce, W.
> Lewis, Eliot and a lot of my stuff that Orage would not have in
> *The New Age*, I wish the young wd. rally round *New Eng. Weekly*.
> (To John Drummond, May 1934)[117]

In later years, when asked for advice from other would-be group
organisers, Pound had some revealing things to say about his own
efforts with the Men of 1914. To James Vogel in 1929, for instance,
he wrote: '*If* you are looking for people who agree with you!!!!
How the hell many points of agreement do you suppose there
were between Joyce, W. Lewis, Eliot and yrs. truly in 1917 . . .?'[118]
Earlier, in November 1928, he had written to Vogel: 'The science
of GROUPS is as follows: at the start you must find the 10% of
matters that you agree on and the 10% plus value in each other's
work'.[119] To John Drummond he stressed an important factor of
the group venture in 1932: 'You have only to note that the best
work of Joyce, Eliot, Wyndham Lewis . . . [has] only got into print
via specially started publishing ventures, outside the control of the
Fleet St. ring';[120] while to Lincoln Kirstein in 1931 he observed: 'life
wd. have been (in my case) much less interesting if I had waited

till Joyce, Lewis, Eliot, D. H. Lawrence, etc. complied with what my taste was in 1908'.[121] What such remarks surely indicate is that Pound acted initially out of spontaneous enthusiasm for what he read from the other three writers, looking for talent and natural literary affinity, and created loyalty by his sheer generosity, coupled to a canny awareness of how to promote writing in the current literary scene. At the same time he had a definite strategic sense and a natural knack for delegating group roles: thus the aggressive Lewis consented to play second fiddle and develop his career within a writing group, somewhat to the detriment of his career as painter: Joyce accepted Pound's definition of him as the novelistic heir of Flaubert, in particular, and shortly renounced his claim to be the new Ibsen or Yeats in order to vie with Lewis for supremacy in the new prose Modernism; while Eliot relinquished his philosophical ambitions and, despite his reservations about Pound's early poetry,[122] collaborated with him to reject 'Amygism' and paired with him to create both new poetic forms and a new critical attitude.[123]

Pound, then, was not only a critic of outstanding brilliance, he was, almost certainly, the most inspired group-leader in English literary history. Coleridge, in the early nineteenth century, had employed instinctive relational dynamics to make Wordsworth birth the 'philosophical' poem he wanted, himself, to write (*The Prelude*). Pound, in the early twentieth century, employed equally instinctual influence to goad into life, most spectacularly, *Tarr*, *Ulysses* and *The Waste Land*. And his own *Cantos*, in important ways, would gain from precisely this diverse and vicarious progeny (see below, pp. 104–11, 138–45 and 178–85). His authority, within the group, depended not only on his gift of encouragement but also on his ability to act successfully as literary entrepreneur. He got Joyce's prose into continuous print when Joyce's own efforts had failed, engineered the first publication of Eliot's 'Prufrock' poems, and acted as Lewis's agent when Lewis terminated *BLAST* and went off to the war. Part of Pound's tactics was to conduct a war of his own – unlike the Great War, one of aggressive advance and consolidation rather than slogging attrition and defence. And while many of the established writers were being marshalled by C. F. G. Masterman and geared into the Allies' war propaganda machine,[124] Pound organised the new male artists (and associated them with feminist writing)[125] as a kind of internationalist counterculture, to whom the War would increasingly appear as an abomination. In group terms, Pound established his leadership as enthusiastic literary agent, editor and inspirer. However, he also led the group (especially when Lewis went to the Front in 1916) in terms of Fight/Flight assumptions,[126] with aggressive assaults on the establishment as his most usual tactic. Thus his sponsorship of the disparate talents of Joyce, Lewis and Eliot was part of a strategy to attack the old culture in terms of the new – which, in itself, gave further identity to the group as a distinctive comradeship of original talent. While *BLAST* had announced the 'end of the Christian era',[127] it was Pound who operated in London, during the war, to try and establish a new culture as the old one steadfastly blew itself to bits. Pound's literary *élan vital* was as geared to advance as that of the French cavalry in 1914; yet he did not have heavy artillery and machine guns to contend with, but an Edwardian literary liberalism which no longer believed in its own role. Assault is of the essence of Pound's critical leadership, and his sponsorship of new writing is characteristically accompanied by denunciations of the establishment:

> The lovers of good writing have 'struck'; have sufficiently banded themselves together to get a few good books into print, and even into circulation. . . . Eliot's *Prufrock*, Joyce's *A Portrait*, and Wyndham Lewis' *Tarr* . . . so there are new rods in pickle for the old fat-stomached contingent and for the cardboard generation.[128]

> In both Joyce and Lewis we have the insistent utterance of men who are once for all through with the particular inanities of Shavian-Bennett, and with the particular oleosities of the Wellsian genre.[129]

> The few poems which Mr. Eliot has given us maintain . . . proportion. . . . After much contemporary work that is merely factitious . . . impotently unfinished and incomplete. . . . It is quite safe to compare Mr. Eliot's work with anything written in French, English or American since the death of Jules Laforgue.[130]

However, the group's dependency on Pound's leadership was founded on a more urgent assumption. Pound's Fight/Flight tactics (partly learnt from Lewis) were essentially protective of, and nurturative for, the group's most profound belief, at both conscious and unconscious levels: that by developing their individual talents within a collective mental project they were birthing a new art for a new age. The whole emotional bonding, conscious endeavour and developing pairings and rivalries within the group were governed by a core Messianic expectation – later to be alluded to, by at least three of them, in terms of the Magi and Epiphany.[131] They were all heirs of Hulme's Annunciation: as in Lewis's evocation of 'POSTERITY', in *Enemy*, Joyce's 'Welcome, O Life!', Eliot's 'the new (the really new) work', Pound's 'MAKE IT NEW'. As we have seen, the whole technological, intellectual and artistic thrust of the early twentieth century was progressive, even millenarian: despite some apocalyptic overtones, the major geopolitical thrust was essentially futuristic. In English literature there had been precursors, new theorisations such as Hulme's, and the early attempt of Lewis and Pound to 'blast' a way through to the future. But during the war years (which fulfilled the prophecies of Apocalypse) the major achievements of Modernism were yet to come, and it was Pound's key role as group leader to hold the group to their major procreative function, despite the worldwide alarums and excursions. He did this by insisting that new writing mattered, and overinsisting that its truth could help change the world. Yet his major function was to hold to his role as approving mentor as the group, itself, strained to bring forth verbal renewal. The progressive was good, the familiar was bad; it was initially Lewis's message but Pound was its group custodian and executor, and its first truly momentous fulfilment would come as the group's futuristic dynamic drew out the potential in its (hitherto) least progressive member. Joyce's *Ulysses* (1917–22) was the first fully-formed child to be born from the interactions of The Men of 1914. But before that advent there arose some complex group-interactions, monitored by Pound but largely begun by Lewisian dynamics. The next chapter will trace this development as the first texts of 'post-Prufrockian' Modernism emerge.

3

The First Heave

A PORTRAIT OF THE ARTIST

Joyce had completed most of the rewriting of his *Stephen Hero*[1] material by the time he began corresponding with Pound. The completed *Portrait of the Artist as a Young Man*[2] ends boldly: 'Dublin, 1904; Trieste, 1914'; however Richard Ellmann has suggested that such symmetry is a construction after the fact.[3] The final chapters of the book were not sent to Pound, to be placed in the *Egoist*, until the summer of 1915 and it is likely that they were, at the least, not finalised until that year. Nevertheless the bulk of this aesthetically-cadenced autobiographical work precedes any question of group influence and must be considered, like *Dubliners*, as the record of Joyce's largely isolated struggle to escape from the late nineteenth century discourse in which his writing was founded. Much has been made of the striking 'child-speech' style of the first page[4] and of the way the overall style develops in discrete stages, representing the disparate discursive influences on the hero as he grows up. However, it has to be said that except for the first page and short last diary-chapter, Joyce's 'shape and ring of sentences', throughout, differ little from Victorian models, and the most celebrated epiphany in the book is distinctly aestheticist in both quasi-religious symbolism and periodic rhythm:

> A girl stood before him in midstream, alone and still, gazing out to sea. She seemed like one whom magic had changed into the likeness of a strange and beautiful seabird. . . . Her bosom was as a bird's, soft and slight, slight and soft as the breast of some dark-plumaged dove. But her long fair hair was girlish: and girlish and touched with the wonder of mortal beauty, her face.
>
> (p. 171)

First offered to the *Egoist* readership months after the eruption of Lewis's Vorticist stylistics in *BLAST* (see below pp. 60–7), Joyce's *tour de force* must have appeared distinctly neo-Paterian and *passé*.

It had been a long struggle for Joyce, in the face of the world's indifference, to transform the rather plodding realism of the *Stephen Hero* manuscript into something to which he would want to sign his name. The origins of the novel had been in an even earlier piece of writing ('A Portrait of the Artist') offered to the journal *Dana* in 1904.[5] Ellmann's description of this – as a combination of essay and story – makes it sound quite like Lewis's early Breton pieces. However *Dana* rejected it and 'Joyce took this reaction as a challenge to make the fictional history of his own life the call to arms of a new age'.[6] It took him eleven years to complete, working as he was on the *Dubliners* stories too. Based on key events in his own life, *Portrait* embodies Joyce's own idea of writing as a form of giving birth. 'In the virgin womb of the imagination the word is made flesh'.[7] At the same time, as Ellmann demonstrates, the whole narrative represents 'the gestation of a soul', beginning with 'amniotic tides' of imagery and developing towards the free flight of the artistic imagination.[8] The hero's 'Welcome, O life!' looks forward to the midwife's exclamation in *Ulysses*: 'Hoopsa boyaboy'. Stephen is, in effect, 'born into' modernity only at the end of the book and his final commitment is to transform the social *status quo* by his own act of aesthetic birthing: 'to forge in the smithy of my soul the uncreated conscience of my race'. The book ends, then, as Joyce's challenge to the world in an essentially futuristic spirit, and the up-beat note of final assertion (so different to the tone of 'The Dead') may well have drawn inspiration from the new contact with Pound and a sense of the spirit of *BLAST*. Certainly the diary-shorthand of the last section is more experimentalist than anything else in the book except the first page. Pound admired the ending most of all, pronouncing it 'splendid' and liable to provoke 'insane hyperboles'.[9] Thus Joyce's autobiography became authenticated by the new group-leader as the stuff of 'the new'.

When Pound reviewed the publication of *Portrait*, in its book-form, he praised its 'swift alternation of subjective beauty and external shabbiness', but he also remarked that 'there is little to be said in praise of [*Dubliners*] which would not apply with greater force to *A Portrait*'.[10] In terms of the futuristic orientation of the work-group, this is a somewhat backhanded compliment. Pound believed in Joyce's talent and would praise him loyally in public, but it was not until the completion of *Ulysses* that he hailed Joyce as specifically Modernist master of the word. And although there are proto-Modernist features in *Portrait*, the greater part of the

writing is more traditionalist than Pound's imagism, Eliot's collage
symbolism or Lewis's prose Vorticism. Only at the end does the
writing, like the hero, escape from the varied discourses of Victorian
Dublin. It is these discourses which the book is centred on and
that it largely replicates. *Portrait* is original in that it breaks up the
normal *Bildungsroman* narrative progression into a series of bold,
almost autonomous key experiences,[11] yet each section is quite
conventional in its narrative exposition and development, mounting typically to some form of climax which provides an 'epiphany'
of liberation (for example the cheers following Stephen's protest
to the rector or the figure of the girl on the strand). Overall, the
novel can be read (and has been read) as a contribution to
the normal *Künstleroman* tradition, with a few unusual stylistic
variations. Although something of a *tour de force* of 'Symbolist'
realism, the novel is arguably no more Modernist than Lawrence's
Sons and Lovers. If Joyce had died in 1916, it is doubtful whether
he would be regarded as part of the Modernist movement at all –
except in terms of Pound's sponsorship. Conrad's earlier *Lord Jim*
(1900) and *Nostromo* (1904) are far more Modernist in technique
than *Portrait*.

This is not to deny the book's fine qualities nor its important
transitional role in Joyce's development. Yet some of its most
memorable parts – the Christmas dinner scene or the hellfire
sermon, for instance – exploit an essentially Victorian discourse to
achieve their success. It is as if Joyce is compelled to recirculate
the discursive tropes he grew up with, using them to represent
the very process of his development out of them, before he can be
free to write as he wishes. Joyce's mature style will be precisely
polyphonic rather than monovocal – and the exploitation of
polyphony begins here as a 'sloughing-off' of styles. The 'anxiety
of influence' remains – Dickens here, Pater and Newman there –
but the movement of the book is to appropriate the influence to
his own ends and leave it behind. By the last section, with its diary
extracts, that process will be complete: 'soul free and fancy free'.
Nevertheless most of the book is dominated by that struggle.

As in *Dubliners*, much of Joyce's power in *Portrait* lies in incisive
realism – and it was this, of course, which led Pound to evoke the
names of Stendhal and Flaubert. Joyce can use langauge in such
a way that it causes the reader to experience almost physical
sensation:

When you wet the bed first it is warm then it gets cold. His mother put on the oilsheet. That had the queer smell.   (p. 7)

A hot burning stinging tingling blow like the loud crack of a broken stick made his trembling hand crumple together like a leaf in the fire: and at the sound and the pain scalding tears were driven into his eyes.   (pp. 50–1)

He drained his third cup of watery tea to the dregs and set to chewing the crusts of fried bread that were scattered near him, staring into the dark pool of the jar. The yellow dripping had been scooped out like a boghole and the pool under it brought back to his memory the dark turf-coloured water of the bath. . . .
(p. 173)

This is a technique which Joyce will combine brilliantly with stream-of-consciousness stylistics in *Ulysses* (as when Bloom gives milk to the cat in 'Calypso') to create a spectacularly Modernist mode of discourse. In *Portrait* such realism is frequently presented (as above) as a canny refinement of classic nineteenth-century practice.

However, Joyce's autobiographical intent ensures that mental constructions as well as sensory perceptions are represented in the book:

He leaned his elbows on the table and shut and opened the flaps of his ears. Then he heard the noise of the refectory every time he opened the flaps of his ears. It made a roar like a train at night. And when he closed the flaps the roar was shut off like a train going into a tunnel. That night at Dalkey the train had roared like that and then, when it went into the tunnel, the roar stopped.   (p. 13)

He wanted to meet in the real world the unsubstantial image which his soul so constantly beheld. He did not know where to seek it or how, but a premonition which led him on told him that this image would, without any overt act of his, encounter him. . . . He would fade into something impalpable under her eyes and then in a moment he would be transfigured.   (p. 65)

If largely constricted by conventions he will later abandon, Joyce's interest in interior associations and fantasies is already apparent here and points forward to the psychoanalytic content of *Ulysses*. However, the restrictive conventions remain. It would take a heightened zeal for experimentation, fostered within Pound's work-group, and the assimilation of a variety of new influences before Joyce could find full expressionistic range for his fascination with the dynamics of the mind.

The symbolism in *Portrait* is also largely trammelled by Victorian discursive conventions. In a curious way, the narrative presuppositions of the *Bildungsroman*, however adapted in the novel, operate to wrench the symbolic passages back into a rhetorical coherence which Joyce had broken with in the earlier, discrete 'epiphanies'. In attempting to write a publishable novel, Joyce becomes, as it were, the revisionist of his own earlier radicalism. At the same time, the urge toward acceptable, connective rhetoric helps steer him back to the well-established rhythms of Aestheticist prose. The sea-girl epiphany has already been cited; but the tendency is inherent in many places. In the following, for instance, the symbolisation of freedom (flight) is undercut by rhythms which reinforce the restrictions the young 'artist' wishes to escape:

> He watched their flight; bird after bird: a dark flash, a swerve, a flutter of wings. He tried to count them before all their darting quivering bodies passed: six, ten, eleven: and wondered were they odd or even in number. . . . They were flying high and low but ever round and round in straight and curving lines and ever flying from left to right, circling about a temple of air.   (p. 224)

It may be simplistic and unfair to compare such cadenced and repetitive rhetoric to the *ostinato*, percussive imagery in Lewis's *Enemy of the Stars* (see below pp. 60ff.), yet the difference between such traditionalist and futuristic writing is striking, and just so do we distinguish, for instance, Stravinsky's *Rite of Spring* from Elgar's *Enigma Variations*. The Men of 1914 would work to create a radically new literature – not produce beautifully-finished Aestheticist set-pieces. Again, the rhetorical orchestration of 'epiphany' in *Portrait* looks backwards rather than forward, for all that its ostensible subject matter concerns the freedom to create anew.

Nevertheless, Joyce's overall self-liberational project remains important as a starting-point for prose Modernism. For the thematic intent is to assert the transformation of both self and society through writing. And the variable prose used throughout the book as a whole indicates Joyce's chosen way of attaining this – through a fluxive, polyphonic style which will eventually, in *Ulysses*, marginalise Lewis's powerful, but monovocal attempts to forge the style of the future. Joyce's ending is crucial here. For the diary extracts represent the moment when author and character merge and are subsumed into a single, interiorised notation which refuses the discourses of others and is self-chosen and self-revelatory. In addition, the extracts represent jottings clearly taken with the intent of storing material for future fiction – so that the 'artist' is shown already at work in his new medium of prose. The language used is no longer borrowed: it purports to express the tone and terms in which Stephen/Joyce habitually thinks *himself*;

> *March 20.* Long talk with Cranly on the subject of my revolt.
> He had his grand manner on. I supple and suave.   (p. 248)

At the same time, just because these are jottings, the style and manner of the writing can vary, fluxively, according to the subject of interest. Thus we have not a monovocal style but stylistic variation:

> In company with Lynch followed a sizeable hospital nurse.
> Lynch's idea. Dislike it.   (p. 248)

> A troubled night of dreams. Want to get them off my chest.
>   (p. 249)

> . . . the images of fabulous kings, set in stone. Their hands are folded upon their knees in token of weariness and their eyes are darkened for the errors of men go up before them for ever as dark vapours.   (p. 250)

> Eyes of girls among the leaves. Girls demure and romping. All fair or auburn . . .   (p. 251)

> Old man sat, listened, smoked, spat.   (p. 252)

> Amen. So be it. . . . I go to encounter for the millionth time the reality of experience. . . .   (p. 253)

It is, then, in the last few pages of *Portrait* that Joyce most particularly asserts his contribution to the new art for a new world. The novel ends with a promise of recreation *ab initio*, and the radical discursive innovations which will be entailed in this project are already demonstrated in terms of the diary jottings. Joyce has finally liberated his writing from the stylistic influence of the nineteenth-century masters and implicitly suggests that the prose of the new century will be informal, collagistic and polyvocal. So the diary extracts point the way forward to the varieties of discursive experimentation in *Ulysses* which will themselves inspire the discursive Babel that is *The Waste Land* and the 'shelved (shored)' voices of the past in the *Cantos* – as well as the fluxive 'woman-tone' of Woolf. Pound was unerring in sensing the importance of the ending of *Portrait*, for it bears within itself the seeds of mainstream Modernism as we now know it. Yet before it was published a different move was being made in the struggle to bury conventional style and begin afresh. The writer who made the move was Lewis, and his way forward was not the way of polyphony but the forging, in his own 'smithy', of a monovocal, Vorticist prose so violently energised that it would sound like the the *macho* voice of twentieth-century society itself.

ENEMY OF THE STARS

There are no absolute origins; the new always manifests itself as a remix from among available genetic lines. Making new is always implicated in remaking. Yet without the urge toward radical origination there would be, perhaps, no creative renewal. *Enemy of the Stars*[12] evidences the passion for sheer, reckless novelty more than any other early Modernist text. In it, Lewis's quarrelsome part-involvement in Marinetti's Futurism[13] springs a textual sport as seminal as it is bizarre. It has, so far, been given little place in official chronicles of the development of literary Modernism – perhaps because of its debatable worth as 'literature' in its own right. However, its importance lies not in some autonomous value but in its fertilising power. Far and away the most striking contribution to *BLAST* 1, its effect on the 1914 group, was I suggest, incalculable, inaugurating both a climate of experimentalism and a mode of scenario which would help energise the first draft of three Cantos, and the second half of *Ulysses*, through *The Waste Land* and *Finnegans Wake* into the major works of Samuel Beckett. There is, arguably, a sense in which all high Modernist texts speak back to the outrageous venture of Lewis's Vorticist 'play'. Violent, lurid, Expressionistic, bombastic yet incisive, it asserts a rapacious masculinist 'yawp' as birth-cry of the new. Against it, beyond the occasional imitation, the rest of the group were to respond in contrapuntally 'feminine' tones, of one modulation or another – whether *vers libre*, stream-of-consciousness, *Wake*speak or whatever. Despite some masculinist countergestures ('Hoopsa boyaboy'), the acknowledged Modernist progeny will be 'feminine': 'Anadyomene'; 'Weialala leia'; 'and yes I said yes I will Yes'.

The setting of *Enemy* itself suggests a birth-site: 'THE RED WALLS OF THE UNIVERSE'; 'FECUNDED BY MAD BLASTS OF SUNLIGHT'; 'PACKED WITH POSTERITY' (pp. 95–8). Yet the scene is also pornographic under a ruthless, if fantasising, male gaze: 'AUDIENCE LOOKS DOWN INTO SCENE, AS THOUGH IT WERE A HUT ROLLED HALF ON ITS BACK, DOOR UPWARDS, CHARACTERS GIDDILY MOUNTING IN ITS OPENING' (p. 97). And the future that is born here (most prescient in a year pregnant with the Great War) is a male twinning whose antagonisms result in a desperate double-death. The initial action looks forward through Orwell's *Nineteen Eighty-Four* vision[14] to anticipate the world of random violence in *Waiting for Godot* and *Molloy*: 'A boot battered his right hand ribs. . . . The second attack, pain left by first shadow, lashing him, was worse. He lost consciousness' (p. 99). Such nightmare preparation inaugurates the main action between Lewis's duo, Arghol and Hanp – a coupling which sets a precedent for other Modernist double-acts: Stephen and Bloom, 'E.P.' and Mauberley, the bisexual Tiresias, Estragon and Vladimir. There is gender ambivalence here (cf. Bloom as well as Tiresias): 'HE BULGES ALL OVER . . . TYPE OF FEMININE BEAUTY CALLED "MANNISH"' (p. 96). But the focus is ultimately on masculine antagonism – both intellectual and physical – leading up to the finale: 'the hand rushed in, and the knife sliced heavily the impious meat'; 'He sprang from the bridge . . . and sank like lead' (pp. 118–19). Destructive endings were to become the hallmark of that doomed era – engraved in spent bones throughout No Man's Land. The Great War – in which Lewis adapted his 'Blasting' as a gunner – led Freud to rewrite his diagram of the mind into a duel between Love and Death[15] and spawned, in literature, a set of destructive endings: the Zeppelin-bombing at the close of Shaw's *Heartbreak House*; Gerald's emblematic icy death in *Women in Love* (a touch of Scott and Oates there); the negative vision in the last section of *The Waste Land* – 'falling towers',

'maternal lamentation' and a Russellean nightmare[16] distantiated
as nursey-rhyme: 'London Bridge is falling down'. If the new art
is Modernism's dream-child, its birth-cry tells of a world where
healthy issue has become impossible.

Such interpretation of Zeitgeist-as-Death-Instinct is diffused
throughout *Enemy* with all the force of a prophecy. Here Pound's
dubious scientific metaphors of the artist as 'litmus paper', 'ther-
mometer' and 'seismograph' achieve an uncanny relevance. In 1914,
Lewis was both more artistically daring than the rest of the group
and more in touch with underlying European antagonisms. In
Enemy, his violent outpourings manifest a sombre awareness which
his prankish editorial Blastings and Blessings serve to obscure.
Before 'D. H. Lawrence's Nightmare' or Shaw's 'Journey to
Heartbreak',[17] before trench-poetry, Pound's disgust and requiem
in 'Mauberley' or Eliot's despair in *The Waste Land*, Lewis's Vorticist
prose speaks a civilisation in death-oriented crisis: 'POSTERITY IS
SILENT, LIKE THE DEAD, AND MORE PATHETIC' (p. 95);
'Europe grows arctic' (p. 96); 'like blood from a butcher's pail'
(p. 98); 'sullen violent thoughts' (p. 100); 'a rapid despair . . .
galloping blackness of mood' (p. 118); 'Preparation for Death'
(p. 116); and, as last words, 'his heart a sagging weight of stagnant
hatred' (p. 119). If, as Lawrence wrote, it was in 1915 that the
'heart' of London broke, Lewis embodied in *Enemy* the terminal
stresses which led to that dire event. Though informed by a hectic
Nietzschean 'gaiety', *Enemy of the Stars* is a dark and portentous
document whose 'wheelwright's yard' scenario is a protowaste-
land, without hope of a Godot. As punishment for being so
viciously prescient, Lewis's piece has been virtually ignored by
literary history. But if it appears still as some grotesque corpse
planted in a still-Edwardian guardian, its 'sprouting' may be a
matter of its galvanising effect on the rest of the group.

The extraordinary style of *Enemy* is its chief achievement. As
drama, it is unplayable in its own terms: and it is perhaps the only
'play' whose described settings are the most arresting feature. If
the occasional metamorphoses anticipate Surrealism, the violent
conflict – however striking – is a species of melodrama. It is Lewis's
wild, lurid, Vorticist descriptions that constitute the challenge to
'POSTERITY'. No one had ever used English like this before:

The Earth has burst, a granite flower, and disclosed the scene.
A wheelwright's yard.

Full of dry, white volcanic light.
Full of emblems of one trade: stacks of pine, iron, wheels stranded.
Rough Eden of one soul, to whom another man, and not Eve, would be mated.
A canal at one side, the night pouring into it like blood from a butcher's pail.
Rouge mask in aluminium mirror, sunset's grimace through the night.
A leaden gob, slipped at zenith, first drop of violent night, spreads cataclysmically in harsh water of evening. Caustic Reckitt's stain.
Three trees, above canal, sentimental, black and conventional in number, drive leaf flocks, with jeering cry.   (p. 98)

Or again:

The great beer-coloured sky, at the fuss, leapt in fête of green gaiety.
Its immense lines bent like whalebones and sprang back with slight deaf thunder.
The sky, two clouds, their two furious shadows, fought.
The bleak misty hospital of the horizon grew pale with fluid of anger.
The trees were wiped out in a blow.
The hut became a new boat inebriated with electric milky human passion, poured in.   (p. 110)

These are founding, phrasal brush-strokes of a writer whom Eliot would later name 'the greatest prose-master of style of my generation' and 'perhaps the only one to have invented a new style'.[18] There was generosity in this late tribute to an ageing and ailing friend, but perhaps, too, an awareness of how Lewis's stylistic strength had forced even the author of *Ulysses* into comparatively reactive (and often parodic) strategies. For all his neglect, Lewis's prose has attained discerning admirers. Hugh Kenner has noted how 'ten words, when he put them together, bore his signature';[19] both Pound and Rebecca West once likened him to Dostoevsky; and Fredric Jameson (whose subtle book on Lewis unaccountably ignores *Enemy* entirely) finds in *Tarr* what was present already in the 1914 play: 'the sentence reinvented with all the force of origins, as sculptural gesture and fiat in the void'.[20] Lewis was 'the arch-Vorticist . . . unmistakably'[21] and the only one to find a literary equivalent to the tensile energy in Gaudier's 'Marble Cat', David Bomberg's 'In the Hold', Epstein's 'Rock-Drill' or his own 'Alcibiades' for the aborted *Timon* series. The style is more radically metaphoric than any contemporary poetry; more aggressively incisive than any contemporary prose. It subordinates grammar and syntax to expressive power; it renders atmosphere in terms of ruthless image, inculcates setting as elaborated idea; it uses an *ostinato* rhythm to break down expectation in jarring vibrations. 'Trace' here is a turbulent wake caused by the passage of violent intellectual and imaginative energy, conjoining the disparate obsessions of a Blake, a Webster, and a Swift. Ruthless antagonism is expressed here as impassioned 'splitting' – Arghol and Hanp, the warring poles of Lewis's own mind.

It was this very verbal energy that galvanised the efforts of the group, and enforced Lewis's influence. Yet influence consists in far more than imitation or the seed of development.[22] It manifests itself as anxiety and effects both defensive refusals and creative appropriations. If *Enemy of the Stars* was the chief proto-Modernist bid of 1914, one of its main effects, I suggest, was to initiate a rivalry in experimental daring which helped propel Joyce toward *Ulysses*, Eliot toward *The Waste Lane* and Pound (through the ambiguities of 'Hugh Selwyn Mauberley', see below pp. 78–80) toward *The Cantos*. And that rivalry shows, in the body of key texts, the bruise-marks of wrestling with Lewis's pre-emptive strike to sire the new art. Pound's attempts to assimilate, and utilise, Lewis's verbal gestures still show in the finalised *Cantos*: 'Palace in smoky light, / Troy but a heap of smouldering boundary stones' (IV); 'Great bulk, huge mass, thesaurus' (V); 'the stench of wet coal, politicians / . . . Standing bare bum, / Faces smeared on their rumps, / wide eye on flat buttock' (XIV).[23] Pound tries for *Enemy's* image-montage and rhythm, yet wholly fails to match the Expressionistic power ('Throats iron eternities, drinking heavy radiance, limbs towers of blatant light' (*Enemy*, p. 100). Pound's earlier attempts to Blast along with Lewis were similarly unimpressive ('Let us deride the smugness of "The Times"; – GUFFAW!'[24]). The long-term lesson for Pound would be that he was never made for macho assertiveness: his finest vein is a compound of lyricism and elegy. He could have learnt that from the confrontation with Lewis's style; to an extent he did, and it liberated his Sapphic voice and the tone of a modern Moschus: that he did not wholly is, maybe, one of the tragedies of *The Cantos* and of his life.

By contrast, Joyce – connoisseur of the struggle with influence – appropriated what he wanted of *Enemy* and the later *Tarr*, and developed a stylistic fluidity destined for ultimate greatness by negotiating with Lewis's formidable 'floating rocks' rather than encountering them head-on. If 'Proteus' in *Ulysses* is reminiscent of *Enemy*'s metamorphoses and self-preoccupied imaginative intellectuality, it is in 'Circe' that Joyce introjects Lewis's descriptive brilliance to his own comic ends: *'Round Rabaiotti's halted ice gondola stunted men and women squabble. They grab wafers between which are wedged lumps of coral and copper snow. Sucking, they scatter slowly, children.'*[25] (p. 350). *'A sinister figure leans on plaited legs against O'Beirne's wall, a visage unknown, injected with dark mercury'* (p. 356); *'With hanging head he marches doggedly forward. The navvy, lurching by, gores him with his flaming pronghorn'* (p. 365). Lewis later felt that Joyce had plagiarised *Enemy of the Stars* in *Ulysses*. It is certainly difficult to believe that the grotesque settings, weird metamorphoses and noe-Vorticist stylistics of 'Circe' are not a quite direct response to Lewis's 'play'. But 'plagiarism' is wide of the mark. Joyce here appropriates Lewis, as Lewis had appropriated Cubism and Marinetti. 'Circe' outbids *Enemy*'s experimentality and transforms its Expressionist melodramatics into psycho-drama burlesque. The 'sinister figure' in the second *Ulysses* quotation, above, is characterised as the early 'Spanish'-Bohemian Lewis: *'under a wideleaved sombrero the figure regards him with evil eye'*.[26] In that chapter, as in *Enemy*, a fight occurs at the end: but it is not lethal, and it is surely a Joycean joke that the same mild-mannered hero who rescues the victim should have saluted the earlier Lewis-figure as 'Señorita Blanca'. Joyce understood the evasive, but tellingly insulting, counter-power of the underdog, as Lewis – seeing mainly the Masculinist overreacher in Nietzsche – did not.[27]

Eliot – 'the Possum' to Pound – was also adept at accommodating others' imaginative energy. His well-known rationalisation of this was to construct, in 'pontifical' prose, a model of the poet's mind as 'catalytic chamber'[28] ('from which, and through which, and into which' one is tempted to interpellate, 'ideas are constantly rushing', as Pound had earlier apostrophised Vortex[29]). He later wrote: 'immature poets imitate, mature poets steal'. Which is still not quite what the subtle Possum did – for he too appropriated, and so well that no one seems to have noticed; perhaps because

appropriation is always a negation of the unneeded, an amplifi-
cation of the desired. Thus: 'coughing like a goat' (*Enemy*, p. 100) –
'The goat coughs at night' ('Gerontion'); 'heavy black odour . . .
deep female strain' (*Enemy*, p. 101) – 'the good old hearty female
stench' (*He Do the Police . . .*[30]); 'VERY WELL ACTED BY YOU
AND ME' (*Enemy*, p. 95) – 'You! hypocrite lecteur!' (*The Waste
Land*, l. 76[31]); 'furious mass of images' (*Enemy*, p. 103) – 'A heap of
broken images' (*The Waste Land*, l. 22); 'crosses yard to the banks
of the canal: sits down' (*Enemy*, p. 99) – 'While I was fishing in the
dull canal' (*The Waste Land*, l. 189); 'a pool of bleak brown shadow,
disturbed once by a rat's plunging head' (*Enemy*, p. 102) – 'A rat
crept slowly through the vegetation / Dragging its slimy belly on
the bank' (*The Waste Land*, ll. 187–8); 'Three trees . . . bleak and
conventional' (*Enemy*, p. 98) – 'And three trees on the low sky'.[32]
None of this can be wholly conclusive – but the overall sense of
an influence is compelling. In *The Waste Land*, alone (that most
exposed of Eliot's productions) key features of *Enemy* – canal, rat,
swamp, bedsitter, cityscape – are adapted to powerful effect. Eliot
wrestled with *Enemy* better than Pound to create his own major
poem, yet he did not, like Joyce, mock Lewis with exhaustive
parody. He transformed the literary energy to contribute to his
own modern-European ingathering. It is noticeable, however – if
only as a demarcation between rivals of genius – that what
in Lewis is imbued with thrust and bombastic intent becomes
transformed in Eliot as a species of paralysis and desiccation.

Enemy of the Stars, then, was the chief imaginative gamble of
early Modernism and constituted, above all, a stylistic *tour-de-force*
which stirred the mutual *politesse* of the Men of 1914 into a genuine
vortex of group-rivalry. Its impact will spark apparent betrayals as
well as tributes and – much later – fuel an elegiac affection in Eliot
and Pound for the man who, in *BLAST*, started the group off,
without knowing that he was doing it, and who sketched or
definitively painted all of them, utilising his other technical brilliance. It remains a gap in the official account of the origins of
modern literature, as Lewis remains the unacknowledged harsh
horizon-line against which Joyce, Pound and Eliot defined themselves, and so found their authentic careers. As his biographer,
Jeffrey Meyers has written: 'it seems just and proper to include
him in the literary mainstream with Joyce, Pound and Eliot'.[33] And
Enemy is, with *Tarr*, the chief text to justify that inclusion – not
just as seminal influence but in its own right as major Modernist

declaration. However, it seems likely that such acknowledgement must wait not only upon a more open critical opinion but also upon a greater general awareness that 'Literature' is not just a matter of unique personalities – but that unique personalities themselves tend to be fostered and defined, if not constructed, within endeavour groups. The 'Lewis' that Percy Wyndham became was fostered by more than one of these, from the Slade onwards. With *BLAST* (as brilliant editor) he also provided a 'container'[34] and vehicle for many others. He yielded to Pound's 'boy-scouting', perhaps to preserve his own self-image as 'mystic'[35] and fathering founder of the new. But the War intervened, and he 'went to it' and eventually painted some striking pictures of it. In the meantime, *BLAST*, and above all, *Enemy of the Stars* was his firstly really radical contribution to the New Age. Both, I believe, have their formative power in the development of this major group – a group important, partly, because *Enemy*'s formidable potency chased them in the direction of their ultimate literary selves.

TARR

During the war and, indeed, almost until the publication of *Ulysses* and *The Waste Land* (1922), Wyndham Lewis remained master of the Modernist literary game. If the appearance of *Portrait* in the *Egoist*[36] had confirmed Joyce's reputation as promising fiction-writer, it scarcely established him as an apostle of the New, except right at the end (see above pp. 59–60). It was the publication of Lewis's *Tarr*[37] (also in the *Egoist*) which completed the challenge of *BLAST* and asserted, at novel-length, a revolutionary prose to express the modern world. If *Portrait* ends by hailing the new that is yet to come, *Tarr* – from its beginning – asserts the new age in spectacularly dynamic prose:

> . . . the small business . . . had driven out terrified families, had hemmed the apoplectic concierge in her 'loge', it had broken out on to the court at the back in shed-like structures: and in the musty bowels of the house it had established a broiling luridly lighted roaring den, inhabited by a fierce band of slatternly savages. (p. 96)

The raw energy of twentieth-century capitalism is here matched by a demonic style, as energetically celebratory as it is drastically satiric. This is a far cry from Joyce's Paterian cadences: ('But her long fair hair was girlish: and girlish, and touched with the wonder of mortal beauty, her face'). It is the difference between secondhand pre-Raphaelitism and revolutionary Vorticism – where Lewis's dynamism is focused through an objectivising gaze, and projected as ruthless literary grotesquerie. Pound, as group leader, hastened to authenticate its Modernist contribution – 'the most vigorous and volcanic English novel of our time'.[38]

Like *Portrait*, *Tarr* affirms the hero as artist. And for all the ironic undermining of the double, Tarr-Kreisler, life-artistry is the chief human source of energy in a world largely ruled by inchoate mechanistic forces. That this 'artistic' energy is out of control, and implicated in masculinist self-destructiveness, is the profoundest theme in a book which anatomises pre-war European aggression, and was completed as Lewis, himself, was waiting to go to the Front (1915). *Tarr* is centred on the aggressive faculty. It constitutes the apotheosis of Adlerian man, as *Sons and Lovers* is that of Freudian man. Its key dynamic is the recoil and flow of anger – both poles imaged at the farcical Bonnington Club, where Kreisler constructs a fortress of chairs in the conservatory, then issues forth for a manic dance, when his partner is forced to trip and then fall, in dress-torn humiliation. Kreisler is the artist[39] as psychopath – the adult rogue male, at large, in a middle class order driven by machinery out of control. He is a bourgeois nightmare – lazy, rapistic, suicidal, parasitical, murderous, a creature of whim without any self-wisdom. He dominates the book, a German on the rampage, and the Englishman, Tarr, is his henchman and rival – as Lewis is both celebrant and satirist in this disturbingly ambivalent textual creation.

Tarr is a kind of *Enemy* writ large. In both the New is birthed, through astonishing prose, as the rampant male, split at the core, a destroyer fuelled by his own self-destruction. The text tells the truth of its time. The underlying antagonisms in Europe which erupted catastrophically in 1914 are imagined here as the darkest of farces. The duel scene is paradigmatic, resonant with all the irony of a 'civilisation' bent upon war: 'The field was filled with cries, smacks, harsh movements and the shrill voice . . . .. exclaiming "Gentlemen! gentlemen!"' (p. 281). The commenting doctor sums it all up: 'this is a brawl not a duel' – and that is before someone gets killed. Masculinity, here, is the issue – ·and the whole Patriarchal order that had made it and created, in turn, what seemed, at the time, the ultimate conflict. *Tarr* is one of the greatest (certainly the earliest) of World War I fictions. With its Germans, Russians, Slavs, Englishmen and Frenchmen, its 'blood and iron' hero,[40] (cf. Kreisler – Kaiser) its feminine (Big) Bertha, its constant manoeuvres of personal strategy, its rape, blows and gunshot climax, it expresses, in neo-Futurist prose, the reality of the contemporary world. Beside it, Joyce's *Portrait* appears narcissistic and marginal – a beautifully-rendered pose in the 'cracked looking-glass of a servant'. *Tarr* offers a comparatively impersonal, if lurid, vision of metropolitan antagonism, emblematic of that contemporary geopolitical rivalry which culminated in the Great War.

For all the ambiguity of his energised irony, Lewis's anatomisation remains persuasive. The book is fixated on the mechanism of maleness, with almost no appreciative tribute to the spirit of femininity, as in Lawrence's work or that of the later Joyce. *Tarr* is about twentieth-century male sexism, with all its anarchic lust, scorn and ultimate self-contempt: 'women . . . there they were all the time – vast dumping-ground for sorrow and affliction – a world-dimensioned Pawn-shop, in which you could deposit . . . yourself, temporarily, in exchange for the gold of the human heart and any other gold that happened to be knocking about' (p. 100). Hence Kreisler, arch-masculinist, 'approached a love affair as the Korps-student engages in a student's duel' (p. 101). The results of this are conveyed in brutal phrases which anticipate Marilyn French or Marge Piercy on similar scenes:

> With the fury of a person violently awakened to some insult he had flung himself upon her: her tardy panting expostulation, defensive prowess, disappeared in the whirlpool towards which they had both, with a strange deliberateness and yet aimlessness, been steering. (pp. 193–4)

> . . . it was all over, the day was lost, she lay convulsed upon her back, her mouth smeared with blood: in a struggle that had been outrageous and extreme . . . Bertha and he had fought out the simple point, mysteriously fierce, like snarling animals. (p. 191)

Despite the ambivalence, it becomes clear that this is a rape-scene –

and it is the key sexual exchange in the book. *Tarr*, then, predicates masculine rivalry and violence in terms of cultural gendering, where women are to be pursued, conquered and humiliated.

It is a complexly disturbing book to read, because of the aggression it expresses at the heart of masculinity. At the same time it focuses on male attempts to subvert the Patriarchal order by resisting the more positive male roles of husband and father. The Wastrel is at the centre of the novel. Kreisler is the chief exemplification of wastrelism – a man who does no work, rapes or seduces women at random, and refuses to acknowledge or provide for his offspring. The novel caricatures his disruptive role through the device of 'rumour': 'Kreisler had to keep seventeen children in Munich alone . . he had only to look at a woman for her to become pregnant . . . a small society had been founded in Bavaria to care for Kreisler's offspring throughout Germany' (p. 93). Kreisler's wastrelism is complicated (and partly explained) by his relationship with his father. Among the first things we learn about him is that his father had married Kreisler's girlfriend. In the course of the book his father also stops his maintenance cheques at a time when he has no patron to sponge off. Paradoxically, then, Kreisler the wastrel can only survive if his father keeps honouring the patriarchal bond. Since Kreisler adamantly refuses the world of work, the stopping of the cheques amounts to a death-threat. So Kreisler projects the threat onto others around him: 'Behind Ernst and his parent stood Soltyk and his stepmother' (p. 121). He believes Soltyk has damaged his relations with Ernst Vokt, his erstwhile sponsor. And it is Soltyk he challenges to a duel and, in fact, kills. Kreisler's murderous aggressiveness is thus tied in with his wastrelism and his attempt to subvert the patriarchal order to his own ends. In this he is typical. Tarr, too, is a wastrel through most of the book – but he justifies this in terms of his Art. And beyond him come a neo-Conradian retinue of scroungers and loafers – Hobson, Soltyk, Bitzenko et al. Lewis's perspective and tone remain ambiguous – he seems to approve Tarr's devotion to art: but the implications of the tale anatomise realities beyond the author's satiric intent. This is an all-male world in which the aggression of all the main figures is directly related to the patriarchal order and the gender roles it has constructed. Attempts to subvert the order only result in heightened aggression and a caricatural heightening of negative male qualities. The connection to war is implicit. This is the bourgeois order as Lewis sees it, and the events encode the implications of its fearful structure.

Yet marriage remains an option in the book. For Bertha, Tarr's mistress, it seems important largely because of what her circle of friends might think. Tarr is her 'fiancé' and if she loses him she loses face. So she is a puppet in the Patriarchal plot and must play her role, and use her female weapons, as Tarr and Kreisler do their male ones: 'the key to her programme was a cumulative obstinacy' (p. 180). But in trying to use Kreisler against Tarr she gets more than she bargains for; as sexual threat, Kreisler's insistence invades her whole living-space: 'it was *he*, the enemy, getting in: she wished to stop him there, before he came any farther: he was a bandit, a house-breaker, after all a dangerous violent person' (p. 184). Much of the action of the novel is ultimately generated by Tarr's strategy of evading Bertha. In the end, however, he marries her *pro forma*, to legitimise the child Kreisler has sired. To an extent, then, both are recuperated into the Patriarchal order – even though Tarr keeps his affair with Anastasya and Bertha eventually divorces him and remarries. In a rather tacked-on last paragraph, Lewis awards Tarr three children from a certain Rose Fawcett, while hinting at a further affair. Meanwhile Bertha, with her 'eye-doctor' lapses into 'brooding serenity'. Despite these gestures towards a conventional *dénouement*, the main thrust of the book is to attack the institution of marriage as inimicable to personal freedom and fulfilment. It queries marriage from the rogue male point of view, as *Women in Love* tries to[41] from the viewpoint of the new woman.

But the impact of *Tarr* is as much in terms of individual scenes and brilliant phrases as in overall theme and plot. Like *Enemy*, *Tarr* is very much a *tour-de-force* of style. Lewis presents the Modernist New as a compound of Expressionism and Futurism, bringing the eye of a Grosz and the wit of a Swift to inform a prose as energised as Carlyle's. So the novel can be savoured for its 'one-liners' alone:

Lowndes was a colleague, who . . . had just enough money to be a cubist. (p. 39)

. . . he gave a hasty glance at his 'indifference' to see whether it were O.K. (p. 48)

The late spring sunshine flooded, like a bursted tepid star. (p. 75)

It was an eye . . . the gland shot a tear into it.   (p. 119)

. . . pumping at a cigarette, reducing it mathematically to ash.

(p. 163)

. . . sex surged up and martyrized him.   (p. 206)

Such writing expresses both process and behaviour in terms of a consistent and radical vision. It is above all a satiric mode of viewing the world as mechanised energy. In this lay Lewis's chief challenge to the early literary group. His Modernism was to be the creation of vivid friezes, capturing contemporary urban life in all its tension and complexity. In its strong style and radically satiric vision *Tarr*, like *Enemy*, constitutes this challenge and effects a textual sport so striking that it pushes the other three writers in a different direction.

There is thus a slight irony in Lewis's 1928 Preface where he suggests that *Tarr* was 'in a sense the first book of an epoch in England'.[42] For in terms of his immediate peers – most especially the other prose-writer Joyce – Lewis's influence becomes largely a matter of repulsion. Yet in larger terms, there is a central strand in twentieth-century English fiction which uses black humour and radical satire as the most persuasive way to render the modern world. The legacy of *Tarr*, then, may be Douglas, Aldington, Huxley, Waugh, Beckett and the two Amises. Most specifically, *Tarr* suggested to those alert to such things, a way of writing about maleness – and especially the experience of war. This was neither stream-of-consciousness nor Lawrentian empathy but satiric distance and stylistic *grotesquerie*. *Death of A Hero*, *Goodbye to All That* and *Parade's End*, for instance, seem very much in the spirit of *Tarr*. And this is fitting since, as I have suggested, *Tarr* is in a sense a war fiction. For this reason the true ending of the text is not the flip *dénouement* given in the last short paragraph but the duel scene and Kreisler's consequent suicide. For whatever Lewis intended about Tarr as hero, it is Kreisler's manic energy which dominates the text, and like Gerald Crich in *Women in Love*, it is his destiny which symbolises the fate of the modern male. Hence the strange blend of black farce, thwarted energy and sexual suggestion at the climax of the duel scene:

Kreisler walked up to them. He was very white, much quieter

and acting with some effort. He stooped down to take up one of the pistols. The doctor aimed a blow at his head. It caught him just in front of the ear, on the right cheek bone: he staggered sideways, tripped and fell. The moment he felt the blow he pulled the trigger of the Browning, which still pointed towards his principal adversary. Soltyk threw his arms up, Kreisler was struggling upwards to his feet, he fell face forwards on top of him.

Believing this to be a new attack, Otto seized the descending body round the middle, rolling over on top of it. It was quite limp. (p. 283)

This speaks of male gendering and modern European history as nothing even in *Ulysses* will do. *Tarr* is Lewis's verdict on modern man. Its message could be summed up in a later phrase of Pound. 'With a bang, not with a whimper'.[43]

POLYPHILOPROGENITIVE

Towards the 1920s, the verse of both Pound and Eliot manifested a degree of uncertainty and took some surprising directions. Both temporarily gave up the characteristic voices they had established – Eliot's self-reflexive irony, Pound's free-cadenced romantic imagism – and tried out new postures and forms. One particular experiment, the adaptation of Gautier's quatrain form to express radical satiric mockery (Eliot's satires, Pound's quatrains in 'Hugh Selwyn Mauberley') has been famously rationalised by Pound in terms of a minor *Rappel à l'Ordre*.[44] Amy Lowell's well-financed takeover bid for Imagism had resulted in a loosening of principles and the publication of 'sloppy' poems (including her own) – scornfully dubbed 'Amygism' by the indignant (and strategically-bested) Ezra.[45] There is doubtless truth in this version (though both he and Eliot continued to write free verses as well as the neo-Parnassian quatrains which were supposed to return discipline to verse). But this scarcely explains the new note of scathing contempt in much of their work. If the Great War provided a specific motive for disgust, the energy and mode of attack are specifically Lewisian. Between *BLAST* in 1914 and the book publication of *Tarr* in 1918, it was Lewis, above all, who dominated Modernist literary experimentation and, through stylistic brilliance, stamped early

Modernism with his own anarchic negativity. This pre-emptive strike sent waves of influence through the entire group, and if Joyce was able to respond fairly swiftly (see below pp. 89–97), it took Eliot and Pound until the next decade to refind their own poetic directions. The earlier meditative lyricism ('we have lingered in the chambers of the sea'; 'The apparition of these faces in the crowd') has succumbed to Lewis's ferocious Blasting. What temporarily emerges is transformation through literary introjection – a verse collusion with Lewis's grotesquely satiric prose:

> A lustreless protrusive eye
> Stares from the protozoic slime
>   ('Burbank . . .')

> Phallic and ambrosial
> Caliban casts out Ariel
>   ('Hugh Selwyn Mauberley')

Both poets attempt to move forward by submitting their talents, in slightly different ways, to the Lewisian spirit.

However, the quatrian phenomenon also evidences a poetic bonding between the two writers as striking as that between Wordsworth and Coleridge in the *Lyrical Ballads* project. If Eliot initially felt that Pound's own poetry lacked substance,[46] he respected him as critic and mentor from the first and in 1917 he published an approving article on his metric.[47] And if Eliot had demonstrated to Pound the importance of Laforgue's work for modern poetry, it was Pound who convinced Eliot for a while that Gautier also had great importance. Eliot had still not recovered the early inspiration which produced the 'Prufrock' poems. These themselves, as has been noted, had developed out of a creative struggle with Laforgue's manner and tone. After the initial contact with Pound, Eliot sketched some loosely satiric verse to keep his name before the public, the 'Bostonian' poems (of which 'Mr Apollinax' is the deftist and 'Hysteria' the most psychoanalytically interesting), and tried his hand at versifying in French – a tactic by no means as successful as Beckett's comparable move in the 1940s and 1950s.[48] But while Pound was trying out early versions of cantos and translating Propertius into satiric free verse, Eliot began to find a distinctive new direction by combining Lewis's anarchic vision with Pound's hunch about the relevance of Gautier. The result was a group of unusual poems (including 'Mr Eliot's Sunday Morning Service', 'Sweeney Among the Nightingales' and the notorious 'A Cooking Egg'[49]) which critics have typically found it difficult to 'place' within the overall Eliotic canon.

The specific influence of Lewis on Eliot has never, to my knowledge, been demonstrated. Before Eliot arrived in England, he knew enough about *BLAST* 1 to parody its stance in a letter written while he was in Germany. As noted above, Lewis was the first editor to publish Eliot in England and it is likely that Eliot would have first met Lewis with a considerable feeling of awe. After *BLAST* 1 Lewis was known as the most dynamic editor and notorious stylistic innovator in London. And while Eliot also respected Pound, it is likely he would have appreciated, early, the comparative differences in reputation at this time. It was Pound's own sponsor, A. R. Orage of *The New Age*, who found *Enemy of the Stars* an 'extraordinary piece of work' while judging other specifically creative contributions to *BLAST* 1 (including Pound's own) 'disappointing'.[50] Eliot read *Tarr* when it came out in the *Egoist* and, upon its book-publication in 1918 reviewed it very favourably indeed.[51] However, the easiest way of beginning to assess Lewis's influence upon the quatrains is contained in a reference in that review, to an essay Lewis had written and left with Pound when he went to the war. The essay was called 'Inferior Religions' and Pound got it published in the *Little Review* in 1917.[52] Eliot wrote of the essay that it constituted 'the most indubitable evidence of genius, the most powerful piece of imaginative thought, of anything that Mr. Lewis has written'.[53] In his editor's note for the *Little Review* publication Pound, too, called the essay 'the most important single document that Wyndham Lewis has written'.[54] Granted the importance that both Pound and Eliot attributed to the piece – in a eulogistic prose they only employed fully for Joyce after the publication of *Ulysses* – it is remarkable that it has been almost entirely absent from the usual accounts of the development of literary Modernism. I shall give a brief description of it here because it seems to me that it was highly influential on the aesthetic thinking and practice of Eliot and Pound in this era.

'Inferior Religions' was written to accompany Lewis's early stories in a book to be entitled *The Wild Body*,[55] and it seeks to explain the principles of satiric comedy which inform the 'Breton' pieces. The version of satiric puppetry outlined in it owes something to Bergson; yet the scornful standpoint, the ruthless formularisation of behaviour, the religious dimension and the incisive Vorticist articulation are Lewis's own. Its metaphysic is essentially Existentialist, part-based, no doubt, on Lewis's reading of Nietzsche. Authenticity is here articulated as 'energy' and its lack in the figures he satirises renders them hollow men: 'A comic type is a failure of considerable energy, an imitation and standardising of self, suggesting the existence of a uniform humanity – creating, that is, a little host as like as ninepins' (p. 316). So, anticipating Eliot's vision of the crowd on London Bridge, Lewis sees his 'puppets' as 'only shadows of energy' caught up in an 'inferior religion' which constitutes a repetition-obsession with trivia. The whole of modern Existentialism from Heidegger through Sartre is inherent in the vision and embodied in characteristic stories in *The Wild Body* – 'Kodacked [*sic*] by the Imagination'.[56] In a wonderful phrase, Lewis describes satiric laughter as 'the mind sneezing'.[57] But such imaginative 'gaiety' cannot blind us to the bleakness of Lewis's vision and his immense intellectual scorn for those who lack imagination. He sees their lives as 'mechanisms' conforming to a 'logical structure' – foreshadowing the geometrical orbits of Beckett's lowlife clowns. And, oddly, his chief exemplum of such mechanistic bad faith is a certain Moran, whose existence powerfully reminds one of Sartre's later figure of the self-deceived waiter who 'plays' at being a waiter: 'Moran rolls between his tables ten million times in a realistic rhythm. . . . He worships his soup, his damp napkins'.[58] The oddity here, as Bernard Lafourcade has pointed out, is that 'there is no extant text with a character bearing this name'.[59] Actually there is – but it is not by Lewis. Jacques Moran is the second narrator in Beckett's *Molloy*[60] ('He asked for a report he'll get his report,' p. 110): and both in egoic cruelty and robotic comicality he is a fully Lewisian figure.

However, the point here concerns Eliot. As he attempted to find fresh inspiration to write, he made use of Lewis's theory and introjected the spirit of 'Inferior Religions' to energise his experimentation with the quatrain form. The result is spectacular in effect, if not a true way forward for Eliot: for the poems are unlike anything else in his work. As Stephen Spender has noted, they have 'a stiff, rigid, static quality not characteristic of his other poems'.[61] Spender goes on to evoke the painting of Francis Bacon to suggest the quality; but he need only have pointed to Lewis's 'Smiling Woman Ascending a Stair' or the 'Tyro' sketches. For

Lewis is clearly the major influence here and the *grotesquerie* (and unpleasantness) of these poems draws directly on Lewis's vision. In particular, Sweeney represents a perfect 'Kodacking' by the satirical imagination:

> Apeneck Sweeney spreads his knees
> Letting his arms hang down to laugh,
> The zebra stripes along his jaw
> Swelling to maculate giraffe.
> ('Sweeney Among the Nightingales')

In such verses Eliot masters two of the most effective techniques deployed by Lewis. The first is the use of Expressionistic shock-imagery: 'Daffodil bulbs instead of balls / Stared from the sockets of the eyes!'; the second, bizarre contextualisation of ironic abstractions: 'Polyphiloprogenitive / The sapient sutlers of the Lord'.[62] Within the taut constraints of the quatrain form, Eliot proved brilliant at being Lewis in verse (something Lewis, himself, never quite managed).[63] The end-metre of the line is used as boldly and harshly as Lewis's painterly diagonal lines of force: and there is a heightened visual sense in parts: ('Paint me the bold anfractuous rocks'; 'Designed upon a gesso ground').[64] The vivid social snap-shots can be as shocking as anything in Grosz – 'A meagre, blue-nailed, phthisic hand'; 'clawing at the pillow slip'; 'Sweeney shifts from ham to ham / Stirring the water in his bath'.[65] Above all, Lewis's vision of characterisation as mechanical puppetry is given incisive expression: 'A saggy bending of the knees / And elbows, with the palms turned out'; 'Jackknifes upward at the knees'; 'promise of pneumatic bliss'; 'The silent vertebrate in brown / Contracts and concentrates, withdraws'.[66] Lacking the haunting verbal music of the 'Prufrock' poems, these satires snarl and jeer as arrogantly as any of the brazen pronouncements in *BLAST*.

Pound, as we have seen, had for some time employed the Whitmanesque 'yawp' to express his own Lewisian introjections. But another strategy he used to negotiate this influence was that of evasion. The years between 1914 and 1920 are the heyday of Pound the translator, and translation, as Pound's comment makes clear (see above p. 37), is a species of mask. To speak in the voice of someone else is a natural defensive move in a game currently dominated by Wyndham's aggressive, masculinist ego. To translate is, as it were, a 'feminine' role, requiring a degree of self-surrender in terms of empathy and the nurturing of textual life. This is the period of *Cathay* and 'Homage to Sextus Propertius' – a time of recycling energies from the past and tentatively trying out modes which will lead to the 'ragbag'[67] polyphony of the *Cantos*. Pound was already aware that to 'MAKE IT NEW' means to *re*new as well as to originate – a truth Lewis never laboured hard to acknowledge. Eliot proclaimed in 1917 that 'no poet . . . has his complete meaning alone'[68] and Ezra had always had a strong traditionalist streak (which Lewis rather mocked).[69] This would eventually make a major contribution to the allusive depth of the *Cantos*, and it is arguable how far their historical resonance may be due to the fact that Lewis had thoroughly outbid Pound in the futurism stakes. However, in the end, the difference between the two men is less to do with the fact that one was more radical than the other (as Lewis would have it) than that Lewis's genius was aggressive and monovocal, and Pound's lyrical and polyphonous. And that polyphony (which with that of *Ulysses* and *The Waste Land* was to become the hallmark of high literary Modernism) was fruitfully fed by Pound's translations of a great variety of poems, from a highly-impressive range of poetic traditions – Provençal, Latin, Greek, Anglo-Saxon, Chinese and so on. The different cadences would all contribute to the later *Cantos*.

However, Eliot's success in adapting Gautier's technique for English verse tempted Pound to try it for himself and led to the writing of his first major Modernist poem, 'Hugh Selwyn Mauberley'. He proved as adept at the quatrain as Eliot, if to rather different (though still satiric) effect:

> The tea-rose tea-gown, etc.
> Supplants the mousseline of Cos,
> The pianola 'replaces'
> Sappho's barbitos.[70]

But 'Mauberley' is a poem of mixed styles, even though the quatrains tend to dominate the first section, and in important ways, it is, as it were, a 'group' production. As the title indicates, it clearly owes a debt to Eliot's 'J. Alfred Prufrock', and especially in the second section there are lines which remind us of Eliot's earlier stance and style: 'Drifted . . . drifted precipitate, / Asking time to be rid of . . . / Of his bewilderment', or 'Mildness, amid the neo-Nietzschean clatter, / His sense of graduations / Quite out of place'. At the same time, the use of the quatrain is a borrow-back of his own original suggestion, now given an English model in Eliot's own poems. Pound appropriates, for his own purposes, the knowing intellectualism and mocking tone that Eliot had used so well:

> Even the Christian beauty
> Defects – after Samothrace;
> We see τὸ καλὸυ
> Decreed in the market place.
> (p. 99)

And Pound's lines, like Eliot's, also bear the stamp of Lewis's theory and vision: 'an image of its own accelerated grimace'; 'this overblotted / Series / Of intermittences'; 'Beneath half-watt rays, / The eyes turn topaz'. Pound, who had overtly evoked his friend in an early canto-draft,[71] allows the bile of the old Blaster to possess his own verse as he castigates the society that had brought about war:

> We choose a knave or an eunuch
> To rule over us.
> (p. 100)

> For an old bitch gone in the teeth,
> For a botched civilisation.
> (p. 101)

The 'Lewisian' contempt here is stronger and more incisive than in anything Pound had contributed to *BLAST*. The war had taught him to hate, and the Lewisian technique showed him how to 'Kodack' the bourgeois puppet-world. Yet Pound had also been reading substantial amounts of *Ulysses*, as Joyce sent him the developing sections, and the varied Odyssean references in 'Mauberley' acknowledge the Joyce-connection too. E.P.'s 'true Penelope was Flaubert', we are told, and it was precisely Joyce's Flaubertian technique that Pound most admired in the novel.[72] References to 'Circe's hair', Apollo, the raised oar on the beach, even 'Anadyomene' connect the poem up with Joyce's chosen mythological base, while phrases like 'The heavy memories of Horeb, Sinai and the forty years' or 'Irresponse to human aggression' may partly have Joyce's mild-mannered Jewish hero in mind. In 'Hugh Selwyn Mauberley', then, the presences of all the Men of 1914 come together, for the first time, in a completed work of art.

Overall, 'Mauberley' is a strange and rather puzzling production, in which the irony sometimes seems out of the author's control.[73] It is also disturbing to meditate on the apparent self-excoriation involved in the burial of 'E.P.' and Mauberley – both, to an extent, Poundian surrogates. It is as if Pound himself would assent to Lewis's caricature of him as ineffective antiquarian, poeticising lyrically in a world of economic chicanery and political anarchy. However, it is clearly a tough-minded Pound who lambastes contemporary society here, in the process of killing off these inadequate personae. What may be involved is a desire to suppress the gentler parts of himself in order to take up arms against an usurious world, but what the overall poem evidences is a degree of self-fragmentation and self-dispersal. The great elegy for the war dead in IV and the haunting end-lyric to Section I, 'Envoi', coexist with the biting satire of the quatrains, the Jamesian pastiches of Section II and the bizarre metrical Vorticism of the second end-poem, 'Medallion'. These stylistic contrasts, together with the wayward irony, undermine the sense of an overall coherence and cause the sequence rather to fall apart into disparate, discrete sections. Pound may have had Joyce's technique of stylistic sectioning in *Ulysses* in mind, here, but 'Mauberley' lacks Joyce's overall consistency of purpose. However, what the poem evidences before *Ulysses* was completed, is the advent of the principle of polyphony. Different voices may speak within the single work. In one sense, the voices in 'Mauberley' are simply those of the Men of 1914 themselves – Lewis's scorn, Eliot's lilting irony, Joyce's rhetorical pastiche and Pound's lyrical tone all speaking together. In hitting upon such polyvocality Pound, as Joyce, has hit upon the key to the high Modernist future.

VORTEX LONDON

Between 1914 and the early 1920s Pound fostered his new literary group and worked hard at building up a sense of group identity. In this he acted as group leader, literary agent, critical interpreter and (at times) surrogate father. His efforts began in 1914 when the association of the four men commenced. However, at that time Pound was still heavily involved with the general projects of Imagism in literature, and Vorticism in the visual arts, and was associated with many of the new talents. Three main developments helped centre his efforts on Joyce, Lewis and Eliot. The first was the break-up of the Vorticist group of artists as different members went off to war; the second, Pound's disillusionment with Imagism as Amy Lowell's influence took hold; the third, the death of his friend, the sculptor Henri Gaudier-Brzeska, on the Western Front. The last event struck Pound hard, and in describing it to Felix Schelling he defensively resorted to British understatement: 'Gaudier-Brzeska has been killed at Neuville St Vaast. . . . One is rather obsessed with it'.[74] Pound channelled his grief (and disgust) into frenzied activity and within a year he had brought out *Gaudier-Brzeska: A Memoir*. After this, he tended to concentrate his hopes and emotional loyalty on the new literary group.

It was about this time that Wyndham Lewis was himself preparing to go to the front. He left his most recent manuscripts with Pound, thereby effectively making him his literary executor – a role Pound had already performed for Gaudier. The two visual artists seem to become rather linked in Pound's mind at this time. In March 1916 he was writing to John Quinn: 'I have certainly GOT to do a Lewis book to match the Brzeska'.[75] The conscious aim here, as always, was to promote the best of the new art; but perhaps the unconscious motive involved both a sense of guilt towards Gaudier and of anxiety for Lewis as he went to the same area of danger. The latter is surely rationalised in one of his several war-years' letters to Lewis: 'I can not see that the future of the arts demands that you should be covered with military distinctions'.[76] The anxiety recurs in an almost parental protection of Lewis in a letter to Margaret Anderson of the *Little Review*: 'Lewis is not to be counted on, NOW; by the grace of God he may come back in due season'.[77] The same letter brackets Wyndham's work with that of Joyce and Eliot and shows the development of the fourway dynamic of the group in Pound's mind. That dynamic remained when Lewis came back from the war and becomes extrapolated in another Poundian venture on Lewis's behalf: 'I have the idea of trying one [book] on "Four Modern Artists"'.[78] The other three were Brancusi, Picabia and – most particularly – Picasso. The inner workings of Ezra's mind show a strange symmetry: as Lewis substitutes for the lost Gaudier, so Lewis's painting career must be construed within a grouping whose dynamic replicates that of the writing group – a four-way vortex with Lewis specifically paired with a coequal rival: Picasso on canvas as Joyce in fiction. It was, I suggest, particularly between 1916 and 1918 that this group symmetry built up in Pound's mind.

The build-up of that 'groupography'[79] can be evidenced in letters of the time. For instance, Lewis, Joyce and Eliot are commended to Kate Buss in March 1916;[80] a day later, Lewis is preferred to Blake in a letter to John Quinn;[81] and a week later Pound is writing to Harriet Shaw Weaver about Joyce's various troubles.[82] In January 1917 all three are conjoined in a letter to Margaret Anderson (see above p. 50); in April, they are all promoted, along with Yeats's poems, to John Quinn; and the next year the same recipient is sent a kind of situation-report on the group-members:

> Poor Joyce is down again with his eyes. Lewis nearly dying of the attempt to paint something bad enough *in the right way*. Eliot has emitted a few new and diverting verses.[83]

It is clear from such letters that Pound not only gave the group literary help and advice but also strong emotional support in the more practical affairs of their lives. He worried about Lewis at the front, and provided an important link with Lewis's 'normal' environment and career; he sympathised with Joyce's illnesses and organised invaluable financial help when he was stranded in Zurich with his family; and he fostered Eliot's self-esteem and even interceded with his family in America when Eliot married against their wishes.[84] Pound was interested in developing a top-class artistic group, and he succeeded in this; he was also, surely, building up a substitute family in which he could play both mother and father (along with his wife Dorothy), cut off, as he was, from his own American family. There were emotional strains attached to such an enterprise, as well as rewards, and he may well have felt that his own work suffered by his efforts for the group. This probably explains his eventual decision to leave London, then Paris, when he embarked on the *Cantos* in earnest – rather than any of the reasons he gave at the time. He had by then expended quite enough energy and understanding on Lewis's feuds, Eliot's nervous depressions and Joyce's Job-like complainings, and needed to spend more time nurturing his own talent and leading his own life. By that time, however, his essential role of group-leadership had been accomplished and the Men of 1914 were already famous in the postwar literary world.

Pound's literary work-group was essentially a construct of the intellectual imagination. Unlike some other artistic groups, the Men of 1914 did not meet together regularly to discuss and plan their literary efforts. On the contrary, they never met, all together, at all. In psychological terms, I suspect, this may well have strengthened rather than hindered the sense of group identity, since the free play of fantasy was rarely constricted by physical presence. Nevertheless, there were, of course, meetings between different members. As we have noted, Pound and Lewis first met in 1910 and later collaborated closely over *BLAST*. In 1914 or 1915 Lewis went to Ezra's triangular flat in Kensington and was there introduced to 'a sleek, tall, attractive, transatlantic apparition – with a sort of Gioconda smile'.[85] This was Eliot, of course, and the two would remain friends for the rest of their lives, despite Lewis's occasional attempts to quarrel with Tom. Pound was, appropriately, the first of the other three members of the group to meet Joyce. After the war, Joyce had returned to Trieste and when Pound was staying at Lago di Garda in May 1919, he invited Joyce to come and visit. The first attempt failed, but Joyce eventually arrived, despite the possibility of thunderstorms (which he dreaded), bringing his son 'to act as a lightning conductor'.[86] It was here that Pound first mooted the strategic advisability of Joyce going to live in Paris. Both writers would, in time, allude to this first meeting.[87] Later in the same summer Pound continued his travels in France and was met in the south by a rucksacked Eliot. Together, along with Dorothy Pound, they explored troubadour country. Again, both men would refer back to this vacation in later work.[88] However, it was in the next year, after Joyce had moved to Paris, that the best-known meeting in the history of the group occurred. Lewis and Eliot arranged a rendezvous with Joyce, bringing with them the symbolic presence of the group leader, in the form of a now-notorious parcel. Lewis's brilliant anecdotage is worth yet another recirculation:

Eliot now rose to his feet. He approached the table, and with one eyebrow drawn up, and a finger pointing, announced to James Joyce that *this* was that parcel, to which he had referred in his wire, and which had been given into his care, and he formally delivered it, thus acquitting himself of his commission. . . .

At last the strings were cut. A little gingerly Joyce unrolled the slovenly swaddlings of damp British brown paper in which the good-hearted American had packed up what he had put inside. Thereupon, along with some nondescript garments for the trunk – there were no trousers I believe – a fairly presentable pair of *old brown shoes* stood revealed, in the centre of the bourgeois French table.

As the meaning of this scene flashed upon my listless understanding, I saw in my mind's eye the phantom of the little enigmatic Ezra standing there (provided by our actions, and the position of his footgear at this moment, with a dominating stature which otherwise he scarcely could have attained) silently surveying his handiwork.

James Joyce, exclaiming very faintly "Oh!" looked up, and we all gazed at the old shoes for a moment.[89]

In such a fashion did Joyce's self-chosen role as group pauper and scrounger become killed by kindness. According to Lewis, neither he nor Eliot were allowed to pay for anything as the three of them dined and wined for the rest of the visit. However, despite the embarrassment of this first moment of meeting, the visit again resulted in mutual comradeship and rivalry which would last for the rest of their lives.

By 1920, then, Pound had succeeded in forming his literary group; and he had even managed to persuade its most spectacularly egotistical member, Joyce, to conceive of his own career in group-terms. Again, Lewis provides the evidence:

. . . he said to us – toasting us obliquely . . . 'It appears that I have the melancholy advantage of being the eldest of the band', or words to that effect. Band was not the word, nor group, but I cannot recall it nearer than this. He referred, of course, to the literary band, or group, comprised within the fold of Ezra Pound – the young, the 'New', group of writers assembled in Miss Weaver's *Egoist* just before and during the War. And of course Pound, Joyce, Eliot and myself were all within about five years of each other in the matter of age.[90]

It is worth recapitulating the relative positions of these writers at that time, since with the book-publication of *Ulysses* and *The Waste Land*, and Pound's final rejection of the London literary scene, the dynamics within the group will shortly begin to change in major ways. In 1920, Pound retained his reputation as the most progress-ive poet, critic and entrepreneur of literature in English, even though Eliot's stock as poet and critic was beginning its meteoric rise. 'Hugh Selwyn Mauberley', published that year, demonstrated, to the discerning at least, that he could be as subtle and 'difficult' as Eliot – and considerably more variable, more *virtuoso* in pastiche, than Eliot had so far shown himself to be (for all the difference between his earlier poems and the satires). Pound was also the acknowledged leader of the futuristically-orientated young writers, who had now survived the war intact and made much pre-war literature appear obsolete. Pound had publicly sponsored *Prufrock and Other Observations*, *A Portrait of the Artist*, and *Tarr*, and was associated, for those who tried to keep abreast of the avant-garde, with the periodical appearance, in America, of the strangest novel since *Tristram Shandy*, Joyce's *Ulysses*. In short, he was poised to take up a position as pope of the new literature, uncontaminated as he was by the Allied war propaganda, and wholly committed to the propagation of merit and experimentalism alone. He had only to stand his ground, wait for the harvest he had so painstakingly prepared and be willing to moderate his combative stance once the earlier struggles and disappointments were things of the past.

Eliot, though still under Pound's wing (emotionally if not intellectually) was now slowly gaining in poetic confidence and critical reputation. The collaboration with both Pound and the spirit of Lewis had opened a new vein in his poetic repertoire and he was about to produce the most spectacularly radical poem of the era. Yet his bank-work exhausted him, his marriage was breaking down (if by stages) and his own *'anomie'* kept him constantly near the brink of nervous collapse. He was beginning to make a name for himself as a cautious but authoritative critic, but he also sensed that he still needed a substantial piece of creative work – on the scale of, say, 'Hugh Selwyn Mauberley' (a poem he much admired) – before his poetic promise became fulfilled and his reputation consolidated. In collaboration with his wife, Vivien, he was already beginning to build up a portfolio of poetic passages and fragments under the working-title of 'He Do the Police in Different Voices'.[91] This was a loosely-structured sequence based, allusively, on Frazerian fertility myths – in particular the story of

the death and rebirth of a year-god – but much of the material
concerned the mental state of his wife and himself. Within two
years, and only after a partial mental breakdown, he would submit
the manuscript to the group leader for emendation – out of which
'Caesarean operation'[92] *The Waste Land* would appear to express a
'generation's disillusionment'. However, in 1920 Eliot was still
playing second string to Pound's poetic experimentation, and
passages in 'He Do the Police' show it to be still partly a species
of group-work rather than pure 'individual talent'. Until 'Ash
Wednesday', at least, Eliot would stay very much within Pound's
Bewegung, in the terms that Pound laid down.

The year 1920 appears as a watershed in James Joyce's career.
Following Pound's suggestion, he left Trieste to visit Paris and
ended up staying there for the next twenty years. Pound had
prepared the ground carefully, interesting people in Joyce's early
work, praising the first chapters of *Ulysses*, finding friends to meet
Joyce and using his contacts (and his own purse) to help establish
him financially. In Trieste Joyce had complained: 'Not a soul to
talk to about Bloom', and he had even mooted dropping the
project.[93] However, Pound was seeing to it that the *Little Review*
kept bringing out the chapters as they were completed, and by the
end of the year Joyce was in the middle of 'Circe', with only three
more sections to go. In fact, Joyce was now turning out the most
brilliant and potentially-celebrated prose of his life – a fact of which
Joyce was self-consciously aware – and in the process producing
the first (and in some ways definitive) Modernist *magnum opus*.
The 'eldest' of the group, as he acknowledged to Lewis and Eliot,
Joyce was also now the most forward-looking and experimentalist.
By the end of the year in which, as Richard Ellmann has noted,
'Pound exercised for the second time a decisive influence upon his
career',[94] Joyce was poised to make his decisive bid for creative
leadership of the Men of 1914. He was now group 'mystic', chief
innovator and father of the New. It is fitting that Lewis and Eliot
should go to visit him in this, the year of his unmistakable
ascendancy.

With Lewis, things were very different. As his biographer Jeffrey
Meyers has put it:

The sudden reputation and notoriety that Lewis achieved in
1914 as the leader of the Vorticists and editor of *Blast* had
disappeared when peace broke out in 1919. Though he had done

some extraordinary abstract pictures and published *Tarr*, he had to some extent to begin all over again.[95]

Lewis's strategy was to retire into himself for a period of incubation: 'I buried myself [and] disinterred myself in 1926'.[96] Although the ostensible reason for this was to rethink his creative career, it is likely that – as in the case of Robert Graves and T. E. Lawrence – he needed time to recover from his war experiences. At the same time, it was in the year 1920 that Lewis's mother – at the core of his intense emotional life – died during the influenza epidemic (which Lewis would later blame on the war itself). Lewis, then, was at his lowest emotional and creative point just when his prose rival within the group was nearly at his highest point. Apart from the critical pamphlet, *The Caliph's Design* (1919),[97] Lewis had published little since *Tarr*. Hence when he met Joyce in 1920 he must have felt at a distinct disadvantage. Joyce seemed to treat him with respect, even at the expense of Eliot ('your friend'), but there was also perhaps a sense of having been somehow assimilated and transcended: 'Joyce . . . had, I am persuaded, read everything I had ever written. He pretended however not to have done so.'[98] Joyce's very 'politeness'[99] may have concealed a feeling of having outdone Lewis's futurist bid already. Lewis does not indicate this in his amusing account of their meeting, but it is noticeable that although he generally claimed to admire the poetry of Pound and Eliot in *Time and Western Man* he would give *Ulysses* (that book specifically) a notorious Blasting (see below pp. 95–7). This spoiling move, I take it, would be Lewis's delayed response to Joyce's appropriation of the role of chief prose Modernist.

In 1920, then, we can see Pound still firmly in control of the group and the direction of its group-work. In this year all the Men of 1914 met each other, once Joyce had taken his vital decision to move to Paris. In the same year, Pound confirmed his own creative leadership, as poet, with the publication of 'Hugh Selwyn Mauberley' – a poem which also, in its polyphonic variability, contrived to bring together the presences of each of the group members. For Lewis this was a time of withdrawal and preparation; for Eliot one of uncertainty and doubtful experimentation; but for Joyce it was a time of productive brilliance. Pound's organisational abilities were now more focused on *Ulysses* and Joyce's welfare than on any other literary career, including his own. He had brought the Men of 1914 through the war years intact: he no longer had to feel anxiety about Lewis being at the front, and he consequently showed less interest in Lewis's new plans and threw his energy into supporting Joyce – the one artist of the four who was really forging ahead. So while the balance of power within the group was changing, they were still united in seeking to create a new art – with Joyce now leading the way. Of course, the new age was no longer what it had seemed in 1914: the war had changed much. Nevertheless, the challenge to express the altered modern world remained, and the group was now poised to produce the Great Decade of literary Modernism.

4

The Great Decade

ULYSSES

The book-publication of *Ulysses*[1] in 1922 inaugurated the great era of literary Modernism. It also marked a major shift in the balance of power within the 1914 group. Whereas Lewis's contribution was supreme in, say, 1917 when Pound and Eliot largely danced to his tune, and Joyce was still perfecting the first three episodes of *Ulysses*, by 1920 Pound and Eliot had become mesmerised by Joyce's masterwork and Lewis had scarcely got back into gear after his war years. The bringing together of the various chapters (many already published in periodical form)[2] into a single volume was, apart from anything else, a triumph of sheer magnitude. Its seven hundred or so pages vastly exceeded any earlier Modernist ventures and, more importantly, its theme and self-assured poise indicated achieved masterwork rather than a mere bid for attention. In terms of the disparate emphases of the group members, *Ulysses* also offered an overall synthesis where extremes could meet: radical experimentality could coexist with allusive resonance; strong stylistic postures could be asserted within a comprehensive polyvocality; and romantic self-preoccupation could be subsumed into neoclassical impersonality. The book also opened a vast mine of themes, techniques and symbols which others could exploit as they chose. In *Ulysses*, the Modernism we know was given birth in comprehensive form. The twentieth-century world could be given most authentic expression by radical technique organised through Epic structuring. From here on Joyce was regarded by the new *literati* as master-mystic rather than mere man, and *Ulysses* as a monument of the complex modern world.

So with *Ulysses* Joyce replaced Lewis as galvanising genius within Pound's group. But did he write the book, and achieve this position without showing a trace of the Lewisian influence – as most accounts suggest? Ellmann's authoritative account of the publication of the first three chapters in *The Little Review* focuses on a reaction to the opening of 'Proteus'. Margaret Anderson, on reading it, said 'This is the most beautiful thing we'll ever have. We'll print it if it's the last effort of our lives'.[3] The crucial words were:

> Ineluctable modality of the visible: at least that if no more, thought through my eyes. Signatures of all things I am here to read, seaspawn and seawrack, the nearing tide, that rusty boot. Snot-green, bluesilver, rust: coloured signs. Limits of the diaphane.   (p. 31)

It is truly wonderful – and it is Joyce. But without Lewis would the author of *Dubliners*, *Portrait* and *Exiles* have come up with phrasal gestures like 'seaspawn and seawrack . . . that rusty boot' or 'Snot-green, bluesilver, rust'? Surely this is an appropriation of the method of *Enemy*. And, indeed further phrases (in the *Telemachiad* alone) seem a transformation of the Lewisian satiric *daemon*:

> A scared calf's face gilded with marmalade.   (p. 7)

> A sleek brown head, a seal's, far out on the water, round.
>   (p. 19)

> Gabbles of geese. They swarmed loud, uncouth, about the temple, their heads thickplotting under maladroit silk hats.
>   (p. 28)

> Dead breaths I living breathe, tread dead dust, devour a urinous offal from all dead.   (p. 42)

Often interiorised, more lyrical if often as gut-direct, here is the same preference for jagged phrasal adjectivality over smooth syntactical sequence, the same compound of grotesque image and ironic intellectuality, and a similar anthropological-satiric gaze – all 'Kodacked by the Imagination'. Already Joyce has introjected and transformed enough of Lewis's method to help lay the rich groundwork of his masterwork.

Perhaps this influence can never be fully proved. It is not certain whether Joyce had seen *Blast* 1, though he is Blessed in it and Lewis (the editor) thought he must have seen it (perhaps sent by Pound?). Yet in the *Wake* there are several apparent references to *Enemy*.[4] And, at least, Joyce certainly received a copy of *Tarr*, even though he sent it for Frank Budgen's opinion before reading it.[5] At the same time, the intertextual evidence seems to me strong,

even granted that in Zurich 'the atmosphere of literary experimentation braced Joyce for *Ulysses*'.[6] If 'Circe' may also owe to Expressionist plays he saw during the War, the phrasal similarities and
satiric gaze seem distinctly neo-Lewisian. Granted that Joyce was
consciously forcing the limits of the English language in this work,
and that he was compulsorily assimilative of stylistic habits, it
would be natural for him to introject the major prose experimentalism (along with Stein's)[7] of that era. The parody of English literary
styles in 'Oxen of the Sun' peters out in pastiche *speech*-habits. But
the latest stage of 'foetal' textual development is diffused through
other chapters of the book as stream-of-consciousness and transformed prose Vorticism. And Joyce continues to interweave the two
veins from the first three chapters onwards, combining fluidity
with phrasal 'rock-drill' and empathy with incisive irony. So
Lewis's literary project had helped Joyce become master of the
modern word.

The *Telemachiad* alone, however, is scarcely representative of
Ulysses; nor is the book as monolithically planned as it is often
represented. Ellmann's caution has rarely been heeded in the
accounts of Joyce's strongest admirers: 'Joyce did not have his
book all in mind at the beginning. He urged a friend later not to
plan everything ahead, for, he said "In the writing the good things
will come"'.[8] If, in a sense, the first three short chapters are the
'Ithaca rock'[9] of the whole, the project of the book is, in fact, an
ongoing stylistic journey. In 'Calypso' begins the major strand of
Bloomian 'stream-of-consciousness' which flows on, in modified
form, through 'Lotus Eaters' and 'Hades' and swirls back past
'Aeolus' into 'Lestrygonians'. But 'Aeolus' marks a stylistic break.
Perhaps Joyce felt that the style was becoming bogged down in
rather samely interior rendering; certainly, this marks the beginning
of a series of radical stylistic variations, which had even Pound
complaining: 'a new style per chapter not required'.[10] At the same
time, the theme of 'Aeolus' is rhetoric and the locale a newspaper
office; Joyce need have searched no further than *BLAST* 1 and 2 to
find his major structuring device for the chapter – the insistent
use of parodic newspaper headlines: 'IN THE HEART OF THE
HIBERNIAN METROPOLIS'; 'DEAR DIRTY DUBLIN'; 'DIMI-
NISHED DIGITS PROVE TOO TITILLATING FOR FRISKY
FRUMPS . . .'. By 'Wandering Rocks', Joyce is making it New,
every chapter, as heartily as the most revolutionary modern could
desire. Of 'Cyclops' he asked Budgen whether the 'episode did

not strike him as futuristic',[11] and in 'Circe', as has already been suggested, the method of *Enemy of the Stars* is transformed into out-and-out Expressionistic vaudeville: 'On an eminence, the centre of the earth, rises the fieldaltar of Saint Barbara. Black candles rise from its gospel and epistle horns. From the high barbacans of the tower two shafts of light fall on the smokepalled altarstone. . . . The Reverend Mr. Hugh C Haines Love M.A. in a plain cassock and mortarboard, his head and collar back to the front, holds over the celebrant's head an open umbrella' (p. 489). Joyce has outgrown *Portrait* to realise that the modern mode is neither lyric nor 'dramatic',[12] but comedic. He will continue to spawn new styles, yet commit himself to none, and complete the long second half of the book in a spirit of parody. From Ibsen and Flaubert he had learnt the power of concise realism, in Dujardin he had savoured the possibilities of interior monologue, in *Tarr*, at least, he had registered the energy of satiric Vorticism – he drew on them all, but rejected all versions of unitone style. The New must speak in disparate voices as 'everything speaks in its own way'.[13] In the latter part of *Ulysses*, the discourse is thus 'feminine': and 'feminine' discourse will become now the voice of the New, as the last chapter presages: 'Yes because he never did a thing like that before. . . .' (p. 608).

Ulysses is the apotheosis of Modernism. Its key strategy is to be inclusive, even when most ironic, and express, by whatever stylistic devices, the heterogeneous plurality of twentieth-century life. For this reason, it is perhaps the fullest, most detailed and most 'presentative' novel ever written, for all that it is confined to one city and limited to one day. It is, simultaneously, an immensely social and deeply psychological book, and its hero is the most rounded and deeply-structured character in English literature.[14] Leopold Bloom is socially constituted by his Dublin environment and, at the same time, he turns the city about himself, indulging his sensuousness in the public baths, his appetite in the shops and bars, his curiosity about female statutes in the Trinity College Library. History impinges upon him – as even more on Stephen – in terms of learnt oddities and social preservation in representative buildings, behaviour patterns and discussions (his disagreement with the 'Cyclops', for instance, is a classic of rival readings of history, based on contrastive tribal experience). At the same time, the mythic parallelism and general allusiveness of *Ulysses* makes it inclusive, beyond its hero's experience or consciousness, of what

Eliot called the 'mind of Europe' – from contemporary literary speculation back to the theological debates of the Christian fathers and, beneath, to Greek myth and Hebrew scripture. 'Metempsychosis' is a key term in signalling the historical plenitude of the work, and the way the events of 16 June 1904 resonate with ardent desires and conflicts which a chronicle-novel could never foreground. If little 'happens' in normal novelistic terms, it is because individual action counts for less than depth-motivation or historical resonance. It is also, perhaps, because the central figure is a 'womanly man',[15] and, as such, less interested in the male world of career and sexual conquest than in relationships, feelings and the pleasures of contemplation. Joyce's Dublin is the opposite of Lewis's Paris ('paralysis' versus dynamism), and Bloom is about as far from being a Kreisler as a man could possibly be. Indeed, on this comparison, the 'Cyclops' is the Kreisler-figure, with both Bloom and Molly a species of Bertha, while Stephen is only a less-detached Tarr. The focus, at any rate, is on the oddly cross-gendered hero and it is around his mild-mannered habits that the largely static, if variegated, modern world revolves. Bloom, as Odysseus, is the wily yet pacific negotiator of the contemporary in all its manifestations – neither propagandist for nor adversary of twentieth-century urban life. Simply, he is at home in it. So, too, *Ulysses* as novel advocates nothing yet, in the end, affirms everything – even those things it makes look most absurd.

The book's implications for the future literary activity of the group are manifold. In terms of the evident rivalry between Lewis's futurism and Pound's comparative traditionalism, *Ulysses* suggested that the Men of 1914 could have it both ways. The birthing of the New could take place within a genetic matrix stretching back to the Greeks – and be given the semblance of structuring thereby. Eliot immediately homed in on this development as vital to the future of literature – in words now famous:

> In using the myth, in manipulating a continuous parallel between contemporaneity and antiquity, Mr Joyce is pursuing a method which others must pursue after him. They will not be imitators, any more than the scientist who uses the discoveries of an Einstein in pursuing his own, independent further investigations. It is simply a way of controlling, of ordering, of giving a shape and a significance to the immense panorama of futility and anarchy which is contemporary history. . . . It is a method

for which the horoscope is auspicious. . . . It is, I seriously believe, a step toward making the modern world possible for art.[16]

This is Eliot, the critic, in his most gravely percipient mood – even appropriating the stately prose of Sir James Frazer to add authority.[17] Whether the 'mythic method' in *Ulysses* actually does provide a means of 'controlling, of ordering' – or indeed whether Eliot's use of it in *The Waste Land* achieves that purpose – is perhaps not to the point here. The mythic dimension points a way ahead (the 'horoscope', the 'step toward making the modern world possible . . .'). The discoveries of Einstein are cited to give the method a finally impersonal importance, to be appropriated by others in the group. And this magisterial compliment is matched, in the full article, by a rogue move which attributes the first consciousness of the mythic method to an Irish writer of the previous generation, W. B. Yeats. Thus, in a stroke, Joyce's method is appropriated for the Men of 1914 at large – a legacy of 'the last Romantic', which Joyce was merely the first to have put to effective use.[18] After this, the Frazerian anthropologising and constant allusion-mongering of *The Waste Land* and then *The Cantos* becomes justified. That Joyce's version of the 'mythic method' is contrastive and comical does not concern this bid to recuperate it for future groupwork in general.

Pound's comparable review of *Ulysses*[19] concentrated on its stylistic plurality and overall balance, before using it as a platform to attack censorship and reiterate his longheld view that: 'A *great literary masterwork is made for minds quite as serious as those engaged in the science of medicine*'. Having praised the first three chapters in a letter to Joyce in 1917 (in Poundian Yankee ideolect),[20] Pound's *Dial* 'letter' commences with an official Blessing: 'All men should "Unite to give praise to *Ulysses*"; those who will not, may content themselves with a place in the lower intellectual orders'. Its place in the 'scout-troup' is assured, and those who disagree with the scout-master's favour are beyond the pale. Joyce is certified as that kind of 'creative writer or artist who does the next job'. In his 1920 review of Lewis, Pound had rated *Portrait* and *Tarr* as coequal, Joyce having the greater stylistic polish, Lewis the more volcanic energy – 'something active and "disagreeable" . . . the percussions of a highly energised mind'.[21] The stylistic quality of *Tarr* is rightly identified as 'hardness, fullness, abundance, weight, finish'. Pound now hails the achievement of the near-opposite in *Ulysses*: 'Joyce's characters not only speak their own language, but they think their own language'; 'This variegation of dialects allows Joyce to present his matter, his tones of mind, very rapidly'; 'Joyce speaks if not with the tongue of men and angels, at least with a many-tongued and multiple language, of small boys, street preachers, of genteel and ungenteel, of bowsers and undertakers, of Gerty MacDowell and Mr. Deasey'. This is the reverse of *Tarr*'s monovocal 'hardness, fullness, abundance, weight'. It is, for Pound, the 'next job' in prose and, altogether, the abundance and 'correspondences' of the novel result as 'a triumph in form, in balance, a main schema, with continuous inweaving and arabesque'. Polyvocality, inweaving and arabesque would become the hallmarks of his own *Cantos*, even though they never achieved consistency in 'form, in balance, a main schema', as he had intended. For Pound too then, though a prose work, *Ulysses* provided a new way forward.

Lewis would not see it that way at all – if only because its method was inimical to his own genius. His main reply came later, in *Time and Western Man* (1927)[22] and, of all the opinions of *Ulysses*, Joyce was to dread Lewis's most,[23] perhaps out of the guilt inherent in his triumph (Joyce was a man who himself detested a 'Usurper'). In the chapter 'An Analysis of the Mind of James Joyce', Lewis acknowledges the *succès d'estime* of *Ulysses*, with occasional complimentary asides, but his main thrust is to murder by dissection. He explicitly dismisses Eliot's reading: 'As to the homeric framework, that is only an entertaining structural device or conceit' (p. 121). With regard to stream-of-consciousness and Pound's point about polyphony he writes: 'the method of *Ulysses* imposes a softness, flabbiness and vagueness everywhere in its bergsonian fluidity' (p. 120). Under the guise of an attack on "time philosophy" (and Einstein is involved as well as Bergson), Lewis asserts his spatial hard-edge against fluidity – so cannily anticipating a tension evident in Pound's own later *Cantos*.[24] According to Lewis, the novelty of *Ulysses* is highly diluted: before citing the precedent of his own *Enemy*, he observes: 'You will find many traces in it of the influence of T. S. Eliot and of Pound's classical, romance, and anglo-saxon scholarly enthusiasms, not to be met with in earlier books' (p. 127). This is a group-dependence charge, coming after earlier accusations of influence from Bergson, Gertrude Stein and Flaubert (he has already dismissed *Dubliners* and *Portrait*). It also, most unfairly, suggests that the book is little more than a mixture

of influences. But the deadliest criticism in terms of the group
project to birth the New, is insidiously metaphoric (and repeated):
'the mechanical and abstract, the opposite of living' (p. 118);
'craftsman rather than a creator' (p. 119); 'superficial appearance
of life' (p. 118); 'cold and stagnant reality' (p. 94); 'the material of
the Past' (p. 100); 'An immense *nature-morte* is the result' (p. 107);
'a great variety of recent influences' (p. 108); 'It is like a gigantic
victorian quilt or antimacassar' (p. 109); 'above all, essentially *dead*'
(p. 110); 'walking clichés' (p. 117); 'the most conventional stuff in
the world' (p. 118). Lewis's chapter is part of a much larger
argument which remains a forthright and challenging attack on
the emergence of Modernism as the expression of relativity and
flux (Ezra included here). But, in group terms, Lewis is here
damning the work which has superseded his *Tarr*. The real thrust
is in terms of the group as birthing-cooperative: 'to create new
beauty, and to supply a new material, is the obvious affair of art
of any kind to-day'. As a leading instance of 'time-philosophy',
Ulysses, Lewis thinks, has completely failed here. As the quotations
show, he accuses it of being fluxive, derivative, clichéd, passé,
stagnant, superficial, dead and – Victorian! Lewis refuses to allow
that any new creation has taken place in Joyce's masterwork. For
him, it is merely a compendium of the dead gestures of the past.

Time and Western Man signals, in effect, what was becoming
obvious in the mid-twenties: that Lewis was out of sympathy with
the direction Modernism had taken since *Ulysses*, and was now
marginalised in terms of remaining group-feeling. His central attack
on Joyce, in the book, constitutes an implicit recognition of the
revolution *Ulysses* helped bring about. Joyce would reply to him
in 'Work in Progress', turning the charge of 'deadness' on Lewis
by making him the anally-hoarding 'Ondt' to his life-celebrating
'Gracehoper'.[25] And Lewis replied, in turn (but less aggressively)
by parodying '*Wake*-speak' in *The Childermass*,[26] and Joyce himself
in *The Apes of God*. So the mutually-appreciative Paris drinking
comrades of the early twenties (see below pp. 83–4) squabbled
publicly about the meaning of the Modernist venture. Yet they
always respected each other and, although for the moment Joyce's
inclusive polyvocality was all-triumphant, and Lewis never recovered after the War his central place as prose experimentalist, he
was to have eventually (and perhaps without his knowledge) an
odd revenge, when Beckett found himself as nouveau Moran after
Joyce's death. Beckett was eventually to gain the Nobel Prize by

transforming Lewisian principles into prose Minimalism.[27] In the
meantime, for all its intelligence and acumen, the piece on Joyce
in *Time and Western Man* is as much a group spoiling-move, by a
marginalised member, as it is a species of disinterested literary
criticism. Despite F. R. Leavis's later (and similar) dismissal of
Ulysses, it remains a major work for most Postmodernist readers.
If its internal games can seem over-scholarly, its love of life is
apparent, its new techniques forward-looking and its balanced
monumentality indisputable. More than any other single Modernist
text (except perhaps *Finnegans Wake*), it constitutes the twentieth-
century mode of representing contemporary life in all its confusing
diversity. It is Joyce's most certain success.[28] In the wake of the
Great War, he had produced a synthesis of the New which
could accommodate plenitude through a plethora of revolutionary
techniques. And in whatever mode – whether irony or acclamation –
he had ended it (as Lewis could never end anything) with a
resounding and persuasive Yes.

THE WASTE LAND

Eliot's extraordinary postwar poem constitutes a verse-synthesis
of Modernist techniques, comparable in resonance, if not in size,
to *Ulysses*, and incorporating and transforming various features
from Joyce's novel. Eliot's engagement with *Ulysses* was more
intense than the mandarin prose of his *Dial* review would care to
admit. As Peter Ackroyd notes, extrapolating Eliot's letter to Joyce
of 12 May 1921, he 'was explaining . . . that, although he wholly
admired the achievement, he rather wished, for his own sake, that
he had not read it'.[29] Eliot, in short, was aware of the strong
Joycean influence as he wrestled with his poem 'He Do the Police
in Different Voices'[30] – shortly to become *The Waste Land*. Eliot –
anguished and short of leisure to write – was collating some old
poetic fragments and by fits and starts creating various kinds of
new ones, in the attempt to achieve a quasi-Epic Modernist poem
with an internal coherence and form. If the confidence of Pound
in his genius encouraged him, the spirit of Lewis (confirmed in
his reading of *Tarr*) influenced him – as did now the achievement
of Joyce in *Ulysses*. So, in a sense, the aims and energies of all
three of the other Men of 1914 meet in *The Waste Land* – the

influence of Pound augmented recently by the collage-poem sequence, 'Hugh Selwyn Mauberley'.

The Waste Land, I suggest, found crucial inspiration from Eliot's reading of passages in *Tarr* and *Ulysses*, in particular. For the opening *tour de force*, Lewis's prose evocation of Paris in summer (perhaps echoing Eliot's own epiphany of Jean Verdenal in the Tuileries)[31] seems particularly relevant:

> The new summer heat drew heavy pleasant ghosts out of the ground, like plants disappearing in winter; spectres of energy, bulking the hot air with vigorous dreams. . . . Visions were released in the sap, with scented explosion, the Spring one bustling and tremendous reminiscence.   (*Tarr*, p. 45)

This complex apostrophe (whose aftermath, in the shop, may have sown a seed for Bloom's first purchase)[32] may well appear, transformed into exhausted Eliotese – Verdenal long since dead – in *The Waste Land*'s magnificent and multi-allusive opening:

> April is the cruellest month, breeding
> Lilacs out of the dead land, mixing
> Memory and desire, stirring
> Dull roots with spring rain.
> Winter kept us warm, covering
> Earth. . . .
> Summer surprised us.

This passage, together with the Hyacinth Girl epiphany and the corpse whose 'sprouting' is an issue, speaks back to Lewis's prewar vigour,[33] after the deluge.

One early *Ulysses* passage seems even more germane to the preoccupations of the poem. It is from 'Calypso':

> . . . *A barren land, bare waste. Vulcanic lake*, the *dead sea: no fish*, weedless, *sunk deep in the earth*. No wind could lift those waves, grey metal, poisonous foggy waters. Brimstone they called it raining down: *the cities of the plain: Sodom, Gomorrah, Edom. All dead names*. A dead sea in a dead land, grey and old. *Old now.* . . . The oldest people. Wandered far away *over all the earth*, captivity to captivity, multiplying, dying, being born everywhere.

It lay there now. Now it could *bear no more.* Dead: an old woman's: the grey *sunken cunt of the world.*   (p. 50)

The underlinings of the key phrases are mine, and indicate what seems to me the relevance of the quotation to *The Waste Land* as a whole. Here are some quotations from the poem which I take to be particular appropriations in the spirit of the passage:

> *The Waste Land.* . . . 'A pool among the rock' . . . 'Oed' und leer das Meer' [empty and waste the sea] . . . 'fishing in the dull canal' . . . 'exhausted wells' . . . 'What is the city over the mountains' . . . 'Jerusalem Athens Alexandria' . . . 'Where the dead men lost their bones' . . . 'old man with wrinkled dugs' . . . 'swarming / Over endless plains' . . . 'By the waters of Leman I sat down' . . . 'empty cisterns' . . . 'Ganga was sunken, and the limp leaves / Waited for rain'.

Such an extrapolation is by no means exhaustive – anyone who knows the poem well could add to it, after meditation on the passage from Joyce. *The Waste Land* is a notoriously allusive poem ('mature poets steal'), but there is no reason to suppose it only alludes to the past. Eliot's own notion of Tradition includes 'the new (the really new) work'.[34] Laudatory reviews show he regarded both *Tarr* and *Ulysses* in exactly this light. One need only imagine, then, what a deeply disturbed man, perhaps drinking too much at the end of a day at Lloyd's Bank,[35] might make of such passages and what profound transformations they might effect, into unique verse, when the tired spirit stirred to create again and his own repertoire of styles found articulation in a rhythm that could speak. Like Pound's Tiresias in Canto I, Eliot's internalised ghosts could speak when enough blood of suffering was spilt on the ground.

More than any other text of the period, *The Waste Land* reads like a group production.[36] Written in the period of Eliot's greatest marital turmoil and personal torment, we can detect Pound's group-family contributing its diverse strengths to produce a poem centred on the near-impossibility of productive issue. The waste land (waist-land) means what it signifies. Yet, put as psychoanalytic metaphor, we might say that, in it, the poet as voyeur (Tiresias)[37] fantasises the insemination of himself from inside the textual womb. In this scenario, Lewis's satirical thrust toils within Joyce's stylistic elasticity to create the new poem as a wail of infantile

impotence. Pound, here, was self-consciously the 'obstetrician'[38] –
who effected delivery of the poetic child thus engendered. Such
an account is, in fact, quite close to the metaphoric game Pound
and Eliot played in their correspondence about the poem. But here
Ezra attempted to usurp the role of father, engendering in the
passive Possum a text-child 'by the Uranian muse begot' – where
Uranian means homosexual[39] There are some lines which suggest
the influence of Pound ('You! hypocrite lecteur!'; 'The river's tent
is broken'; 'Red and gold / The brisk swell / Rippled both shores'),
but the primary living influences in the poem are the Lewis of
Enemy, *Tarr* and 'Inferior Religions', and the Joyce of *Ulysses*.

I have already suggested ways in which *The Waste Land* scenario
looks back to details of the prose-setting in *Enemy of the Stars* (see
above p. 66). The details given could, doubtless, be added to.
However, I want to argue more generally for the diffused and
transmuted influence of both *Enemy* and *Tarr* and, in particular,
the appropriation, at times, of the satiric stance and tone embodied
in 'Inferior Religions' – an appropriation which would not survive
Eliot's conversion to Christianity, but which is manifest in *The
Waste Land* as in the quatrains. The satiric mode seems to have
been a primary feature of the new fragments of 'He Do the Police'
from 'First we had a couple of feelers back at Tom's place'[40] onward.
However, I shall argue only in terms of the edited *Waste Land*,
since that is the text which has become familiar, and indeed
canonical. Pound's edited version retains quite enough Lewisian
grotesquerie to justify the idea of powerful influence, struggling
with other influences and impulses, to express the modern world
in highly unusual verse. The Lewisian vein is diffused throughout
the poem. In 'The Burial of the Dead' we have the satirical portrait
of Madame Sosostris[41] ('Kodacked' by the ear rather than the eye)
and the grotesque corpse in the garden; in 'A Game of Chess' the
sardonic rendering of the pub scene perfectly expresses 'inferior
religion'; in 'The Fire Sermon' we find a canal scenario, the
evocation of Mrs Porter (a 'Breton' if ever), the robotic Mr Eugenides
and a seduction scene as dingily mechanistic as Kreisler's rape is
dynamically horrific – with the typist responding similarly to
Bertha;[42] and in 'What the Thunder Said' there are the neo-
Expressionist 'hooded hoardes', the exploding city (cf. 'The Earth
has burst, a granite flower'),[43] and the Vorticist-Surreal imagery of
the woman playing the fiddle on her hair, the baby-faced bats and
the upside-down towers in the air. Such instances demonstrate

the complex blend of ironic ruthlessness and anarchic (sometimes apocalyptic) grotesquerie that was Lewis's early creative legacy.

Against this satiric intensity work wholly contradictory strands of pathos, nostalgia, sudden lyricism and elegiac diminuendo. It is here that the Joycean precedent of polyvocal metamorphosis is essential to the poem as mélange (a reality which Pound appreciated, tightening the contrasts even further). The satiric cutting edge of the quatrains is here: 'One of the low on whom assurance sits / As a silk hat on a Bradford millionaire'. But within the whole poem such objectivising scorn must coexist with empathetic lament: 'I think we are in rats' alley'; 'O City city'; 'burning burning burning'; 'These fragments I have shored'. Like Joyce, Eliot has utilised what he needed of Lewis's satiric daemon but contains its monovocal stridency within a developing multivoiced orchestration, which utters the indepth meditations of the broken 'mind of Europe'. *The Waste Land*, like *Ulysses*, works by stylistic montage, and combines ironic observation with empathetic interiority within an overall continuum of aesthetic patterning. The influence of *Ulysses* on *The Waste Land* is scarcely disputed now. In his scholarly work on the poem of 1983, Grover Smith summarises the main details over some pages.[44] One of the most persuasive factors is the correspondence between Stephen's meditations on the corpse washing around the coastline in 'Proteus' and the varied references to seawater, drowning, fishing, sailing, etc. in *The Waste Land* – both Joyce and Eliot haunted by the Shakespearean magic of: 'Full fathom five thy father lies . . .'. There is also the bisexuality of Tiresias (as of Bloom and Bella Cohen), the mutual incorporation of untranslated foreign phrases or the shared delight in snatches of popular song. However, it is not my intention here to add to the list of possible 'borrowings'. It is, I believe, overwhelmingly in the matter of overall discursive strategy – the attainment of a 'feminine', polyphonous, stylistic flexibility – that *The Waste Land* owes to *Ulysses*. The precedent of *Ulysses* took away the necessity of choosing between the Laforguean note of 'Prufrock' or the Gautier-Lewis tone of the quatrains (or any other monovocal style) and allowed the Possum to become brilliant poetic parrot, in a work which expresses the modern world as Babel.

However, Eliot's engagement with the implications of *Ulysses* was not merely passive. If subconsciously (and perhaps sometimes consciously) he introjected both key themes and overall stylistic strategy, he was also mentally engaged with the meaning of the new techniques and seeking – in rivalry as well as imitation – to appropriate them for his own poetic purpose. The discussion of the 'mythic method' is much to the point here. If, to a degree, Eliot misread the implications of Joyce's Homeric parallelism, he did so in terms of his own interests – the creation of a new poem, which could be related to the anthropological world of primitive religion which had fascinated him since his Harvard days.[45] In effect, the 'mythic' substratum of *The Waste Land* is a bid to go further back and deeper than *Ulysses*. Joyce's book is above all a compendium and satire of textuality. It alludes to an epic, *The Odyssey*, conceived at that time as having been written by a single poet. It was above all a primary instance of written narrative – an art which in the nineteenth century was appropriated from poetry by the power of the novel form.[46] Eliot sees the 'mythic method' primarily as a means of transcending narrative and hence bringing to birth a new art. This *Ulysses* had not really done, for all its stylistic pyrotechnics, since it still proceeds chronologically through its allotted day while also alluding (though unevenly) to Homer's narrative epic. *The Waste Land*, in a sense, aims to get behind written narrative altogether. Its allusions reach down, behind stylistic postures, to the shared world of essentially oral culture: the realm, not of writing, but of myth, ritual and even dance.[47] *Ulysses* is a spoof on the abstracted, individualised and chronological nature of written narrative: *The Waste Land* is ultimately an evocation of the sensuous, communal and cyclic world of preliterate religion. The ceremonies of the dying King, the sacrificial Goddess and the return of Spring are evoked as the authentic condition of man from which two thousand or so years of writing (say Petronius to de Nerval)[48] have separated us. At the same time, with its gramophone, its snatches of 'radio' song, its jazz rhythms and its cinematographic scenarios, the poem alerts us to the death of the hegemony of literature, without the new media providing a means to return to the sacral realm which existed before writing. Though the poem is inevitably *written*, its appeal (and many of its innovations) concern the world of the ear – opera, popular song, slang, chant and incantation. It endeavours to return poetry to its oral, vatic base – thereby (among other things) marginalising the realm of prose fiction. Where Joyce satirises the evolution of English style, Eliot returns us to the world of primal utterance ('la la'; 'Co co rico'; 'DA'; 'Shantih shantih shantih') and the historic trace of 'Indo-European' language in Sanskrit. *The Waste Land* thus outbids

Joyce's Odyssean move by plumbing deeper than the Western text into the oral realm of mythology. Joyce, I believe, instinctively understood this[49] – and his reply would be in the infinite mythic murmurings of *Finnegans Wake*.[50]

Yet where Joyce's novel affirms, Eliot's poem seems to deny. In this *The Waste Land* is closer to *Tarr* than to *Ulysses*, articulating a contemporary male death-wish played out on the dead body of the earth-mother ('empty cisterns and exhausted wells'). In this, like 'Hugh Selwyn Mauberley' too, the poem is born from the impossibility of giving birth and tells us that, in reality, we do not exist. Beyond Eliot's 'private . . . grumbling',[51] then, *The Waste Land* exemplifies the way the urge to artistic birthing has collided with the realities of the Great War. Paul Fussell is right, I believe, in seeing it, in a sense, as a war poem,[52] whose theme spills over into the postwar situation. Molly Bloom can assent to life because she lives outside of masculine history and rejects the patriarchal order in asserting her sexual being; in *The Waste Land* the equivalent earth-goddess has no adulterous option while men are preoccupied with death: 'Ganga was sunken, and the limp leaves / Waited for rain'. Nevertheless, the poem is open-ended and the possibility of change and of rain remains to the end. Written in the aftermath of world catastrophe, Eliot fully expresses the nightmare of history and the poem effects both lament and a warning. If the 'hypocrite lecteur', together with the Fisher King, cannot 'set [his] lands in order' the world cannot be saved from its appalling plight. Yet the thunder's commands are repeated, at the end, as a challenge: not a textual description or prescription, but an oracular verbal command with the force of *Kerygma*: 'Datta. Dayadhvam. Damyata'. *The Waste Land* looks to its readers to reassert 'feminine' values of empathy, nurture and self-balance, and so remake history in a reborn world.

Thus the poem expresses a horror of impotence and yet looks to renewal – and is itself a new birthing. It is the first fully-Modernist poem and Pound called it 'the justification of the modern movement'[53] thus proclaiming what Joyce evaded[54] – its certification as family child on a par with *Ulysses*. Pound's main contribution, as legend now attests, was right at the end. He detached the living form from the tissue that surrounded it and performed the 'Caesarean' section.[55] 'Complimenti, you bitch' he wrote to his friend when the text-child was born, 'I am plagued by the seven jealousies'.[56] Yet he had his role and rejoiced at the result. The group had now produced the Modernist 'verse-epic', and it proceeded to take the literary world by storm. For Pound himself it confirmed the shape and method of his own life-long epic, the *Cantos*: not '*Émaux et Camées* and the State Bay Hymn Book'[57] but collage polyphony on the model of *Ulysses* and *The Waste Land*. Yet granted the overall 'ragbag' construction, there would still be a place in the *Cantos* for Lewis's vision and painterly phrase.[58]

THE DRAFT OF XVI CANTOS

The most productive poetic influence of *The Waste Land* appears in the *Cantos* of the man who edited it – although Beckett's *Whoroscope* (1930) introjects its manner to try out an ultimately false direction.[59] This is wholly fitting, for the method of 'Hugh Selwyn Mauberley' helped provide a precedent for *The Waste Land*, as it was the Poundian skill which produced its final shape. It is above all the neo-Joycean polyphony of Eliot's poem which helps solve the problems Ezra found with his 1917 version of three cantos.[60] There was no need now for the monovocal presence of a controlling author to pull together the 'ragbag' – stylistic montage could stand by itself. So *The Waste Land* helped inspire that fluxive, onward pulse of Poundian creation which flowed through the rest of the twenties, and for another three decades, to result as some eight hundred pages – *The Cantos*. Yet, through much of that period, a tension is evident within the polyphony between Lewisian hard-edge (Gaudier, Epstein, Confucius, et al.) and the 'musical phrase'[61] of Imagism (Sappho, Catullus, H.D.). The former comes coded as 'rock-drill' and 'marble': the latter sometimes 'ooze', sometimes 'ply over ply'. The tension would never be fully resolved. Simply, the poet's energy eventually ran out and *The Cantos*, like *The Waste Land*, is finally left in the hands of the reader: 'I have brought the great ball of crystal;/who can lift it?'[62]

Lewis had figured as a presence in the earliest drafts and the original second canto overtly invoked the brash phrases of *Enemy*: ·

Barred lights, great flames, new form; Picasso or Lewis[63]

In the revised version of *Draft of XVI Cantos* (1925), the phrasal rhythm remains but the name has gone:

> Sleek head, daughter of Lir,
> eyes of Picasso
> Under black fur-hood, lithe daughter of Ocean.
>
> (p. 6)

This epiphany is now introduced by a line that seems to speak back to *Ulysses*: 'Seal sports in the spray-whited circles of cliff-wash' ('A sleek brown head, a seal's, far out on the water, round', *Ulysses*, p. 19). However, the influence of Lewis lingers on in the *XVI Cantos*, and Pound remains particularly fond of the phrasal brush-stroke: 'Scene for the battle only, but still scene, / Pennons and standards y cavals armatz', or 'Black azure and hyaline, / glass wave over Tyro'.[64] In particular, Lewis's satiric daemon is evoked and emulated whenever there is Blasting to be done:

> foetor, sweat, the stench of stale oranges,
> dung, last cess-pool of the universe,
> mysterium, acid of sulphur . . . .
>
> (p. 62)

> And before hell mouth; dry plain
> and two mountains;
> On the one mountain, a running form,
> and another
> In the turn of the hill; in hard steel
> The road like a slow screw's thread.
>
> (p. 68)

If Pound's Inferno scenario is modelled on the landscape of *The Waste Land*, the rhythm and something of the eye of Lewis are involved in the style, and the first two lines of XVI (immediately above) anticipate the first sentence of Lewis's own Inferno (*The Childermass*, 1928): 'The city lies in a plain, ornamented with mountains'.[65] Just as Dante was something of a shared obsession with the Men of 1914 (cf. the Lakeland School or The Rhymers) so their visions of hell (and sometimes of paradise) speak to each other across the texts: 'Hades' – *The Waste Land* – Hell cantos – *Childermass*; the later texts informed, too, by the landscape of the Great War.

It is in the 'Hell' cantos[66] that Pound shows his greatest debt to

Lewis – not only in terms of phrasal rhythm but in terms, also, of
the ruthless grotesquerie of 'Inferior Religions':

> The pimply and hairy skin
> > pushing over the collar's edge,
> Profiteers drinking blood sweetened with sh-t,
> And behind them . . . . . f and the financiers
> > lashing them with steel wires.
> > > > > > (p. 61)

The politicians, newspaper men and 'usurers' of XIV and XV are
'Kodacked' in their behavioural machinery – 'inferior religion' here
being the dragon-whirl of money-value endlessly chasing its own
tail.

But if Pound has learnt from Lewis he has also learnt from Joyce.
Even in Hell there is a touch of Bloom ('Oblivion, / forget how
long, / sleep, fainting nausea', p. 66), while the major method of
associationism, throughout the cantos, is scarcely imaginable
without the precedent of stream-of-consciousness. The model here
is Stephen's superintellectual mind unravelling itself at length, in
chapters like 'Proteus' and 'Scylla and Charybdis', one thought
sparking another, replete with learned quotations, allusions and
further associations, departing from and returning to the realm of
sense-impression. It would be tedious to demonstrate this at
length – but this is a brief example:

> Ear, ear for the sea-surge;
> > rattle of old men's voices.
> And then the phantom Rome,
> > marble narrow for seats
> 'Si pulvis nullus' said Ovid,
> 'Erit, nullum tamen excute'
> > > > > > (p. 24)

Here is the comparable thing in *Ulysses*:

Day by day: night by night: lifted, flooded and let fall. Lord,
they are weary; and, whispered to, they sigh. Saint Ambrose
heard it, sigh of leaves and waves, waiting, awaiting the fullness
of their times, *diebus ac noctibus iniurias patiens ingemiscit.* (p. 41)

Pound, of course, had carefully read and commented on drafts of *Ulysses* as they were sent to him, and always remained most impressed by the earlier chapters, with their exact rendering of sense-impressions and their patterned interior associationism, so it is natural that their influence should show tellingly in his later verse. Joyce had liberated literature from the Subjective–Objective dichotomy (as Romanticism never could) and his associational method passed quite directly into *The Waste Land*, *The Cantos*, *Mrs Dalloway* and beyond. Each writer more or less transmuted the method to personal ends, but one cannot help wondering how much the élitist allusions of high Modernism are due to the fact that Stephen Dedalus (unlike Bloom or Molly) is endowed with Joyce's own neoscholastic mind. Certainly, Stephen's abstruse preoccupations with such as Sabellius, Hamlet, the Vikings and God the Father acted as a precedent for Ezra's transdecadal meditations on such as Venus Anadyomene, the Chinese, Sordello and Scotus Erigena. The effect of *Ulysses* upon his own work was dynamic and lifelong; in the immediate postwar period it found him an ultimate hero and life-model not to be found, after all, in the pages of Browning – Odysseus, the man 'with no name'.[67] And the new first canto begins the great project with a translation, of a translation, of the Homeric hero's visit to Tiresias in Hades, just as Joyce's rationale for the method in 'Sirens' provided him with a 'fugal' suggestion of structure to offer the baffled Yeats as he read the early parts.[68]

'These fragments you have shelved (shored)' (p. 28): the Possum also is 'part of the process', and, as the cantos develop, an uneasy recoil and flow of sympathy in Eliot's direction is evident – quite similar to the equivalent relationship between Lewis and Joyce. Pound knew his own verse-strengths well enough to avoid the lure of the Eliotic line, but a common ear for the prose of James can produce, in VII, a tone that seems to look back to 'Gerontion' and on to 'Ash Wednesday':

> And the old voice lifts itself
>   weaving an endless sentence.
> We also made ghostly visits, and the stair
> That knew us, found us again on the turn of it,
> Knocking at empty rooms. . . .
>
> (pp. 24–5)

At the same time, in XII their shared benefactor John Quinn is evoked as spokesman for the story of the bisexual sailor – the anecdote mimics their private fantasy of 'pairing' on *The Waste Land* and it is especially a joke for Eliot that the hospital officials hand him a baby: ' "Here! this is what we took out of you" '.[69] And, of course, Pound the 'surgeon' was merely using cutting techniques inherent in *The Waste Land* manuscript – which he now adopts to create a collage-poem of his own. The basic principle is Eliotic juxtaposition:

> Drear waste, the pigment flakes from the stone,
> Or plaster flakes, Mantegna painted the wall.
> Silk tatters, 'Nec Spe Nec Metu'
>
> (p. 12)

The sectional collage of 'Hugh Selwyn Mauberley' has been adapted here to break up even the line, through the example of *The Waste Land*.

Yet the first XVI cantos constitute a very individualised field of ingathering. Like Joyce and Eliot, Pound has introjected and transposed to effect his own creation. He has also done so at such ongoing length that he virtually appropriated the method, and Eliot would in future abandon polyphonic collage and return to the meditative, if fluid, line and strive for a more conventional structure. *The Cantos* will take verse-mosaic as far as it can usefully go – and probably much further: in the meantime, the first ones published try out a range of voices and themes and push back the frontiers of poetic convention. I am not much convinced by the proferred *schemas*[70] – Pound's or anyone else's. There is no *Ulysses*-type scheme here (and that itself scarcely serves to structure the plenitude of Joyce's novel). Pound's 'navigation' was even less oriented than that of Odysseus himself, as he zigzagged home from one amazement to the next. There can be no real Ithaca for a Modernist poet like Pound and, unlike Eliot, he found no place to return to and 'know . . . for the first time',[71] though he endured 'dark seas' and did indeed 'lose all companions'.[72] And this finally directionless venture is evident from the first XVI cantos. We move off from Greek myth to Venice and El Cid, and so on to Provence, the Renaissance, the Middle Ages, Malatesta's Rimini, Confucius, then hell – all shot through with allusions that resonate not just the 'mind of Europe' but 'Spiritus Mundi'. We have Pound as translator, chronicler, evoker or denouncer; there are snatches of lyric, Uncle Ez anecdote, and diary-reminiscence. We find, in short, whatever seemed needed as Pound was writing. And in this – *contra* Lewis – Pound is the Modernist *par excellence*. Whatever the material – whether ancient or modern, Western or Eastern – the method is radical because it refuses the illusion of overall order. Unlike James Joyce, or Eliot as critic, Pound never pretended that his vast, heterogeneous collation was really a species of rational structure. In this, he was following the true implications of *Ulysses* and *The Waste Land* – not purposive plot, but art as odd patterns emerging from chaos.

What died in such writing was the old Aristotelian notion of structure; what was born – as Lewis deplored – was a post-Einsteinian space-time continuum where pattern, not purpose, was the golden rule. And the patterns themselves could be quite discontinuous and random: 'ply over ply' (p. 15) or 'Passion to breed a form in shimmer of rain-blur' (p. 27). In this the past, as the present, was grist for the mill, since ends and beginnings were now conflated and the present was only the 'trace' in the text. Pound, above all, is the poet-'translator', bearing illuminations forward and across. 'The past should be a light to the present and the future', he would write,[73] and what mattered was to keep words alive, like the air-borne 'blossoms of the apricot';[74] or like Odysseus with Tiresias, to make the dead speak: 'the husks, before me, move, / The words rattle' to reactivate virtùe – 'Being more live than they, more full of flames and voices' (p. 27). Energy, here, was the key – not mere novelty. So Pound was developing a form of poetic recycling where living, verbal ecology was all – outside the old structures of space and time. In the *Cantos* voices, discourses, speak irrespective of space and time and resonate life out of Waste Land deadness. If Pound only partly knew what he was after, he had been at it some time. 'All ages are simultaneous' are almost the first words of his first prose book (*The Spirit of Romance*, 1913). If *Ulysses*, for him, had ended the 'Christian Era',[75] it had also ended the era of orthodox Greek thought. After Aristotle, Bergson and Einstein – as before him Heraclitus or Homer. *The Draft of XVI Cantos* asserts the reality of the new world of simultaneous, yet discontinuous, information – as resonant and life-related as Eliot's lost oral culture. The task for the poet is to pick up pattern, where pattern emerges, and keep the words going, keep remaking them new.

Yet a horror of 'deadness' informs the continuum. In this, Pound was a man of his time, and the first sequence ends with the First World War. As old 'scout-master', already one duty is elegy – for the older Imagist workgroup and for Blasters who had not survived:

> And Henri Gaudier went to it,
>   and they killed him,
> And killed a good deal of sculpture,
> And ole T.E.H. he went to it. . . .
>
> (p. 71)

The old Western paradigms had changed and a new mode of art had been born – but what could be made of worldwide war? As in Lewis, Lawrence and Freud, Thanatos appears as a rival to Eros, but in Pound – shocked out of aestheticism and trying to think, beyond his means, for a key to renewal – this will be linked with a theory of money. It was already there in the Great War fragment of 'Hugh Selwyn Mauberley' – 'usury age-old'. In the Hell cantos, especially, both become further linked (in satiric logic) with excrement, sexual perversion and arid scholarship. So far so good, but a 'theory' of money, a programme of reform, fits badly into a 'space-time' verse-sequence. In the first XVI Cantos there is little problem. The *virtù*, for instance, of a resuscitated Malatesta speaks jauntily forth as valour, sexuality and the love of beauty – beyond any notions of Social Credit. If the seeds of a later dogmatic preachment are evident, their origin in death (where they both begin and end, outside the middle sections with their 'palpable design')[76] is the major and valid theme to be set in contrast to goddesses and 'lights' – the fragmentary glimpses of a new *Paradiso*. Death is already the negative pole in a palimpsest aiming to renew the meaning of living. Death means 'stench', 'oblivion' and 'petrification'. And its chief symbol already is war. There is irony in that such an avant-garde sequence should end with moves forward that end in mass-death:

> and that the advance was beginning;
> That it was going to begin in a week.
>
> (p. 75)

However, the cantos still affirm the possibility of fruitful advance: 'And then went down to the ship', it begins. In this, like *Enemy*,

Ulysses and *The Waste Land*, it is a poem about birthing the New – and one which, as much as *Ulysses*, affirms the possibility of a cosmic 'Yes'. Like *The Waste Land*, it is meaningfully born from the group, its author a medium as well as a magus, through which their joint voices can mingle, with others, in Messianic expectation. But where *The Waste Land* keeps all in doubt, Pound – as Eliot's activated reader – hastens to put his lands in order as affirmative ingathering. Although the first sequence ends with a death, it merely prepares for a sensuous renewal: 'So that the vines burst from my fingers . . .'[77] And already a pattern of courageous creation, in adversity, has been established: Odysseus, E.P., El Cid, Malatesta or Confucius made to relive that life might go forward. In the new space-time discourse (collaged from a clamouring of voices), the life pulses forward, lamenting its dead, and excoriating the killers, yet as intent on salvation as Augustine or Blake (p. 76). Motion through resonance is all. Words, like Shelley's winged seeds, are set into movement, uplifted, and Pound, the poet, has 'tried to keep them from falling' (p. 60).

THE CHILDERMASS

In *The Pound Era*, Hugh Kenner recounts an amusing anecdote about Pound visiting Joyce in Paris. Finding his old friend surrounded by an entourage of admiring acolytes, he acidly asked one pallid disciple whether he was essaying an *Iliad*, or perhaps another *Divina Commedia*. The young man was a certain Samuel Beckett MA – whom Pound was to meet again some thirty years later, at a performance of *Fin de Partie*.[78] At that time, in the late twenties, however, someone had already written a kind of prose *Inferno* – not one of the Joyceans, but Joyce's friend and arch-rival Wyndham Lewis. And in that work Lewis parodied the style of Joyce's ongoing 'Work in Progress', which Beckett was to commend in *Our Exagmination*.[79] . . . As we have noted, Lewis tried to take apart the achievement of *Ulysses* in *Time and Western Man*. Yet clearly he had also registered its success, and the fittest response to a large prose-epic would be to write an even larger prose-epic. Lewis's would be called *The Human Age*, made up of three related volumes – *The Childermass*, *Monstre Gai* and *Malign Fiesta* – and would stretch, in terms of publication dates, between 1928 and 1955. Apropos *Time and Western Man*, it would attempt to rescue fictional prose from 'time-philosophy' and its 'baby-language'. The mode was science fiction, the scenario the afterlife, and the inevitable Lewisian duo two men killed in the Great War.

If its opening is reminiscent of Pound's Hell cantos, it is even more an appropriation of the scenario of *The Waste Land* and *The Hollow Men*. And although it also has clear connections with the setting of *Enemy*, the difference in mood between the two works is striking. *Enemy* is spectacularly dynamic, while *The Childermass* is made out of deadness and desecration. It is now as if the spirit of the Possum has overwhelmed Lewis's energy as he tried to come to terms with the 'inferior religion' of postwar civilisation. The roles are reversed. Yet Lewis's satiric precision and eye for detail remain, as does his use of the *image juste*:

> The western horizon behind the ridge, where the camp ends inland, but southward from the highroad, is a mist that seems to thunder. A heavy murmur resembling the rolling of ritualistic drums shakes the atmosphere. It is the outposts or investing belt of Beelzebub, threatening Heaven from that direction, but at a distance of a hundred leagues, composed of his resonant subjects. Occasionally upon a long-winded blast the frittered corpse of a mosquito may be borne. As it strikes the heavenly soil a small sanguine flame bursts up, and is consumed or rescued.   (p. 9)

Lewis's 'desert' scenario is characterised by Eliotic properties – mist, thunder, murmurs like ritualistic drums, wind, purgatorial flame ('burning burning burning'), and into it come two figures who openly proclaim their Eliotic credentials: 'One would say one was hollow!' (p. 12); yet only Lewis could have built up the scene with so cosmically indifferent a gaze, and 'the frittered corpse' and 'sanguine flame' are typically Lewisian brilliances. Eliot, in fact, was notably exempted from the rubbishing which Lewis devoted to the work of Joyce, Pound and many others in *Time and Western Man*. Later on, Lewis would take issue with some of Eliot's more dubious critical pronouncements,[80] but still show great respect for the author of '*Ara Vos Prec, The Waste Land* or *Prufrock*', in an essay which begins: 'There is no person today who has had more influence upon the art of literature in England and America than Mr. T. S. Eliot'.[81] It was Lewis, of course, who had first published some poems of Eliot in England. By the twenties Eliot's 'influence upon the art of literature' had extended to Lewis himself. Eliot had introjected Lewis's *Enemy* scenario and theory of satire, and given back to him a Dantesque vision of modern life as limbo-land which Lewis could construct into a panoramic dystopia. Returned from the shattering realities of the Western Front, and scornful of the artistic pretensions of both Bloomsbury and postwar Paris, he devised his *Divina Commedia* out of the very 'time-philosophy' he attacked. And he began it firmly in Eliot's territory: 'Beyond the oasis-plain is the desert' (p. 9).

However, in an important sense, *The Childermass* could not possibly have been the book it is without Joyce. In fact it is scarcely too much to say that the whole novel is an elaborated response to *Ulysses* and the earlier parts of 'Work in Progress'. Even the parodies of Gertrude Stein ('He's been most fearfully tiresome when he likes and he's been tiresome too but who doesn't when they're not?' etc. p. 44) are, in fact, pokes at Joyce whom Lewis (rather improbably) accused of imitating Stein's method. There are quite a few overt jokes directed at his old drinking-companion. Thus Pullman, the more robust of the two leading figures, is given a specifically Joycean history at one point: 'When war was declared I was in Trieste – in Spandau, I should say, at the Berlitz, teaching' (p. 99). Just before this there is a passage which speaks back to Joyce's pyrotechnics in 'Circe' which had themselves spoken back to *Enemy*: 'Exit Fathers like a cohort of witches, turning tail at sight of the bristling righteous phalanx of incestuous masculine matrons, with hittite profiles, hanging out like hatchets just clear of the chest, Eton-cropped, short stout necks firmly anchored in asthmatic lungs, with single eyeglasses, and ten diamond corking-pins representing the decaceraphorous beast of the deliverance. . . . (p. 97). At another point Joyce's 'Bello' is invoked (pp. 278–9), while the whole situation of the characters is described as 'this posthumous odyssey' (p. 138).

However, the most specific and elaborate sally occurs when Pullman and Satters (his side-kick) are listening to the Bailiff, a Punch-like figure who runs the whole show. The Bailiff, who regularly harangues these hollow men of the afterlife, is given to neoJoycean metamorphoses. In one of the most extraordinary of these, his voice modulates from stage 'negro-talk' to pastiche *Wake*speak:

hit's hit hit in me brain-pan and bin an mixt all the lettas!

Ho Christ Chris hiffit hazzent mixt . . . hall the wordies up in
me old tin brainpot wot I dropt in two at a time dayin dayout,
at word-wide pains scrapped and scraped smelt-out sniffed-in
collectioneered coined let slip and held tight got right side up
an arse-overtip and toppled into me lucky-dip. . . .   (p. 173)

There follow some five pages or so more of this kind of thing. If
the parody is not quite resonant enough really to beat Joyce at his
own game, Lewis certainly has considerable fun at his rival's
expense: 'seabird-girl sob-slobber' (so much for the great epiphany
in *Portrait*); '"dublin-pubmumper on the rivolooshumshighbrow-
lowneck-racket"'; '"Master Joys of Potluck, Joys of Jingles, whom
men call Crossword-Joys for his apt circumsolutions"'; '"Deedal-
dum cum Deedaldee"' [Dedalus or 'Steve']; '"Neggs-in-progress"
and "wirk-on-the way"'; '"that synthetrical spirit of the bloody
bog orange man"'; '"Joys being jokey for sportive in roman"';
'"since s'help me Jayzers oiv sed all I haz to say and there's an
end of the matter"' (pp. 174–8). Lewis systematically uses 'ant' for
'and' throughout the passage, with variants sometimes – 'ant add'
or 'odts ents ant' (odds and ends). Presumably this is related to
Joyce's reply to *Time and Western Man* in *Transition* (also 1928)[82]
where he makes Lewis the Ondt in relation to his Gracehoper (see
below, pp. 127–9).

The Childermass is a response to the phenomenon of Joyce in far
more ways than such direct evocations. In a meaningful sense, the
Bailiff is Joyce himself as (for Lewis) chief spokesperson of the
whole 'time-philosophy', with its space-time continuum, its anti-
heroic hollow men and its pervasive 'baby-talk'. As Pullman
explains to Satters, when confronted with the insubstantial images
of this 'afterlife': '"The waves are years, the water is 'Timestuff',
as they call it"' (p. 40). The Bailiff appears both as the magician
and apologist of the whole chimerical scenario. In it, there are
friezes of historical scenes – a man at the plough, a sexual pursuit –
in diminishing perspective: this seems to relate directly to Lewis's
charge that *Ulysses* is 'an immense *nature-morte*' (*Time and Western
Man*, p. 107). At the same time, the way characters can change
dimension and appearance, in arbitrary metamorphosis, is related
to Joyce's technique in 'Proteus', 'Cyclops' and 'Circe' in *Ulysses*
and the method of 'Work in Progress' as a whole. If there is a

paradox in the view of 'time-philosophy' as simultaneously *passéist* and totally fluxive, Lewis had worked hard to justify it in *Time and Western Man*. In *The Childermass*, both appear naturally together in an Erewhon which is wholly artificial and essentially static. Beyond a few moments of sudden violence, the mass of its half-people are kept as contended and infantalised as the majority in Huxley's later *Brave New World*. So the satiric implication of the fiction is that 'space-time' writers such as Joyce, for all their merits, collude with the New Physics on the one hand, mass technological democracy on the other, to accept, or even consecrate, a social status quo where there is neither concrete substantiality nor spiritual identity. In a sense, one might say that Lewis here creates a scenario in which he recruits the vision of Eliot (and the Pound of the hell cantos) to invalidate Joyce's affirmation of the eclectic banale.

However, in another sense, *The Childermass* demonstrates an extension of the perceptions of *Enemy*, 'Inferior Religions' and *Tarr*, modified by the horrors of war and the trivialities of twenties' capitalist consumerism. There are random outbreaks of brutality – Satters's battering of Pullman, or the decapitation of Barney – and varied representations of mass-entertainment – the Hollywood scenario and antics or the demogoguery of the Bailiff. The masculinist drive of *Tarr* has largely drained away here: the male characters are sometimes 'feminised', usually infantalised, and – with spectacular exceptions – aggression and imaginative energy have been dissolved into mechanistic habituation. To a degree, this paralysis has infected the narration itself. The opening vision is compelling, some of the scenes unforgettable, and the stylistic brilliance recurs to the end. But the second half of the book resolves into extended debate between the Bailiff and all-comers, especially the Hyperideans who are Lewisian antagonists of the status quo. The daemon of philosophical contention begins to overwhelm the fictional vision and, despite the Ubuesque antics of the Bailiff, the science fiction fantasia gives way to neo-Shavian dialogue. In a way, this is faithful to Dante's poem. But it does not make for compelling prose-fiction in the twentieth century – nor does it seem faithful to the imaginative scenario of the beginning. Lewis could have left the arguments to *Time and Western Man* and his many other polemical works. Certainly, he should not have allowed his *Inferno*, so vivid in places, to resolve as a noeplatonic talk-shop. Joyce, it has to be said, never quite made that mistake – though there are precedents

('Ithaca'; parts of the *Wake*) to lure Lewis's counterblast in that
Aeolian direction and onto the rocks.

Nevertheless, there are innumerable brilliances in *The Childermass*
which – beyond its patent significance as a move in the development
of Modernism – cry out against its virtual 'exclusion from the world
of letters'.[83] If *Tarr* set a precedent for war literature and postwar
social satire, then *The Childermass* is, among other things, a key
work for post-Wellsian science fiction, whether male dystopia or
female utopia – or vice versa. There are also many quite recent
films – not to mention TV fantasies – which owe, if only in
subterranean ways, to Lewis's *Divina Commedia*. *The Childermass*
established a classic version of 'The Hollow Men' as sci-fi limbo,
marrying Wells with the Conrad of *Heart of Darkness* and Eliot's
Waste Land to suggest what we are by illuminating where we could
be. At the same time, the achievement, as in *Enemy* or *Tarr*, is
evident in stylistic gestures still unrivalled by any other twentieth-
century prose stylist: 'The ass pumps an ear-splitting complaint
into its downy snout, scouring the loud sound up and down in an
insane seesaw' (p. 25); 'sounds rise on all hands like the sharp
screech of ripping calico, the piercing alto of the slate-pencil, or
the bassooning of imposing masses, frictioning each other as they
slowly turn in concerted circles' (p. 42); 'Tapping on the flags of
the court with a heavy stick, his neck works in and out as though
from a socket, with the darting reptilian rhythm of a chicken'
(p. 130); 'Barney's body falls stomach upwards, the head bounding
against the fence, the trunk gushing upon the pavement' (p. 193);
'Dense centripetal knots or vortices of people collect marginally,
beneath the wall or beyond the path, but a march is kept up where
the ground is even by an active inquisitive crowd of promenaders
passing each other back and forth like the chain of a funicular'
(p. 239); Love hidden in one of the crevices of Crawshaw's mistress,
the shadow of Plato's Cave and the Spirit of Night who dosses
with Bysshe somewhere east of Suez' (p. 284). As in *Enemy* and
Tarr, such powerful combinations of image and ironic abstraction
are *tours de force* which can, if necessary, stand on their own. At
the same time, although the debate-sequences of the second half
paralyse the action, the quality of the argument can be breathtaking.
Such ultraconscious excellence of rational discourse serves as a
counter to Joyce's primal punning and symbolic concealment in
the 'semiotic chora'[84] of *Wake*speak. In both scenario and argument
Lewis insists on conscious control, as opposed to Joyce's evocation

of the collective unconscious – whose slogan could almost be: where Ego was there let Id be. Despite parodic concessions to Joycean polyphony, Lewis reasserts Masculinist monovocality to keep satirical control of his 'time-philosophy' nightmare. *The Childermass* is a highly rationalist ironic placing.

Yet the novel is largely forgotten. There are weaknesses in its construction to help account for this neglect – it is neither consistent narrative nor cohesive drama. Yet the marginalisation of the work is probably due more to Lewis's political reputation in the thirties and his refusal of the Joycean version of the modern. *The Childermass*, altogether, is not a sufficient counterweight to *Finnegans Wake*, yet in the end it effected its own form of revenge on the master of polyphony. For in its stark scenario, comedic apparatus, and infantalised dialogue it set a precedent for a future Nobel prize-winner. No student of Beckett – and especially of *Waiting for Godot* – could miss the seminal importance of the following sample of quotations from *The Childermass*:

'Oh do let's not part.'   (p. 31)

'I simply can't go on any longer.'   (p. 31)

'Charlatan!' – a count of three – 'Outsider!'   (p. 62)

'Supposing we pinch each other that might enlighten us.'(p. 73)

'We are evidently not affected by the same laws as this leaf.'
                                                                        (p. 105)

'You want me to put those things on?'   (p. 119)

'It's no use kicking.'   (p. 119)

'I'm damned if I'll put up with you any longer.'   (p. 120)

'Shall we go now?'
Satters does not move.   (p. 121)

'I'll forgive you, shall I?'   (p. 122)

'Bracing his little legs in bandy equipoise, and hauling with all his might Pullman gets under way, marching step by step, Satters in tow. . . .'   (p. 124)

'The numerical identity of a particular existent, then, as it is catalogued in philosophy – am I right? – is not our affair at all.'
                                                                        (p. 150)

'He's about to dance!'
'Stop him! it's not decent! . . .'   (p. 217)

'Shall we go?'   (p. 240)

'Can't we go, Pulley? . . .'
'Step out. Pick your feet up. If you must go nowhere, step out.'
                                    (p. 320 – last words of the book)

If there is no single precedent for Lucky here, the Bailiff is a
convincing prototype of Pozzo, while Satters and Pullman are dead
ringers for Estragon and Vladimir – infantile and dependently
conjoined in frictional male companionship, in a wholly *Absurde*
universe. So Joyce's greatest disciple finally became his own man-
of-words by the ultimate betrayal – choosing the precedent of
Lewis, the rival, to find his own way. In this sense, *The Childermass*,
not the *Wake*, would be the gate to a Postmodernist future.

VORTEX PARIS

Ezra Pound stayed in Paris from the winter of 1920 to the autumn
of 1924. As I have argued, this period constituted the most
productive time of group activity for the Men of 1914, and Pound,
always susceptible to millenarian possibilities, proclaimed the
'end of the Christian era'.[85] Pound's move necessarily heralded a
shift of central placement for the group's interaction – from war-
obsessed London to gay, postwar Paris. Pound had persuaded
Joyce to come to Paris to live, and both Eliot and Lewis would visit
him there. These Paris years also coincided with the publication of
the three major group-works – *Ulysses*, *The Waste Land* and the
early *Cantos* – which would determine the forms and themes of
high Modernism in literature. During these years Pound was at
the centre of the dynamism which produced these works, not only
encouraging Joyce's efforts and editing the manuscript of *The Waste
Land* but also laying the foundations of his own extraordinary life-
poem. The book-publication of *Ulysses* was the emblematic event
of this time of intense achievement and Joyce, himself, rejoiced[86]
in the symbolic fact that the writing was completed on Pound's
thirty-fifth birthday. The Men of 1914 were coming of age, in all

senses of the phrase, and Ezra Pound retained his centrality as
leader at this moment of emergent greatness. His move to Paris
brought him close to the author of *Ulysses* just as Joyce was
achieving his Modernist supremacy. In the early twenties, Pound's
presence in Paris was an outward and visible sign of the transformation of imaginative thrust which had occurred since Lewis went
to war, and Joyce – studiously evading all war-issues except his
own exile from Trieste – forged ahead with his major novel in the
artistic neutrality of Switzerland.

Pound claimed that Paris was the most promising arena for
experimentality at this time – and this was almost certainly the
case. Postwar literary London was dominated by English middle-
class cliques, like the Bloomsbury set and the Sitwells – a phenomenon Eliot perhaps found conducive to the renunciation of his
'personality' but which Lewis would later denounce with all the
vituperation at his command;[87] postwar artistic Paris, by contrast,
was galvanised by international, Bohemian geniuses – a spectacle
that American writers, in particular, hastened to adore and imitate.
Pound, the sponsor of Joyce, relished the cosmopolitan 'laboratory'[88] of imaginative ideas where Picasso, Brancusi and Diaghilev
could rub shoulders with Cocteau, Madox Ford and Antheil, and
Hemingway, McAlmon and other fellow-countrymen help to swell
the scene. Pound remained amazingly alive to future possibilities
in all the arts – a fact the war-weary Richard Aldington judged
jejune[89] – and, while still fervently sponsoring the careers of the
Men of 1914, he interested himself in the work of many different
artists in the French capital. The main thrust of his interests here
achieves a strange symmetry with the type of vortex he had
fostered since the death of Gaudier. His chief interest in new artists
in the early twenties focused on Brancusi, Cocteau, Picabia, and
Hemingway. If the sculptor Brancusi is, in a sense, a replacement
for Gaudier, then we have a new painter, poet and novelist to
correlate with the new Pound of the *Cantos*, on the model of
Lewis, Eliot and Joyce. The fourway dynamic is, if nothing else,
suggestive – it is as if Pound unconsciously retains the patterning
of the most significant group of his life whenever he seeks
newer artistic relationships. As we shall see, for all his later
acknowledgement of the godfathers of Modernism – Yeats and
Ford most particularly – it is the fourway dynamic of the 1914
vortex which will stay with him, most profoundly, until the variable
voices of the *Cantos* finally peter out into silence.

Between Pound's renunciation of England and his departure for
Rapallo in 1924, his sponsorship of the Men of 1914 remained
his dominant personal and literary concern, despite his newer
interests. By getting Joyce to live in Paris, he was not only able to
fuss over his friend's family problems, and encourage the onward
progress of *Ulysses*, but he was also able to share in the glory when
the book was published in 1922. As we have seen, his review of
Ulysses was almost entirely celebratory and announced in public
the kind of praise he had given to the developing sections in
private, for example of 'Circe' – 'enormous – megascruptious-
mastodonic'.[90] At the same time, he remained close to Eliot, and
in editing *The Waste Land* so deftly he performed the single most
significant act of literary collaboration of the entire period of group
interaction. Eliot's emotional trust, as well as his respect for
Pound's editorial brilliance, is evidenced by the fact that he
accepted Ezra's suggestions almost entirely – even when they
were questionable, such as the excision of the admirably-chosen
epigraph: 'The horror! The horror!'[91] At a time of mental exhaustion
and confusion, Pound's support and admiration for his work was
one of the most stabilising factors in Eliot's life. Between 1918 and
1922 Eliot often visited Pound for rest and relaxation[92] when his
health was poor and his marital life nearly unendurable; it was
only after Pound's well-intentioned attempt to get Eliot out of the
bank to write (the 'Bel Esprit' enterprise)[93] that Eliot became
somewhat more cautious about Ezra's judgement – for public
disclosure of the abortive venture embarrassed Eliot considerably.
Lewis, of course, was far too independent to allow Pound to
mother him, as he did Joyce and Eliot, even though Lewis's artistic
efforts had received a setback where the other three writers were
forging ahead. However, Lewis visited Pound in Paris (once
meeting Hemingway in his flat),[94] drank with Joyce there and
remained on respectful terms of friendship with Eliot in London.[95]
As noted, Lewis was trying to start his literary career afresh, and
tended to closet himself in his studio in Adam and Eve Mews.
However, and especially in Paris, he remained something of a
roisterer; at the same time, his name as a writer was still highly
respected by the discerning. It was Joyce himself who, when Lewis
was flirting with a prostitute on one of their drinking evenings,
gently reproved him with the words: 'Remember you are the
author of *The Ideal Giant*'.[96] (Joyce's own ideal giant, H. C.
Earwicker, would interestingly preside over a dream-empire where

'riverrun' flowed, fluxively, 'past Eve and Adam's'.[97])

As the above Parisian anecdote indicates, there was an inherently male resonance to the bonds between Pound's group-members. To say this is not to deny the conscious appreciation and respect that each member felt towards certain women: Lewis for Rebecca West, Pound for H.D., Eliot for Virginia Woolf, and Joyce (if only because of her sponsorship) for Harriet Weaver. However, group activity tends to bring out the inherent masculinism in men – as it strengthens the feminism of women. Early in their relationship Pound alluded to Lewis's exploitative sophistication with street-women;[98] Joyce made no bones that the symbolic organ in 'Penelope' was 'the cunt'[99] (and Molly was always more a male celebration of woman's bodily 'Yes' than a psychological gift to feminists); Lewis emphasised his virility by inviting two prostitutes to enliven his drinking sessions with Joyce; and Eliot de-emphasised his wife's contribution to 'He Do the Police' in colluding with the fantasy that *The Waste Land* was the text-child of Pound and himself.[100] It is strange, in fact, that the most evident sign of sexist group-solidarity was a pornographic poem written by the future Anglican layman whose later line – 'The communication/Of the dead is tongued with fire' – would be carved in stone on the floor of Westminster Abbey. Eliot's poem was called 'King Bolo and His Great Black Queen'. Peter Ackroyd, Eliot's excellent biographer (in as far as he has been allowed to be), describes it as 'comic verses . . . with allusions to buggery, penises, sphincters and other less delicate matters'.[101] This Eliotic token of male bonding was pressed upon the other members of the group. In 1915 Pound passed it on to Lewis who refused to publish it in *BLAST* because of the words which ended in '-Uck, '-Unt or '-Ugger'.[102] Later the Possum also confided in Pound about circulating the poem to Joyce. In 1922 Pound wrote back to Eliot in suitably lewd terms: 'You can forward the "Bolo" to Joyce if you think it won't unhinge his somewhat sabbatarian mind. On the hole he might be saved the shock, shaved the sock'.[103] This delicate matter of male initiation in coarseness intrudes into the *Waste Land* correspondence – indicating its importance to Eliot as a bonding-rite.

Pound's Paris years represent the heyday of interrelationship between the Men of 1914. However, in 1924 Pound decided to leave the city, as earlier he had decided to leave London. The motives behind this decision need some consideration, if only because of its distintegrative effect on group activity and encounter

from the mid-twenties onward. There were reasons of health –
Pound had suffered a touch of pneumonia – and also Dorothy
Pound's objections to Paris winters. There was also the fact that
Pound felt out of place among the hectic partying and, above all,
drinking of the artistic set (especially the wild Americans of the
'lost generation') – Pound was always abstemious about alcohol,
even though he had once mocked Joyce for a similar, and most
uncharacteristic, abstemiousness.[104] Politically, Pound was beginning to move to the right just as the newest Paris movement,
Surrealism, was proclaiming its dubious left-wing credentials as a
revolutionary force. At the same time, he maintained that 'France
has no writer of first magnitude'[105] – an arguable assessment, but
anyway Joyce, Madox Ford and Hemingway were all in Paris, it
was full of top-rate artists and musicians, and Rapallo could
scarcely boast a writer of any kind until Pound went there. His
friend Eliot suggested that Pound was inherently nomadic[106] – yet
after this he lived in Rapallo for all the remaining interwar years
and returned to it on release from St Elizabeth's Hospital many
years later. It is clear that Pound savoured the possibility of a
milder climate and that the spirit of Italy called to him more
powerfully than the current futurist stunts in Paris (perhaps Lewis's
charge of essential 'antiquarianism' is born out here). However,
the predominant reason for the move – conscious or unconscious –
was surely that Pound sensed he must devote less energy to
other men's work and more to his own. Largely through his
entrepreneurial efforts the names of Joyce and Eliot were now
prominent as literary masters of the New – yet the *Cantos* were
coming out only in dribs and drabs, and in little magazine form.
Further, Pound had little time for Joyce's *Pomes Penyeach* and none,
so he intimated, for the elaborate connotative allusiveness of 'Work
in Progress'.[107] His relations with Joyce began to cool (to Joyce's
dismay) and henceforth he would tend to praise Lewis at Joyce's
expense (see below p. 140). Yet the most important motive was
surely enlightened self-interest. As Hemingway put it:

> So far we have Pound the major poet devoting, say, one fifth of
> his time to poetry. With the rest of his time he tries to advance
> the fortunes, both material and artistic of his friends. He defends
> them when they are attacked, he gets them into magazines and
> out of jail. He loans them money. He sells their pictures. He
> arranges concerts for them. He writes articles about them. He

introduces them to wealthy women. He gets publishers to take their books. He sits up all night with them when they claim to be dying and he witnesses their wills. He advances them hospital expenses and dissuades them from suicide. And in the end a few of them refrain from knifing him at the first opportunity.[108]

There is enough truth in this generous tribute to make it a persuasive account; one wonders whether the grateful Ernest may have taken it as his duty to point out the situation to Pound himself. Whether or not, Pound's major role as sponsor of new writers ended when he left for Italy. He did not drop the old members of the group but neither was he disposed to fuss over them as he once had. His departure to Rapallo marks the beginning of a parting of the ways. As we shall see, however, even such differences as opened up between the four men served merely to fuel the ongoing intertextual dynamics within their works.

The first signs of this parting of the ways were Pound's repudiation of the style of 'Work in Progress' and Lewis's attack upon *Ulysses*: perhaps predictably, the break-up centred on the work of James Joyce, now the most spectacularly lionised of the Men of 1914. Eliot, whose *Waste Land* had created almost as much stir in England as *Ulysses* had in France and America, did not join in either repudiation. He remained overwhelmingly impressed by the achievement of *Ulysses*, published part of 'Work in Progress' in the *Criterion* in 1925, and at Faber brought out *Anna Lyvia Plurabelle* (1930), *haveth Childers Everywhere* (1931) and *Two Tales of Shem and Shaun* (1932).[109] In fact Eliot used his good offices as magazine editor and book publisher to benefit all three of his group-friends. *Cantos* IX–XII were published in the *Criterion* of July 1923, and Eliot also printed some of Pound's political and religious musings in the magazine in the Thirties, as well as bringing out *Ezra Pound: Selected Poems* (with an introduction by himself[110]) and the collected *Cantos* (1954 and after) at Faber and Faber. Similarly, although Lewis tended to use his own publishing contacts (frequently abusing his advances by not producing the goods on time – or at all), Eliot brought out two draft chapters of *The Apes of God* in the *Criterion* (1924) – despite their libellous nature – and would later write a foreword to the posthumous second edition of Lewis's *One Way Song* (1960). Eliot, then, was the man who took over Pound's centralising role in the group once Pound had left Paris for Rapallo. And as Eliot grew to become the most authoritative critic in

England, as well as its greatest living poet, his continued regard for Joyce, Lewis and Pound, and his public approval of most of their ventures, helped maintain a sense of group-affinity – despite the growing differences between the members.

5

Lost in the Labyrinth

The beginning of 'Work in Progress'[1] marks Joyce's ultimate rendezvous with history and himself: the style is almost wholly unique. If, as I suggested, *Ulysses* constitutes a stylistic journey – starting with a synthesis of late Flaubert, Dujardin and Lewis in the *Telemachiad* and progressing, through parodic metamorphoses, to the remarkable Molly-spiel of 'Penelope', *Finnegans Wake*[2] (when ended) will elaborate a flexible, yet self-consistent, species of stylistic stasis. Joyce has found a discourse which is wholly his own yet can, thereby, utter a species of the voice of the collective unconscious. And where, as noted above, *Ulysses* is essentially a satiric compendium of written stylistic positions, 'Work in Progress', from the beginning, elaborates a written variant of essentially oral and mythic culture. Joyce, we might say, has taken the challenge of *The Waste Land* on board, and used its probes backward to the mythological unconscious to elaborate his own massively mythic world-discourse. It is notable, over the book as a whole, that the parts of that poem which most fascinate him are the primal and collective cries which he reappropriates: 'by the waters of babalong' (p. 103); 'we weep now with them. O! O! O!' (p. 158); 'Shaunti and shaunti and shaunti again!' (p. 408); 'Cocorico! . . . Cocoree! . . . Echo, choree chorecho!' (p. 584); 'Sandhyas! Sandhyas! Sandhyas!' (p. 593). After the precedent of *The Waste Land* Joyce, too, now reaches behind Greek narrative to resonate tribal myth and 'Iro-European ascendances' (p. 37). It is fitting, therefore, that already in the second paragraph of the whole, he should allude to Eliot's appropriation of his book by Lake Leman ('Helviticus committed deuteronomy', p. 4), 'sternely' (Stearns) transforming his comic affirmation into communal disaster. It is an appropriation he will return to 'anent Tiberias [Tiresias?] and other incestuish salacities among gerontophils'[3] (p. 115) and transform Eliot's ceremonious opening into riotous Joycespeak:

'Midwinter (fruur or kuur?) was in the offing and Premver a promise of a pril . . .' (p. 110).

One of the earliest pieces of 'Work in Progress' transcribes Joyce's feelings about Eliot's appropriation at complex length: in *Finnegans Wake* this stretches from page 35 to page 40 or so. In his *Reader's Guide*,[4] William York Tindall merely points to the reference: 'ildiot repeated in his secondmouth language as many of the bigtimer's verbaten words which he could balbly call to memory' (p. 37). It seems to me there is a lot more reference to Eliot in the whole passage about Earwicker's meeting with 'the Cad' (cadet – the young pretender). Here are some: 'Ides-of-April morning', 'the wastes to south', 'ten ton tonuant thunderous tenor toller'[5] (p. 35); 'reconstricted out of oral style into the verbal for all time with ritual rhythmics', 'the honours of our mewmew mutual daughters'[6] (p. 36); 'saluting corpses, as a metter of corse', 'a musaic dispensation about his *hearthstone*',[7] 'a supreme of excelling peas' ('Shantih' – 'the peace that passes understanding'[8]), 'your rat wi'fennel' (p. 37); ''tis a leaman's farewell' ('waters of Leman', 'O you who turn the wheel and look to windward'[9]), 'eys dry and small',[10] 'Ecclectiastes of Hippo',[11] '(my bravor best! my fraur!)' '(mon semblable, – mon frère!',[12] p. 38); 'the Cock, the Postboy's Horn'[13] (p. 39); 'the Little Old Man's' ('Gerontion', p. 40). The meeting of the two figures is set in a park in Spring at midday. The Cad asks 'how much a clock it was'. This alludes both to Eliot's reference to the 'horoscope' in his review of *Ulysses* and to its publication in *The Dial*.[14] On one level the confrontation is almost a duel – perhaps with *Tarr* in mind. But it concerns 'building' in language and ends as literary appropriation – a kind of Oedipal overthrow associated also with Joyce's legendary meeting with Yeats ('I have met with you, bird, too late',[15] p. 37) – partly, too, because Eliot had attributed the discovery of the 'mythical method' to the older Irishman ('there is not one tittle of truth, allow me to tell you, in that purest of fibfib fabrications' p. 36). In a sense ildiot defeats Earwicker and takes his wife (Ezra, and the body of 'the New Free Woman'[16]). 'Edzo' (p. 39) may here be Pound to Eliot's 'Treacle Tom' ('come off the hulks, both of them awful poor') who in the first revised cantos was 'having a gurgle off his own along of the butty bloke in the specs' (p. 39). There seems, too, to be references to Joyce and Lewis drinking with Eliot in Paris ('a bottle of Phenice-Bruerie '98', p. 38) as well as to Joyce's belated visit to Pound in Sirmione ('*I come, my horse delayed*', p. 40).[17] But the main thrust of the meeting concerns the way Eliot stole Joyce's thunder in *The Waste Land* ('DA', 'DA', 'DA') and ends with reappropriation on p. 44 – 'klikkaklakkaklaskak . . . kot!', as *Wake*speak types back verbal-orally to *The Waste Land*'s 'rhythmical grumbling'. Thus Joyce returns the honour of appropriation, pressed down and running over in verbal fluidity – often with a mind (should they have ears to hear) to 'the laetification of siderodromites and to the irony of the stars',[18] (p. 160).

In this work, Joyce is way ahead of the field again – birthing the New, in wholly original prose, astride the grave of the past – and needing no one but himself (and his growing disciples) to do anything but admire. There is no longer much place for the old 'scout-master', Pound the 'wonderworker' of yesteryear and, indeed, 'Esra, the cat' (p. 116) is rarely a presence in the whole – the less so, perhaps, because Pound was wont to wash his hands of Joyce's entire new project.[19] But another of the Men of 1914 becomes an antagonist against whom 'Shem the penman'[20] will devote more than one counterblast ('Blast yourself and your anathomy infairioriboos!' (p. 154)) – most especially for anatomising the Joycean consciousness in 'Spice and Westend Woman'[21] (p. 292). If he rather feared that 'churchwarden' Eliot might nobble the 'Noblett's surprize' (p. 306) for literature over his head ('Thou in slanty scanty shanty!!!'[22], p. 305), he could certainly not forgive the author of *The Lion and the Fox* ('Lyon O'Lynn . . . played fox and lice', pp. 148–9) for publicly rebuking his masterwork as 'temporiser', (p. 154). Even before the Ondt's putdown, Lewis (both 'Leonem' and 'raskolly Gripos') is made into Shaun, antagonist of Shem the 'Mookse'. So the author of *Enemy* ('mein goot enemy! or Cospol's not our star', p. 155) and *Tarr* ('Rats! . . . Rots!', p. 154) becomes Englished and spatialised (Joyce 'trespassing on the space question', p. 160) and punningly counter-'embousch'ed for the sour grapes of his gripe. The deep hurt of his attack is evident for all Joyce's effort to maintain diplomatic relations: 'Us shall be chosen as the first of the last' (p. 156). And within the polysemous texture of ambiguities runs the thread of a fairly coherent defence. For example, Joyce evokes the names of those Lewis associates him with as 'time-philosopher' – 'Bitchson' (Bergson), 'Miss Fortune' (Gertrude Stein – 'who the lost time we had the pleasure we have had our little *recherché* brush with', p. 149)[23], hence Proust[24] ('*recherché*) and 'Winestain' – (Einstein, p. 149). Joyce does not want to be lumped with anyone as a creature of 'impulsivism' and his style is not equatable with Stein's, granted that 'speechform is a mere sorrogate' (p. 149).

The eleventh part of Chapter VI of the *Wake* appears to be dominated by the dispute with Lewis.[25] There are – as always in the work – complex metamorphoses of character and apparent point of view, but granted that – as Tindall's *Guide* says – it concerns 'a learned defence of space against time, eye against ear, stone against tree',[26] then *Time and Western Man* is far more relevant than Tindall, for instance, makes it. It cannot be said that Professor Jones simply is Lewis (no character simply 'is' in the *Wake*); nor is he specifically either Mookse or Gripes (who exchange roles anyhow). But Jones's defence of space is notably Lewisian and in so far as the Mookse has 'eyes but cannot hear' and the Gripes 'has ears but cannot see',[27] we have a dialectical polarisation of the main issues between Lewis and Joyce. Jones's disgressions complicate the matter considerably but the space-time issue dominates such pages as 148–50 (with a sideglance at Eliot – 'the sword-swallower, who is on at the Craterium') and 153–61, while references to 'the bailiff's distrain' and 'Seter satt huc sate' (Satters?) on 153 seem to suggest Joyce has looked at *The Childermass*[28] too. At any rate, the issue resolves in Joycean affirmation at the end: 'My unchanging Word is sacred . . . the rite words by the rote order' (p. 167). On the way, there are a variety of in-jokes. I take Joyce to be 'foxy' to 'leonine' Lewis; the advent of the 'woman of no appearance (I believe she was a Black with chills at her feet)' (p. 158) surely refers to Lewis's critique of Stein's *Melanctha* (a black girl with 'child' language)[29] and, at this point, the woman rescues the Mookse (here Joyce associating himself with the 'Moo-Cow' of *Portrait*?) and 'plucked down the Gripes'; while references to the 'jus' of the Gripes may refer to the old drinking days of Joyce and Lewis – as well as to the Jews. Altogether there is a national distinction between Ireland and Irishness and English persecution (Nicholas Breakspear as Pope condoning the conquest),[30] on the one hand, and Welshness (the 'Wilsh'), on the other: Lewis was English but (like Prof. Jones) has a Welsh name, while Lewis's rationalist attack on Joyce's subversion of English style becomes a repeat of the old Anglo-Irish quarrel. In a subtly diffused way, the references to Jews, women, blacks and children pick up an undertone in *Time and Western Man* that Lewis scarcely disguised. For in his denunciation of a style he associated with jazz, women (Stein, Loos), Jewish thinkers (Bergson, Einstein), 'dementia'[31] and children's talk, we see a complex Nietzschean paradigm of the discourse of the slave impinging on the domain of the master – 'Western Man'. The impulse behind this is evident in his comment on Charlie Chaplin that the public approves the *'little-fellow-put-upon'* but the 'fact that the giants were always vanquished . . . never, of course, struck the Public as pathetic, too' (*Time and Western Man*, p. 82). Lewis speaks for the Western man (just after his greatest fall in the Great War); he is not much interested in the underdog – in the experience of being Jewish, black, feminine, schizophrenic or childish. And Joyce's situation of the 'dime-cash problem' (p. 149), as repeated motif, also locates another aspect of Lewis's attack – that he was against the commercialised democracy of the twenties, the world of public entertainment, sexual adventure and everchanging fashion. For all his giant élitism, Joyce (creator of Bloom) was all for the little man and his *petit bourgeois* mores and morals.

Joyce returns briefly to the Lewis issue at the end of another Aesopian fable – this time that of the Ondt and the Gracehoper.[32] The 'Accident Man' (p. 418) is clearly occidental Lewis ('your mocks for my gropes'). But where the earlier struggle seems to end on a note of self-pity – Jones's rejection of Shem the exile ('were he my own breastbrother . . . still I'd fear I'd hate to say!', p. 168) – he concludes here with an affirmation of 'my . . . risible universe' and a pointed salute to his old friend:

> *Your genus its worldwide, your spacest sublime!*
> *But, Holy Saltmartin, why can't you beat time?*[33]

Joyce, then, is able to incorporate Lewis's attack into the matter and method of his dreambook and he continues to Gracehope away in the fluxive, multimeaninged style he has elaborated. Doubtless he might have ended up with some proximity to *Wake*speak without either Lewis or the larger group: yet in terms of the dynamics of rivalry between the two prose stylists there is, perhaps, a way in which Lewis's cornering of monovocal rationalist discourse has pushed Joyce towards the semiconscious babble of the *Wake*, as earlier it had pushed him toward the parodic polyphony of *Ulysses*. Joyce has his revenge on the Ondt – yet few, beyond Beckett, could have detected how thoroughly. *Time and Western Man* was public polemic and scored an overt hit: the comic rebuttals in the *Wake* are private encodings, the rhetorical strategy of 'silence, exile, and cunning'.[34]

The achievement of the *Wake* is monumental and wholly daunting. The ongoing sections of 'Work in Progress' took the idea of birthing 'the new, (the really new) work' further than anyone would want to go again, and in that sense its appearance meant the end of the main group-project.[35] If its neoScholastic quirkiness set a precedent for the Pound of, say, the Pisan Cantos, it shunted Lewis back to more populist[36] fiction (bar the parodies in *The Childermass*) and perhaps helped Eliot to 'turn again' in a direction which favoured tradition more than novelty. In a sense, it is an act of deliberate self-isolation. No *Waste Lands* or cantos were ever likely to spring from the reading of this multilingual private labyrinth. At the moment of his greatest acclaim, after the appearance of *Ulysses*, Joyce set himself to do what he had always wanted – create a book out of himself which was finally for himself. As the Irish godfather of the Men of 1914 (and Oedipal butt in the *Wake*) had written: 'A man in his own secret meditation / Is lost amid the labyrinth that he has made / In art or politics'.[37] Joyce had deliberately chosen the figure of the labyrinth for his Daedelian project, and to demand a reader's 'whole life'[38] to understand it was merely to want to make of the reader another (but passive) James Joyce. The birth of the New, here, means Messianic omnipotence with which no Oedipal rival could ever contend – as Beckett came to perceive. It seeks to subsume the whole group-effort (Esra, Ildiot, and Leon the Ondt) into the assertion of 'joyicity' – and the making of the ultimate maze.

The style, here, is more to the point than any neoVicoan plan, since whatever research can yield, in the end the style remains always with us. It bespeaks the core of the Modernist project – to make it new as a mode of literary *re*newing. Encouraged by the group, still notionally under Pound's tutelage, Joyce now opens his wordhoard to include the sounds and half-meanings of language in general. The aim (like that of the *Cantos* overall) is an organised field where all tongues and times can be conjoined in a luminous paradigm of the Modern. And it starts in the first fragment written[39] – its opening verbal gesture agreeably akin to Pound's 'so that' ending to revised Canto II:

So anyhow, melumps and mumpos of the hoose uncommons, after that to wind up that longtobechronickled gettogether

> thanksbetogiving day at Glenfinnisk-en-la-Valle, the anniversary
> of his finst homy commulion . . .   (p. 380)

The sentence continues apace, neoMollyean in this; essentially
paratactic as most of the *Cantos* will be. The vital difference,
however, to Pound's search for ideogrammic facticity will be its
insistent, allusive ambiguity: 'hoose uncommons' or 'finst homy
commulion'. Such (chameleon) communion of some million, million connotations among differences will become hallmark of the
whole – a final refusal of the cult of the concrete and 'presentative'.
Joyce has moved on from the role of successor to Flaubert (or
Lewis); he has discovered the unique and final language to birth
the Joycean Messiah (whose death brings resurrection – Finnegan,
fin-again). For, as he said to his brother, Stanislaus, in 1936: 'The
only thing that interests me is style'.[40]

Yet even the earlier versions of 'Work in Progress' evidence an
ambition, beyond linguistic revolution, to construct a thematic
masterwork – both of the age and for all time. The developing
sections speak of the great age of 'History', now extended to
ethnology and myth. If limited in focus, it out-thinks Spengler (for
whom 'decline' and death is the main agenda) and outflanks Jane
Harrison, and others post-Frazer, by remythologising demytholi-
gisation-discourse.[41] Its highly Postmodernist theme is the rebuilding
which must always take place where deconstructive experts are
having a field day. And that is about where the finished work
starts:

> Oftwhile balbulous, mithre ahead, with goodly trowel in grasp
> and ivoroiled overalls which he habitacularly fondseed, like
> Haroun Childeric Eggeberth he would caligulate by multipli-
> cables the alltitude and malltitude until he seesaw by neatlight of
> the liquor wheretwin 'twas born . . . a waalworth of a skyerscape
> of most eyeful hoyth entowerly, erigenating from next to
> nothing. . . .   (pp. 4–5)

The later Pound might have appreciated how 'erigenating' (originate, Scotus Erigena) is connected with neat/*light* and the city (cf.
Pound's Ecbatan) built with 'trowel' (trow = know, too) out of
fond seed (and found seed) 'overall'). This will be Joyce's mode of
essaying to 'keep the petals from falling' and his ongoing venture
to build the 'city' out of 'confusion, source of renewals' in a great

'palimpsest'.[42] We shall return, in Chapter 6, to discuss the contribution of Joyce's 'next step', in terms of completion. Whatever Pound thought at the time, 'Work in Progress' was also, in a sense, group-work, pitched forward toward some future synthesis in which all reality could be subsumed in Modernist art.

TO TURN AGAIN

In London, T. S. Eliot faithfully published such sections of 'Work in Progress' in the *Criterion*, or at Faber, as were sent to him from Paris. With Pound now in Italy, it was left largely to him to keep the ideals of the Men of 1914 alive. He did this by bringing out contributions by all of them in his periodical, and later by publishing *Finnegans Wake* and Pound's *Selected Poems* and *Cantos* at Faber. In the mid-twenties Eliot's literary reputation in England was far greater than that of the other three. Copies of *Ulysses* had to be smuggled in from France and it was not yet highly regarded in England.[43] But *The Waste Land* had achieved not only a *succès de scandale* but was quickly gaining academic recognition – especially in the new English Department at Cambridge.[44] At the same time, the publication of his early critical essays, and his presence in the *Criterion*, made him the leading authority on the new literature. The Possum had become high priest of Modernism. Yet he was not a happy man. As his marriage deteriorated further and his personal desolation increased, he became less interested in a purely aesthetic rebirthing and increasingly absorbed in the struggle for spiritual renewal. Joyce's punning disparagements of Eliot's verse in 'Work in Progress' could scarcely have touched him, if he had noticed them. He was beyond the 'King Bolo' days of intense group interchange.

As Pound's group began to dissolve into the disparate preoccupations of its constituent members, Eliot attached himself first to the Woolfs' Bloomsbury and then to the Anglican Church. Yet his path now seems an essentially solitary one. If 'The Hollow Men' (1925) develops some of the negative implications of *The Waste Land*, it does so in a very different style and manner and by 'Ash Wednesday' (1930) the radical experimentalism of *The Waste Land* has been very largely discarded. 'Ash Wednesday' is self-confessedly a pivotal poem. There is virtually no trace in it of Lewisian grotesquerie, Poundian collage or Joycean polyphony. Here the plaintive personal voice becomes subsumed into the language of collective liturgy: 'And let my cry come unto Thee'. It is as distinctly a solitary production as *The Waste Land* is a species of group expression. And because of its closeness to the discourse of religious communion, it constitutes, in a way, a renunciation of the group project for a specifically literary renaissance. Writing, alone, was no longer enough. In the light of this, the earlier 'Journey of the Magi' takes on a peculiar interest. For in it, in disguised form, we see Eliot reviewing – as from another life – the shared aesthetic adventure of the Men of 1914.

'Journey of the Magi' (1927) is in a form Eliot had flirted with before,[45] the dramatic monologue, here slightly complicated as a dictated letter – 'but set down / This . . . .' It is about the Magi (no number given) and their encounter with a birth which seems like death. Written by one of the Magi, from a position of brooding dissatisfaction ('no longer at ease'), it recounts hard travel, memories of happier days, a perplexing encounter and a lingering feeling of confusion and regret. Its characteristic pronoun is the group-collective 'we', but it ends on a note of personal isolation: 'I should be glad of another death'. It is, then, a poem about lost group-experience, and it is powerfully reminiscent of another poem on the same subject – Rihaku's 'Exile's Letter', translated by Pound in *Cathay* (1915). 'Exile's Letter' is, for me, the most moving of all Pound's translations. It is similarly written in letter-form, with an intermediary: 'I call in the boy . . . / To seal this'. The poem is also about intellectual peers: 'Intelligent men came . . . / made nothing of sea-crossing or of mountain-crossing, / If only they could be of that fellowship'. It, too, involves journeying – though on more than one occasion – and evokes, among other things, 'hard going' (cf. 'cold coming'), 'late in the year, / in the cutting wind from the North' (cf. 'Just the worst time of the year . . . the weather sharp'), a valley with 'bright flowers' (cf. 'temperate valley'), a 'dynastic temple' (cf. 'summer palaces'), and 'vermilioned girls' (cf. 'silken girls'). The end of 'Exile's Letter' concerns the dissolution of a group of comrades:

> And then the crowd broke up . . .
> And if you ask how I regret that parting:
> It is like the flowers falling at Spring's end.

It ends, as noted above (p. 38), with a masterly stroke of imagistic

understatement: 'And send it a thousand miles, thinking'. Just so,
no doubt, did the Possum now correspond with the old 'scout-
master', some thousand miles away in Rapallo!

Where Rihaku's poem speaks with gusto of the old days, Eliot's –
frequently using a similar paratactic mode – recalls discomfort and
perplexity. The other magi are never described; they are, as it
were, subsumed into the collective experience: 'Then at dawn we
came down to a temperate valley. . . .' There is a strong group
sense of shared effort against odds ('A hard time we had of it')
and of mutual expectation, disturbed by conventional mockery:
'the voices singing in our ears, saying / That this was all folly' (cf.
Pound's earlier 'and all this is folly to the world').[46] In the valley
are 'three trees', looking back to *Enemy* as well as forward (as it
were) to the Crucifixion, and a 'running stream' happily close to
the first word of the future *Wake* ('riverrun'). The 'tavern' recalls
the tavern-gift in 'Exile's Letter'[47] and perhaps the nights with
Lewis and Joyce in Paris – as the journey-sequence ('And the
villages dirty and charging high prices') may well encode experiences touring in France with both Ezra and Wyndham, on separate
occasions. 'Six hands at an open door dicing for pieces of silver'
may transcribe a fear of betrayal by the others in the gamble of
making it new – with the 'open door' the birth-canal of the literary
future. But whatever else, it is the imagistic 'perfect symbol'[48] in
preparing for transition between 'no information' and 'finding the
place'. And so to the event: 'it was (you may say) satisfactory'.
Well yes – *Portrait, Tarr*, 'Mauberley', *Ulysses, The Waste Land, The
Draft of XVI Cantos* and 'Work in Progress'. Yet Eliot's caution is
right: for all their endeavours, quite what had been changed, and
what could be made of the war that had marginalised their
Messianic dreams of renewal? Even the drained and repentant
Possum 'would do it again'; but the question remains as probe of
the whole Modernist project from *BLAST* to *The Childermass* (also
1927): 'were we led all that way for / Birth or Death?' There was
birth, we are told, but it was 'hard and bitter agony for us' and
much like 'Death, our death'. How far the others – especially
Joyce – would have agreed with this verdict is a moot point,[49] and
it is partly a reworking of the deepest ambivalences in *The Waste
Land*. Yet both 'Hugh Selwyn Mauberley' and *The Childermass* create
new life in a scenario of burial or limbo and *Finnegans Wake* will
press the paradox to abstruse *absurdum*. At this point Eliot refrains
from attempting to resolve the equation. Yet he gives enough to

the past group-endeavour in the ambiguous ending: 'I should be glad of another death'.

If the poem aims to re-enact the general experience of the Men of 1914, as a parallel to Eliot's new thinking about Incarnation, it is also surely a specific gift to his old mentor Ezra Pound, as Eliot adopted, in public, the role of English Magus of the new literature – a role which Pound had renounced. The relationship to 'Exile's Letter', in particular, is important here. Eliot's postwar disillusionment transforms Pound's nostalgically companionable translation into a kind of exhausted puzzlement, where the good times 'on slopes, the terraces' are banished to a prior world, which only the unrepentant Ezra will continue to recycle as 'Dioce whose terraces are the colour of stars'.[50] Yet the sense of an uncharacterisable solidarity is here – especially in respect to the brother-poet: 'There were times we regretted . . .'; a note that will recur in the future *Cantos,* and be evidenced in Eliot's fidelity to his friend throughout the years in St Elizabeth's hospital and beyond. Pound would recognise this and repay the debt of feeling after Eliot's death: 'deserving more than I ever gave him . . . let some thesis writer have the satisfaction of "discovering" whether it was in 1920 or '21 that I went from Excideuil to meet a rucksacked Eliot. Days of walking-conversation. . . .'[51] Yes – and perhaps, at evening, 'a tavern with vine-leaves over the lintel' and the talk probably at the expense of 'the old dispensation'. This 'thesis writer' would wish merely to reconnect a modern Christian verse-classic with its precedent-poem, in the context of an aesthetic group-venture which Eliot was now dissociating himself from with sombre deliberation and regret.

'Ash Wednesday' completed, in a sense, this rueful parting of the ways. It is a poem of 'turning', in the Andrewes sense, which no doubt involved all that Eliot had lived until then – the 'lost sea smell' of his Boston days as well as the postwar prerogative 'Redeem / The time'. Dante[52] is the bond here with the other poet-member of the dispersed group, as Rihaku (and Browning) had been in 'The Journey'. The 'Sovegna vos' of IV (Daniel to Dante – as Dante to Daniel in 'il miglior fabbro') speaks forward towards Pound's later 'dove sta memoria' (Canto XLVI), where 'Nothing matters but the quality of the affection'. Yet the issue is 'to turn again'. At the beginning Eliot is still distracted, 'Desiring this man's gift and that man's scope' – Lewis, Pound, Joyce, surely, as well as dead masters. Yet this Magus seeks to no longer 'strive towards such things' and tells himself he is content with 'the infirm glory of the positive hour' (literary fame as his life falls apart?). He renounces the 'blessed face' of the old Muse yet memorialises the Modernist achievement: 'what is done, not to be done again'. It is perhaps wayward to associate the three devouring leopards of II, and the three stair-turnings of III with the threatening 'six hands dicing' of 'Journey', but altogether the land will be divided 'by lot' and (by 1930) 'we have our inheritance', even if that meant a 'journey to no end'. The 'years that walk between' have affected a restoration 'with a new verse' of 'the ancient rhyme' – individual talent thus subsumed in Tradition – but 'our exile' lies ahead and Eliot is concerned to renounce the 'spent word' in favour of 'Word without a word' in V. Canto VI evokes a priestly 'father' in place of the old 'scout-master' and in his presence the 'lost heart' poignantly looks back:

> And the weak spirit quickens to rebel
> For the bent golden-rod and the lost sea smell. . . .

Beyond this, the 'voices shaken from the yew-tree drift away' and 'the other yew' (yew – you?) must now reply. The new 'yew' must be summoned, phoenix-like, out of the ashes of the burnt-out soul, as the poem births a new 'turn' by implying that this is scarcely possible. The past, including the group-past, is laid to rest, yet the presence of Dante – 'Our peace in His will' – offers requiem, in friendship, to Pound in particular, before the poet merges himself in the common liturgical voice.

That ecclesiastical voice becomes the chief note in Eliot's creative work for some time – and not favourably so for his poetic reputation. It becomes, for instance, irritatingly pompous in 'Choruses from "The Rock"':

> All men are ready to invest their money
> But most expect dividends.
> I say to you: *Make perfect your will.*[53]

One might applaud the intention, but not the effect: the 'pontifical' tone has migrated from the early essays to infect a verse once notoriously ironic, fluent and self-knowing. Yet the new *Bewegung* of Anglicanism provided the matrix for a further and final flowering of Eliot's genius. By sponsoring *Murder in the Cathedral*, the Church commissioners opened the way for *Four Quartets*, whose earliest lines were to consist of nondramatisable offcuts from the original script. In the meantime, there was the play itself. *Murder in the Cathedral* (1935) is, in a sense, an offering to Eliot's new spiritual group and is thereby, to a degree, a betrayal of the old work-group, the Men of 1914. Just as Eliot, the critic, will now argue against the essential premise of Pound's group, that the 'really new work' has an autonomous importance irrespective of any value-schemes within it, so, as poet-dramatist, he now puts his talents in the service of a religion to which the aesthetic must finally be subservient. In thus celebrating the martyrdom of St Thomas, he is also martyrising himself – the 'old Tom' whose *Waste Land* had been called 'detached from all beliefs'[54] and whose true successor will be another Becket(t) – Samuel from the land of Shem Joyce. Yet, in one sense or another, Eliot had been connoisseur of death wish from his earliest Laforguean try-outs. What matters is the right kind of death – for in that will lie a rebirthing. Standing in the way of this will be tempters who are also potentially assassins:[55] there are, of course, four of them – one of whom tempts Thomas with his own unredeemed thoughts. It would be totally inappropriate to allegorise the tempters – as, say, Pound, Lewis, Joyce and the old Tom respectively. Very rarely does literature operate so crudely.[56] Yet the four-way dynamic does seem significant, and the combination of temptation and fantasised betrayal and assassination of Eliot, post-'Ash Wednesday', seems psychoanalytically suggestive at far deeper levels than dramatic convenience. The first tempter alludes to the 'gay' old days of male friendship and sensuality ('King Bolo') in language close to that of the Pound of *Cathay*: 'Laughter and apple-blossom floating on the water' (p. 246); 'float as sweet as blossoms'. The second tempter counsels: 'Power is present. Holiness hereafter' (p. 248), as Lewis spent much of the interwar years writing political pamphlets. The third tempter warns that 'real friendship, once ended, cannot be mended' (p. 251) which may relate to Eliot stealing Joyce's thunder and the betrayal insisted on in 'Work in Progress'. And the fourth tempter counsels just such an unredeemed self-immolation which through the death-scenarios of *The Waste Land* and 'The Hollow Men' was primarily to win him the Nobel Prize – that martyr's crown of the aesthetic realm. The collective charge of the tempters – 'Lost in the wonder of his own greatness' (p. 256) – has its own *frisson* in a world where Lewis and Pound were now marginalised and Joyce lost in his incomprehensible labyrinth, nearly blind and quite shortly to die. So, too, the three knights who perform the killing accuse him precisely of betraying their cause: 'The man who cheated, swindled, lied; broke his oath and betrayed his King' (p. 266). The whole issue must remain speculative and operate, anyway, in that uncertain borderland between conscious invention and unconscious drives. Yet granted the way that Eliot 'turned' – thus appalling the Bloomsburys too,[57] who had printed *The Waste Land* – it would be surprising if Eliot felt no guilt towards the ideals of 1914, which he was now renouncing in public. Meantime, he kept on as good terms with his old friends as he could – refusing to quarrel with Lewis[58] and commissioning his portrait from him, and keeping the words of Joyce and Pound alive and well at Faber. Yet something was lost in the new 'blessed Thomas' who, Pound would say, now tended to disguise himself as Westminster Abbey.[59] For the moment, the greatest intensity of his talent was lost; as the Sermon[60] has it: 'I do not think I shall ever preach to you again' (p. 262). But he would – speak if not preach – and in a meditative cycle, structured like music, where five thematic sections are varied four times.

NUEVO MUNDO

Abroad, in the Italian town of Rapallo, Ezra Pound was now as lost in his personal labyrinth as Joyce in the maze of 'Work in Progress', Eliot in his spiral ascent to 'the Word without a word' or Lewis in his complex manoeuvres against assorted 'Apes'. His attempts to set up a new literary group, by means of letter,[61] could never succeed as the old group had, back in the London days. Besides, the old group-leader had himself 'turned': giving birth to a new art was no longer enough after the Great War and in view of the economic and political problems of the twenties and thirties. Ezra became converted to a theory of money which few could accept (although Eliot would help promote it[62]) and he became increasingly isolated and cumulatively cranky. Already, in 1928, he had written in the *Exile*: 'Quite simply: I want a new civilization'.[63] There were many writers and intellectuals who felt the same at that time, but for no one else was Social Credit and the Italy of Mussolini (Pound's current formula) an attractive option. His desire for radical change of the banking system, in particular, was heartfelt

and honourable; but in venturing out of the realm of aesthetics –
where his flair was already legendary – and into the world of
economics and politics, he lacked real maps and eventually landed
himself in positions which no average Douglas-supporter[64] could
endorse, let alone the ageing Men of 1914. He was on a road which
led to the idiosyncratic speeches to American troops, on Italian
radio, in wartime; and so to the Disciplinary Training Center, at
Pisa, the threat of execution as traitor, and eventual incarceration
in St Elizabeth's Hospital, Washington. In self-chosen exile, Pound
dreamed of birthing a new world commensurate to his poetic
imagination, and in doing so eventually courted an isolation worse
even than 'final / Exclusion from the world of letters'.

Pound's new project was embarked on with the best of motives.
He had seen the Great War casually terminate the lives of men like
Gaudier, Hulme and Owen who (even) peacetime Europe had
neither subsidised for their talents nor recognised as socially
valuable. The war section of 'Hugh Selwyn Mauberley', together
with the 'Hell' Cantos,[65] are key pointers to Ezra's new awareness.
Something was rotten in the world, and it was the duty of the
writer – the birther of renaissance – to identify and condemn it.
For this reason, he found Joyce's Olympian egocentricity, and his
tinkering (as he felt it) in the 'Safety Pun Factory'[66] of 'Work in
Progress', not only incomprehensible but repugant as Europe
stumbled on from crisis to crisis. It is surely encoded in one of the
Chinese cantos:

> The highbrows are full of themselves
> learnèd, gay and irrelevant
> on such base nothing stands.
>
> (LIV, p. 278)

or:

> 'Writers are full of their own importance.'
>
> (LIV, p. 279)

Perhaps, indeed, the feeling is already present in canto XXXVIII,
the great diatribe against armament manufacturers and salesmen:
'and the Pope's manners were so like Mr Joyce's, / got that way in
the Vatican, weren't like that before' (p. 187) – in the context of
'Metevsky's' (Sir Basil Zakaroff's?) visit to Catholic South America,

on a selling mission. Certainly, outside the cantos of the late twenties and thirties, which rarely allude to Joyce, Pound made plain his antipathy to Joyce's post-*Ulysses* apotheosis as orchestrator of panoramic ambiguity. As he wrote to Joyce himself in 1926: 'nothing short of divine vision or a new cure for the clapp can possibly be worth all the circumambient peripherization'.[67]

'Circumambient peripherization' sums up the difference between Pound's current, and future, pursuit of a concretely factive language (directed toward active change[68]) and Joyce's arcane collation of multilingual ambiguities to mytholise the present as dream-transformation of the unchangeable, and ever-recurrent past. In practice, this led Pound to prefer Joyce's rival when it came to literary recommendations. To the administrators of the Guggen-heim Foundation, he wrote:

> Wyndham Lewis, I consider without exception the best possible 'value' for your endowment. . . . His mind is far more fecund and original than let us say James Joyce's: he had at the time of publishing *Tarr* or *The Enemy of the Stars* a less accomplished technique, BUT he has invented more in Modern art than any living man save possibly Picasso.[69]

Pound did not feel toward Lewis the ambiguous rivalry he did toward his fellow-poet Eliot, and despite some rough treatment in *Time and Western Man* (to be partly repudiated in a reference to 'the admirable "Cantos"' in *Men Without Art*,[70] he continued to rate Lewis's work very highly. When it was published, he considered *The Apes of God*, with *Ulysses*, as 'one of the great books of the century'[71] and he would later feel that *Self-Condemned* should have won Lewis the Nobel Prize.[72] And, indeed, beyond the overall debt of the Odyssean motif and general stylistic polyphony, it is the influence of Lewis's rather than Joyce's technique which continues to inform the cantos at times. Pound's notion of the telling image and ideogramme was still often expressed, in practice, through a transformation of the phrasal strokes in *Enemy*:

> Chrysophrase,
> And the water green clear, and blue clear;
> On, to the great cliffs of amber   (XVII, p. 76)

tin flash in the sun dazzle	(XXI, p. 99)
Pearl, great sphere, and hollow	(XXIX, p. 141)
Green, black, December	(XXXVIII, p. 190)
Smoke, smell of sea coal, of stagnant and putrid water	(LXV, p. 369)

In general, the spirit and stance of Lewis seem present whenever radical satire invades the flow. And, perhaps, one of Pound's most celebrated prophetic denunciations may well owe to the repetitive condemnations of *Blast* 1 and 2 ('BLAST . . . ENGLAND'; 'CURSE' / *the flabby sky* . . .'; 'OH BLAST FRANCE. . . .' Thus, reappropriated, the voice of canto XLV ('With Usura'):

> With usura hath no man a house of good stone . . .
> with usura
> hath no man a painted paradise on his church wall . . .
> with usura
> seeth no man Gonzaga his heirs and his concubines . . .
> with usura, sin against nature. . . .   (p. 229)

Eliot, both friend, poetic rival and publisher, is less discernible than we might expect in the interwar cantos. There are one or two *Waste Land* echoes: 'Give! What were they given?', (XX, p. 94; cf. '*Datta*: what have we given'[73]), or '(three children, five abortions and died of the last)', (XXXVIII, p. 187; cf. 'She's had five already, and nearly died of young George'.[74] There is also one, well-known, surfacing of antagonism to the new English Magus:

> And if you will say that this tale teaches . . .
> a lesson, or that the Reverend Eliot
> has found a more natural language . . . you who think
>   you will
> get through hell in a hurry . . .
>   (XLVI, p. 231)

However, altogether, Pound keeps a considerable distance from his old protegé in the cantos themselves, at this time. In XLVIII, for instance, there is no sense that during the Mt Segur visit he

was on holiday with Eliot,[75] except for the somewhat Eliotic lines
'and the stair there still broken . . . / where now is an inn, and bare
rafters' (p. 243). And much earlier, in XXIX, he has effaced Eliot's
presence (though substituted the coded figure of Arnaut Daniel)
in lines alluding to the same vacation:[76]

> So Arnaut turned there
> Above him the wave pattern cut in the stone
> Spire-top alevel the well-curb
> And the tower with cut stone above that, saying:
>   "I am afraid of the life after death."
> and after a pause:
>   "Now, at last, I have shocked him."
>
> (p. 145)

Pound did not, indeed, 'understand . . . / This love of death that
is in them' (p. 145), if *love* of death was what, in fact, ailed Eliot as
they sat 'by the arena' in Verona. Later he would experience the
feeling of living death himself, at Pisa, and only nine lines into the
first canto written out of that experience (LXXIV), we have a move
back towards his old friend: 'yet say this to the Possum. . . .'
(p. 425).

In the meantime, the cantos of the thirties, in particular, evidence
the desire of Pound to seek out his own 'periplum', with little
guidance from past group mapping. This is most evidently so in
the cantos on banking, and American and Chinese history. These
are essentially dedicated to social 'risorgimento'. As such, they
represent a major recantation of the ideals of the Men of 1914. The
younger 'scout-master' of that group had been quite doctrinaire
about the view that art was doctrineless. Art 'never asks anybody
to do anything, or to think anything, or to be anything', he
had written.[77] Comparing Western with Chinese music, he had
suggested: 'It is, perhaps, a question of whether you want . . . an
obsessed personality to "dominate" an audience'[78] – ironic words
in terms of the later preachments. And again: 'the difference
between propagandist literature and "serious literature" is that
propagandist literature starts with a ready made solution. It belongs
to the era of theology and dogma'[79] – or, perhaps, the era of
politico-economic turmoil! Pound might, at the time have argued
that he was providing evidence rather than arguing or preaching.
There is much truth to this in the case of, for example, the Jefferson-

Adams cantos. Yet it is not true of the 'Usura' canto, for instance, and the 'ideogrammes' or 'luminous details' in many other cantos are clearly selected to condemn capitalist practices and promote alternatives to them. Pound's new opinions and practice are his reaction to the postwar realities: poets and novelists should now be 'writing about money, the problem of money, exchange, gold and silver'.[80] This attitude becomes focused as a project to reactivate the motives of the American Revolution, in the draft of cantos XXXI–XLI, *Jefferson: Nuevo Mundo*. The anti-capitalist impulse had been there since, at least, 'Hugh Selwyn Mauberley' and develops between the 'Hell' cantos (XIV–XVI) and various other cantos between XVI and XXXI. Pound would remain faithful to his choice of an Italy that Mussolini now ruled with increasing autocracy and Imperialist ambition. But it is significant that his first major 'block' of chronicle-cantos (partly based on Eliot's gift of his Jefferson books[81]) should concern the 'half savage country' he had been born in, at the crucial moment of its birth as an individual state.

The primary technique of these cantos is the opposite of the tropes of high Modernism – as we generally define it. These cantos use few images or symbols, almost no ambiguity, and can be regarded as polyphonous only in the context of *The Cantos* as a whole. Basically, Pound becomes verse historian, using the words of his subjects – Jefferson, Adams, van Buren, Chinese emperors, etc. – to substantiate his version of events. As such, his stance as American political exile in the Italy of the twenties or thirties is comparable to that of Gore Vidal in the eighties – except that the latter is far more politically-informed and in no way advocates Fascism. Pound's 'history' was now dominated by his notions about money, and his discourse was informed by his post-Vorticist theories about writing. The 'ideogrammic method'[82] exploits precisely the denotative power of words, predicated (naively to the Postmodernist mind) on a quite exact correspondence between sign and thing: 'screw more effectual if placed below surface of water' (XXXI, p. 153); 'Bills discounted at exorbitant rates, four times or three times those offered by the Midland (XXXIII, p. 163); or 'Japs burnt the salt words at Hai men / Oua-chi led troops against them' (LVII, pp. 314–15). This is the absolute opposite of the method of 'Work in Progress'; it is as if the interwar cantos are a deliberate counterforce to the direction into which Joyce was taking Modernism. Against the multi-meaninged dance of *difference* ('circumambient peripherization' to Pound), the cantos insist on

'clear terms' to effect a 'constatation of fact'.[83] Pound, one might
say, has here turned his back on 'feminine' polyphony (the norm
in the era of Joyce, Stein, Loos and Woolf) and embraced Lewis's
commitment to the 'objective' Masculinist world of facticity. So
Lewis's 'spatialised' History meets with Williams's American prag-
matism ('no ideas but in things')[84] to help form a discourse anchored
in the real:

> "30 million" said Mr Dan Wester "in states on the Mississippi
> "will all have to be called in, in three
> "years and nine months, if the charter be not extended. . . .
>
> > (XXXVII, pp. 183–4)

Or in the didactic Confucian mode:

> Sun up; work
> sundown; to rest
> dig well and drink of the water
> dig field; eat of the grain
> Imperial power is? and to us what is it?
>
> > (XLIX, p. 245)

By such means, primarily,[85] Pound sought to create a new socio-
economic reality in the interwar years. 'Wrong from the start',[86]
one might feel – granted the way it drew him to Fascism. But the
impulse, at least, was worthy, and if Pound read European realities
all wrong, it was partly because – at root – he was a child of the
American New World. '"The revolution," said Mr Adams, / "Took
place in the minds of the people"' (XXXII, p. 157): perhaps so, and
thus not as a result of a lone individual's theory. As poet embarked
on his 'tale of the tribe', Pound's isolation could have been
beneficial, but not if the long 'poem including history'[87] was
directed at social renewal in a complex political ferment between
two wars. Had he stayed in London, the 'march of events'[88] and
the opinions of friends he respected could have curbed his excesses
perhaps – as Lewis was forced to climb down from his early naivety
about Hitler. But Pound was out on his own, for most of the time,
lost in a world of Ming, Adams and the *Monte dei Paschi* – where
most current news would be Axis propaganda. It is supremely
ironic that he could not see real wood for the trees, in a Europe
where, quite soon, precisely under threat was: 'common law of

England, BIRTHRIGHT of every man here and at home' (LXVI, p. 384). But so he wrote on, befuddled by the very seas of history he was seeking to navigate through 'to splendour', and eulogising ultimate deals that 'Muss' and his friend, the Fuhrer, were intent on destroying. 'Vai soli'[89] (woe to the lonely) was a truth he was living already: but his cantos would not know it until after the coming war. The last English words in the pre-Pisan cantos still acknowledge only one genuine enemy: ' "Ignorance of coin, credit and circulation"!' (LXXI, p. 421). Pound's attempt to birth a new society, through collated historical 'ideogrammes', would end in 'a death, like our death'.[90]

THE APES OF GOD

Throughout the twenties, Wyndham Lewis was trying to rebuild his writing career after the interlude of his war service. As in the case of *Time and Western Man* and *The Childermass*, Lewis saw this project partly as an attempt to wrest Modernism back from the direction Joyce, most particularly, had drawn it towards. However, like Pound and Eliot, he also felt now that an aesthetic rebirthing was no longer enough. The Great War had taught him that politics was too important to be left to the machinations of professional politicians, and works like *The Art of Being Ruled* (1926) and *The Lion and the Fox* (1927) represent (at book-length) his intervention in the political arguments of the time. And just as *The Childermass* is a political fable, as *Inferno*, so there is an underlying political dimension in his most exhaustive reply to *Ulysses* and 'Work in Progress' to date (granted that *The Human Age* was uncompleted) – *The Apes of God* (1930),[91] a quite massive and devastating attack on artistic pretensions of the time. Although – as we shall see – Lewis has his usual fun at the expense of Joyce (and Eliot and Pound), his real target is the world of moneyed, aesthetic dilettantism: as he saw it, the world of Bloomsbury, the Sitwells and postwar Paris, which had swamped the efforts of the Men of 1914 with third-rate imitation and posturing. These are the 'apes' which the absentee-mentor Pierpoint, and his lieutenant Horace Zagreus, seek to expose and whom the ingenu Dan Boleyn will be introduced to as a cautionary education.

There was much scandal, and brandishing of libel-suits, hypothetical or actual, attendant upon the final publication of *The*

Apes of God,[92] six years after two chapters had been tried out in
Eliot's *Criterion*. However, whatever the legal niceties involved *re*
some brilliantly descriptive *tours de force*, this does not seem to me
a *roman à clef* in any simplistic sense. For instance, the comic picaro
'Dan darlin'', if physically modelled on the young Spender, seems,
at times, a joke for Joyce (Boleyn – Boylan, cf. Zulu Blades – Blazes;
threats to complain to his cousin Stephen in Dublin; the Bloomian
gender-transmogrification at Lord Osmund's Lenten Party). He is
also, at times, a type of younger Lewis ('There was a world . . .
where a mob of persons were engaged in hunting to kill other
men, in a battle-park, beneath crackling violet stars', p. 435), and
at times, perhaps, he is a figuration of the young Samuel Beckett
torn between the rival voices of Zagreus and Ratner (Lewis
and Joyce, *at times*). From at least *Enemy* onwards, Lewis had
experimented with bizarre character-mélange and metamorphosis –
an art that Joyce had introjected into 'Circe' and made a central
principle in 'Work in Progress'. At the same time, while as 'The
Enemy' he was undoubtedly settling scores, he was in the end
more interested in creating a kind of Modernist *Dunciad* – something
permanent – rather than tying his satire down to current animosities
or loyalties; and he drew, in diverse ways, on whatever material
was available. Thus the external characteristics of Eliot seem to
contribute both to the American novelist, Horty ('"dry" prim
smiles', p. 290; '"Sardonic" smile', p. 319; 'a final gathering up of
reservations, concessions, indifferences, into one ball of possible
factors', p. 309), and of Sir James [Frazer?] Follett – ('*Those are pearls
that were his eyes* he heard . . . in the accents of Haarlem', pp. 45–6),
who, in his 'editorial' role, is exposed to the 'genius' of
'absolutely the *youngest* generation' (p. 47); '"Is it in free verse? I
suppose so"' (p. 46). At the same time, Dan Boleyn surely sits, at
one point, for a preliminary study of Lewis's oil-portraits of both
Spender and Eliot:

> . . . the head had sagged forward, the elbows swung idly inward
> upon the ribs, a stoop had crept up the back and buried each
> shoulder, two fists foregathered limply upon a mere lap of
> dejected thighs, legs had quitted their muscular self-constriction
> (muscles gone to roost) . . . as tame as two dangling extremities
> of tackle out of commission . . . his eyes met gloomily upon a
> point between two nostrils – resignation had deposited the hands
> like unoccupied gloves beneath the navel at the table-level.
>
> (pp. 407–8)

The phenomenon of Ezra Pound is similarly dispersed, allusively, within the texture of the book. The name Horace Zagreus, for instance, combines the two main facets of Pound's career to date: that of the social satirist and critical exponent of *Ars Poetica* (Horace), and that of the dionysiac evoker of Greek deities ('ZAGREUS! IO ZAGREUS!', canto XVII). Here Ezra may be Zagreus to Lewis's Pierpoint ('Inferior Religions', etc.) just as, in another sense, Zagreus may be Lewis to T. E. Hulme's Pierpoint. Complex assimilation and dispersal are central to *The Apes of God*, as to *Finnegans Wake*. And the energy of the old 'scout-master' is appropriate grist to Lewis's satiric mill. So there are occasional allusions to Pound's poetry: '"*TROP LONGS* HIVERS!"', p. 389 ('Spring . . . / Too long . . .'[93]); 'Horeb and the Forty Years', p. 259 ('Sinai, Horeb and the forty years'[94]); '"Helen of Troy is my mistress"', p. 345 "('Eleanor, ἐλέναυς and ἐλέπτολις!"'[95]). Pierpoint's verse-aesthetic is identical with that of the early Pound:

> 'I impart a musical art. The last thing you must look for is the message of an orderly sentence – the significance lies in the impact of the image . . . it gets you in the guts like a bomb or it doesn't.' (p. 402)

At the same time, Pound's ideas about fiction – drawn from his reading of Flaubert, Stendhal and the Goncourts, and leading to his high praise of *Ulysses* – is specifically refuted by Zagreus/Pierpoint:

> 'We were talking of that sort of Fiction . . . which derives principally from Flaubert – "scientific", "objective", Fiction . . . the work usually of a writer for the salon and the tea-party (and not of a chemist in a laboratory . . .) . . . The Fiction produced in this manner becomes more *personal* than ever before' (p. 272)

> *'The "impersonality" of science and "objective" observation is a wonderful patent behind which the individual can indulge in a riot of personal egotism, impossible to earlier writers, not provided with such a disguise. . . .'* (p. 273)

There are specific responses to Joyce's riposte to *Time and Western Man* in 'Work in Progress'. Thus: Osmund (Osbert Sitwell?) on 'lions' on page 404, etc., Julius's gripe that 'all is not sweet' (on p. 407), the counter-accusation 'no you old cask of *sour-grapes* – Vinegar-man!' (p. 467), and the description of Ratner: 'as bitter as sour-grapes hung a hundred light-years away up *in an old star* could make an embittered fox' (p. 562; – my italics indicate the reiteration of an old debt to *Enemy*). There are also, surely, references back to the phenomenon of *Ulysses* (which had usurped Lewis's early literary pre-eminence as influence): the pub lunch (pp. 81–2); the ('Bello') female tyranny of pp. 237 ff.; the Bloomian prurience of p. 244 ('with sun-kissed silken legs all-clear to the tenderloin'); the Mulliganesque advocacy of 'the old Greeks – the Greeks of antiquity' against Lionel Kein's Stephen-style meditation on the Vikings (p. 256); the denunciation that 'the "great novels" of this time are *dramatized social news-sheets*' (p. 275); 'the liver in place of the heart' (p. 348) – cf. Bloom's love of the 'inner organs of beasts and fowls',[96] and his meal of liver:[97] the apotheosis of Lord Osmund (on p. 371) as 'the goat-like profile of Edward the Peacemaker' (cf. Bloom in 'Circe' as *bareheaded, in a crimson velvet mantle trimmed with ermine, bearing Saint Edward's staff, the orb and sceptre with the dove . . .*;[98] or the following dialogue in relation to Stephen's theory in 'Scylla and Charibdys', and the general father–son motif in *Ulysses*:

> 'A trinity complex?'
> 'Yes a Trinity complex' . . .
> 'But who is the Father? How does he —?'
> 'No, he says he does not know who his father is.'
> 'And the Son?'
> 'He, of course, is the Son.'
> 'He must be quite mad.'
>
> (pp. 382–3)

It is difficult to know how far Lewis is merely playing a game with his old friend, or, in fact, trying to goad him into emnity. Just as Zagreus, at one point, appears as a 'visiting Magus, and they sat with their four backs to the wall' (p. 393), so Zagreus claims Julius as his 'Jinn' (p. 348) and alter ego for Lord Osmund's Lenten Party, with the biographical thrust that Jimjoo's disguise ('the few necessary things') is contained 'there . . . in that brown paper parcel' (p. 346; see above, p. 84). If, at one point, Lewis mocks Joyce's stylistic method ('A little child picked a forget-me-not. She lifted a chalice. It was there. *Epiphany*', p. 166), as Ratner types his novel, at other points he returns to the more general charge of *Time and Western Man* that Jimjoo is flabbily subjective, indulging the 'rat-like *libido* in all its cloacal windings!' (p. 563). The adjective 'cloacal' is used more than once, here associated with 'love-sick blondes' (a reference to Lewis's connection between Joyce and Anita Loos' *Gentlemen Prefer Blondes* in *Time*),[99] and via Einstein (p. 565), Lewis identifies Ratner's 'vulpine craft' with 'SEX in all its many forms', the 'great hobby and profitable business of his earthly days'. Hence the accusation that his writing proceeds from 'the gonadal glands of internal secretion' (p. 562). As usual, Lewis (through the mouth of Zagreus) offers his alternative: 'Satire to be good must be unfair and single-minded. To be backed by intense anger is good' (p. 472). And Lewis uses Joyce's own Rabelaisian gusto to mock Joyce's Bloomian sponsorship of the underdog: 'at the service of all oppressed classes – women, miners, children, Jews, horses, servants, negroes, frogs, footballs, carpets during Spring-cleaning, Zoo-reptiles, canaries and so forth' (p. 473). Lewis can be awful – yet he remains appallingly amusing.

Yet if, in some sense, *The Apes of God* is Lewis's London-opus in response to Joyce's Dublin-magnum, its aim, as noted above, is less to bury Bloom than to demolish the pretensions of the Sitwells and those of Bloomsbury. In Pierpoint's 'Encyclical' this is made clear:

> those prosperous mountebanks who alternatively imitate and mock at and traduce those figures they at once admire and hate.   (p. 131)

This anticipates Lewis's accusation that Virginia Woolf had plagiarised *Ulysses* in *Mrs Dalloway*, thinly disguised as Rhoda Hyman in *The Roaring Queen*.[100] He continues:

> In *Bloomsbury* . . . [amateurism] takes the form of a select and snobbish club. Its foundation-members consisted of monied middleclass descendants of victorian literary splendour . . . . In their discouragement of too much unconservative originality they are very strong . . . . They yield to none . . . in their organized hatred of *living* 'genius' . . . . *Bloomsbury* is really only what is called 'old Bloomsbury', which is very moribund – the bloom is gone.   (pp. 131–2)

It is Lytton Strachey (in the approximate guise of Matthew Plunkett) rather than Woolf herself who bears the brunt of Lewis's attack here. The onetime lover of *'Dante-young'* (Dan Boleyn) has a lisp, a Bloomsbury 'blink', a young girl admirer (Carrington?) and goes to a Germanic psychiatrist who commands: '"You will follow my programme, yes, upon your return to Blumensbury?"' (pp. 90–1). However, the Sitwells are given a much rougher time than the Bloomsbury group and in 'Lord Osmund's Lenten party' there seem to be quite specific caricatures: this long chapter of the book is almost *à clef*. The chief butt, Osmund (Osbert Sitwell) is a figure out of Rowlandson:

> Lord Osmund is above six-foot and is columbiform. His breast development allies him also to that species of birds whose males are said to share the task of sitting and feeding the young with their mates. The pouter-inflation seems also to give him a certain lightness – which suspends him like a balloon, while he sweeps majestically forward. His carefully-contained obesity may be the reason for his martial erectness. Or rather, there can be no other reason for the evocation of that god. (p. 366)

Edith Sitwell and others are caricatured as ruthlessly. But the most telling satiric punch springs less from such setpiece visual cartooning as from the superbly-rendered fatuous dialogue – which looks forward to the Beckett of the fifties:

> 'I don't believe our ears have played us false!'
> 'In this matter – I believe they haven't!'
> 'I am not positive – but I should be surprised if they had deceived us!'
> 'For once I do believe that mine has proved trustworthy!'
> 'It is a miracle if mine have!'
> 'Not more so than with mine!' (p. 379)

Or again:

> 'Can't your hear!' bayed Lady Harriet.
> 'There is not a moment to be lost!' Lord Phoebus exclaimed.
> 'No my lord!'
> 'Yes there is not a moment to be lost!' Lady Harriet boomed as well, planted beside her cadet. 'Don't stand there gaping

at Lady Truncheon you sheepshead!'
'Yes don't gape at Lady Truncheon!'
'Didn't you hear what was said! Take her ladyship at once
to Mrs Bosun's closet – *there is not a moment to be lost!*'   (p. 510)

Some critics have questioned whether such characters justify Lewis's massive and sustained bombardiering.[101] Yet this could also be objected against similar caricatures in Dryden, Pope or Swift. It is less individual 'personalities' that are at issue here than grotesque variations on a type of snobbish parasite, masquerading as significant artist. With characteristic verve and brilliance, Lewis has constructed a modern *Dunciad*-in-prose, through variations of Modernist techniques he had pioneered. Against the charge that it is static one might reply that – as in the case of Pope – that is part of the point, and it is certainly not as static as its natural rival, *Ulysses*, whose recent critical *apotheosis* has placed it almost beyond such charges. The tie-up with the General Strike, at the end, is not as convincing as Lewis would have wished it to be. For the *literati* satirised here appear to be too removed from general sociopolitical realities in England to be symptomatic of much beyond their own futility. Yet as a carnivalised comic monument to aesthetic pretension and coterie-apishness it is a *tour de force*, and makes the writings of such as Huxley or Waugh appear lightweight. I would argue that *The Apes of God* is Modernism's greatest satire (*Ulysses*, I take it, is much more than satire) and, as Pound thought, is fictional masterwork. Like *The Waste Land*, and sections of *Finnegans Wake*, it moves towards a thunderous unmaking of established Western culture:

Then came the first soft crash of the attendant cymbal – it was the prelude of thunder. And in the gutter the crazy instruments at last struck up their sentimental jazzing one-time stutter-gutter-thunder.

> Whoddle ah *doo*
> When *yoo*
> Are *far*
> *Away* . . . .
> Whoddle ah *doo*
> Whoddlah DOOOO!   (pp. 649–50)

ENTRE DEUX GUERRES

'So here I am, in the middleway, having had twenty years –
/ Twenty years largely wasted', Eliot wrote at the end of the
thirties.[102] The thirties had been a decade of relative group-
dispersal, for all the varied meetings of group members in Paris or
London, the continuing correspondence between them and the
centralising force of Eliot the publisher, now known as the 'Pope
of Russell Square'.[103] Geopolitical realities had changed again,
drastically, between the mid-twenties and the late thirties and, of
the Men of 1914, only Joyce would continue to insist on the
aesthetic realm at the expense of any social commitment: Pound,
Lewis and Eliot would all commit themselves to social causes,
with varying degrees of stridency, and with different degrees of
inclination to the Right. As has been noted, Eliot's renunciation
of a purely aesthetic position was primarily a matter of religious
conviction, and while he adopted a reactionary pose, and articulated some unpleasantly doctrinaire views, it has to be said that
he also fostered the careers of the new generation of poets –
Auden, Spender and MacNeice – whose commitment was explicitly
to the Left. Eliot had ostensibly started *The Criterion* to foster the
best in new thinking and new writing – a role he extended to his
publishing activities at Faber from 1927 onwards – and while this
originally provided a forum for Pound's old group, in particular,
it also promoted newer writers bent on colonising the territory
the Men of 1914 had discovered – and from quite different
presuppositions. This was, in a vital sense, faithful to the spirit of
BLAST, yet both Lewis and Pound had changed their ground (and
in different ways from Eliot) and, together with the old *camaraderie*
and the appreciation of Eliot's promotional efforts, the sense of 'a
kind of betrayal' (Ackroyd's phrase)[104] was also in the air. Eliot
had separated himself from his wife, and in critical-creative terms
he had separated himself from Joyce, Lewis and Pound, for all
that he sponsored their new work. For his relaxation and fantasy-
life he cherished, in 1935 and onward, a new fourway male-family
where he was no longer 'Possum', but 'Elephant' to 'Tarantula'
(John Hayward), 'Coot' (Geoffrey Faber) and 'Whale' (Frank
Morley).[105] Nevertheless, when he came to publish the poems he
had originally started for Frank Morley's children,[106] he would call
it *Old Possum's Book of Practical Cats*.

Lewis, who had largely buried himself between 1918 and 1926,

'disinterred' himself in the late twenties to Blast assorted foes –
real or imagined – and denouce the direction Modernism had taken
since *Ulysses*, which included some unkind words about all the
other Men of 1914. However, he seems to have approved of Eliot's
overall direction (and, as we have seen, appropriated much of his
vision) and in the thirties, having nailed the chief 'Apes' in artistic
London, he was more in a mood to celebrate the achievements of
the old *Bewegung*. The four are brought together, with slightly
amateur whimsicality, in the verse of his *One Way Song* (1933):

> I seem to note a roman profile bland,
> I hear the drone from out the cactus-land:
> That must be the poet of the Hollow Men:
> The lips seem bursting with a deep Amen.
> I espy Ezra, bearded like the Kaiser,
>   . . . and James Joyce
> For the third time his thirteen poems deploys.[107]

There are other intertextual evidences of group-influence in the
poem[108] (which Eliot republished after Lewis's death), yet the most
specific Lewisian references to the Men of 1914, in the thirties,
come in *Blasting and Bombardiering* (1937), the last sections of which
constitute a reparative gift to the rival group-members he had
criticised so trenchantly, and is a notable celebration of their
collaborative effort. The Introduction shows a specifically postwar
standpoint, with the shadow of future war in mind. Lewis writes,
'My book is about a little group of people crossing a bridge' (p. 2);
these are characterised, most specifically, as the 'Men of 1914'
(p. 9) whose work 'shows you the origin of all the ideas that are
in the ascendant today' (p. 12) and his 'act of salvage' commemo-
rates 'this group rather than that' who (compared to the 'Blooms-
buries') 'mean a great deal more apart than they would with their
somewhat irregular contours worn smooth in log-rolling and
in back-scratching' (p. 14). Much of the book is about Lewis's
experience in the Great War, and the Conclusion briefly discusses
Auden, Isherwood and others of the newest dispensation, but Part
V is a wonderfully evocative description of the 1914 mood and
Lewis's first meetings and friendship with Joyce, Pound and Eliot.
It is essential to any in-depth understanding of literary Modernism –
most especially of the 'young, the "New" group of writers
assembled in Miss Weaver's *Egoist* just before and during the War'

(p. 292). And in the late thirties, too, Lewis who had earlier both sketched Joyce and made a caricature of 'The Duc de Joyeux', painted brilliant portraits of both Pound and Eliot. Lewis had criticised his friends incisively: yet as his biographer has put it: 'the great writers – Joyce, Eliot, Pound – sustained by a belief in their art, acknowledge the truth of his criticism and remained his friends. Others . . . waited to take their revenge'.[109] Doubtless, too, these 'greater writers' would have acknowledged that in *Blasting and Bombardiering* it was Lewis who celebrated their group venture more positively and boisterously than any of them.

However, the late thirties found Pound, in Italy, distancing himself from the old *camaraderie*, and when he communicated with his old friends it was less now to encourage than to lecture and hector. He wrote to Eliot in 1936: 'The number of putrid pigs in England is so large . . . . I did not instantly expect to find the EVIL one lurking under yr. weskit. But so was it':[110] to Joyce in 1937: 'NOW: about Haupy. I *will* NOT. And fer various reysons . . . NO sane man *likes* wrappin [sic] up parcels. It wd. do you no bloody good'; and to Lewis in 1939: 'If you see Eliot, take a monkey wrench and find out *what* the hell Morley means to do in N.Y. (if anything save sink into the damnbience'.[112] It is true that he modified his directives with old group-witticisms: 'J-J-J-Jayzus me daRRRlint'[113] (to Joyce); 'Waaal Possum, my fine ole Marse Supial'[114] (to Eliot); or simply 'Dear Wyndham: I have buried pore ole Fordie in (of all places) *The XIXth Century and After*'.[115] However, there was something sinister, as well as unfriendly, in his refusal to write something further on Joyce's behalf (as Joyce had, earlier, for him) in 1934: 'There is too much future, and nobody but me and Muss / and half a dozen others to attend to it'.[116] 'Muss' was, of course, Mussolini and for all Joyce's aloof aestheticist élitism, one cannot but applaud the distance he put between himself and the two most chronically mistaken of the Men of 1914: to Harriet Weaver he wrote in the same year: 'I am afraid poor Mr Hitler-Missler will soon have few admirers in Europe apart from your nieces and my nephews, Masters W. Lewis and E. Pound'.[117]

But by the late thirties Lewis, at least, was retracting his earlier tolerance of Fascism (most intelligently reconsidered in *Fables and Aggression* by the Marxist critic, Fredric Jameson), as vigorously as he could without appearing wholly ridiculous. His fine novel *The Revenge for Love* (1937) works out his complex, later political views with respect to the Spanish Civil War and its English protagonists.

Yet Pound was committing himself more and more to Mussolini's Italy and its attendant pretentions and moral evil. Later he would acknowledge that: 'I lost my center / fighting the world'.[118] But he virtually lost his soul, too, and even the later penance and self-excoriation cannot quite atone for some of his views at the time. John Tytell's recent biography brings out the worst of Pound at this time – as Noel Stock's *Ezra Pound* did not sufficiently. Here are some instances: 'Pound insisted that his daughter wear the Fascist uniform to school in Gais, though the only others who did were the children of government functionaries' (p. 242); 'the Jew part of the Bible is black evil' (p. 243); 'The function of Germany, as I see it, in the next forty years' art is indispensable. Nowhere else is there a force toward a purgation' (p. 254 – written in August, 1939!); and on 6 October 1941, in an early broadcast for the fascist radio: 'Mr Churchill and that brute, *Rosenfeld* [Roosevelt] and their kike postal spies and obstructors distress me by cutting off my normal mental intercourse with my colleagues' (p. 262). Of his closest literary 'colleagues', Joyce was exiled to Zurich because of the Nazi lust for war, shortly to die there, Lewis exiled in Canada and desperately lonely because of the war, and Eliot an air raid warden, distracted from writing poems, not now by work at Lloyd's Bank, but by the need to protect Londoners, as far as possible, from the bombs rained on it by people with views like that of the onetime 'scout-master'. Only, after the war, when Pound was in confinement, and still under possible threat of death, would surviving 'colleagues' – Eliot and Lewis among others – want to campaign for him. Truly: 'And as to why they go wrong, / thinking of rightness . . . .' (canto CXVI, *ibid.*, p. 797): such was Ezra Pound in the late thirties and early forties.

James Joyce, racked by illnesses through much of the thirties, and now with his daughter Lucia in permanent mental confinement (despite the administration of C. G. Jung among others), was about to publish the most spectacularly 'really new work' of literature, *Finnegans Wake*, as the decade drew towards its end. Despite Pound's early repudiation of the style of 'Work in Progress' and Lewis's concerted attack on his writing in the twenties, Joyce had by no means lost contact with the other Men of 1914, for all his other, often newer, friends. Just as his recorded dreams register the presence of both Lewis and Pound,[119] so in the late twenties all three supported Joyce's case against Samuel Roth's piracy of *Ulysses* in America (Pound slightly grudgingly so, on a matter of principle),[120] while there remains a sense of group-acceptance in his slightly puzzled comment that: 'the more I hear of . . . the brilliant members of Pound's big brass band the more I wonder why I was ever let into it "with my magic flute"'.[121] The group-influence evident in 'Work in Progress' is demonstrated in other ways in his life. There is, for instance, his parody of *The Waste Land*, sent to Harriet Weaver and beginning: 'Rouen is the rainiest place getting / Inside all impermeables, wetting / Damp marrow in drenched bones';[122] or his comment, 'Pound's book of Cantos is out, a most magnificent thing in gold and scarlet';[123] or his use of Lewis's friendship in 1930 to try and promote the tenor John Sullivan, via Lady Ottoline Morrell.[124] Ellmann's biography attests that Joyce 'took to his bed' when he feared 'Eliot's turning against his new work as Pound and Lewis had done',[126] that he welcomed Eliot's offer to pray for his ailing eyesight,[127] that he admired Pound's *Cathay* and *Lustra*,[127] in particular, and – more importantly – that when his father died, in 1931, he wrote to both Pound and Eliot about his feelings for John Joyce.[128] Lewis, because of the force of his criticism, was owned more easily in the coded word-wrestling of *Finnegans Wake* (see further, below pp. 158–65) than in public comment, letters or meetings. Lewis himself, who was always adversarial, perhaps sensed that he had been too hard on his old drinking-companion: according to Jeffrey Meyers, when Ellman interviewed him in the fifties he 'emphasised their friendship and said that Joyce had always visited him when he came to London'.[129] Whatever else, as we shall see, 'Wyndhame'[130] became a key imaginative foil in the masterwork that became the *Wake*.

The 1930s must rate as one of the most fraught and divisive decades for the creative intelligence in the last two hundred years. The newer generation of writers – from Auden to Campbell, Isherwood to Waugh – expressed this dialectically, while Orwell tried to play *honnête homme* in the middle. The Men of 1914 had been born in the 1880s, educated in the 1900s, turned around by the Great War and achieved their Great Decade in the twenties. They were ill-equipped to register the strains of another decade, and to keep balance between the original project – to birth the aesthetic New – and the more recent social requirement: to take political sides. They reacted in different ways: the two original futurists (Lewis and Pound) veered to the Right, looking now for innovation as *Rappel à l'Ordre*; the subtle self-doubter (Eliot) made Right-on noises yet maintained an important political scepticism;

and the aesthetic egoist (Joyce) loftily ignored the barking 'dogs of Europe'[131] – less to 'cultivate a garden' than to fantasise a historical jungle (the *Wake*). Yet Joyce, who continued amorally faithful to the original group-aims in a wholly changed situation, would personally suffer more in the thirties than any of them. 'We're going downhill fast', he said to Beckett in 1939;[132] 'What is there to get up for?', he would ask petulantly;[133] and in Zurich 'he arrived broken and sick, prematurely aged, among the scenes of his past strength.'[134] In the thirties, all the Men of 1914 became 'lost' in 'the labyrinth': and in 1939 the poetic godfather of the group, who coigned that phrase, himself died. The most spectacular poet of the new generation, W. H. Auden, memorialised the event: 'Earth receive an honoured guest;/William Yeats is laid to rest'.[135] Meanwhile the interim generation – Joyce, Lewis, Pound and Eliot – awaited the future with trepidation. They were a bit like Yeats's version of the Magi – 'the pale unsatisfied ones'[136] – still baffled by the 'uncontrollable mystery' of a birthing they had both witnessed and participated in, but whose growth, within a changing environment, they could not control.

6

These the Companions

RIVERRUN

Finnegans Wake was published in London and New York on 4 May 1939. Joyce had insisted on as early a date as possible since, as he put it in terms of his usual priorities: 'War is going to break out, and nobody will be reading my book any more'.[1] The *Wake* is the supreme and ultimate example of the Modernist urge to 'MAKE IT NEW'. It is also a cardinal demonstration of new birthing as renewal of the past, since it is dominated by allusions to Anglo-Irish and world history – even if history here appears as a species of hysteria. Yet its style makes it 'as modern as tomorrow afternoon and in appearance up to the minute' (p. 309). It constitutes, in a sense, the nearly psychotic counterdiscourse of the artist in a world increasingly taken over by technological master-discourses out of control:

> This harmonic condenser enginium (the Mole) they caused to be worked from a magazine battery (called the Mimmim Bimbim patent number 1132, Thorpetersen and Synds, Jomsborg, Selverbergen) which was tuned up by twintriodic singulvalvulous pipelines (lackslipping along as if their liffing deepunded on it) with a howdrocephalous enlargement, a gain control of circumcentric megacycles, ranging from the antidulibnium onto the serostaatarean.
>
> (p. 310)

Joyce's neo-Vicoan conscious control of the vast linguistic echo-chamber has, I think, been overstated. Language, history, mythology, twentieth-century complexities and his own personal psychic tensions have, in the end, taken Joyce over and rendered him the vatic stutterer of civilisation's myriad discontents. Although it is very funny, the book is also a frightening caution – the ultimate exemplification that 'the falcon cannot hear the falconer' and hence 'the centre cannot hold'.[2] Dream-speech, here, is a species of nightmare: a 'mere anarchy'. It is human – as schizophrenia is –

and one admires the ludic patterning insisted on within the mayhem. Yet it is disturbing, as all wild associationism is,[3] because we can sense the rage for order battling against final fatuity: 'A way a lone a last a loved a long the' (p. 628) – return to first base and try it all again!

The grim contention with others – Wellington, Swift, Berkeley, Yeats, Stanislaus, Jesus et al. – is manifest as unresolved anxiety of influence: just as much so when 'the big four' (p. 384), the gospellers of the new, are involved:[4] 'their ears for the millennium and all their mouths making water' (p. 386). This may have its celebratory element as when the 'senators four' (p. 474) or 'four claymen' (p. 475), characterised as 'three kings of three suits and a crowner' (Pound the last?) appear as Joyce's Magi, present at a Messianic birthing: 'Yawn in a semiswoon lay awailing and (hooh!) what helpings of honeyful swoothead (phew!), which earpiercing dulcitude' (p. 474). The new boy speaks a 'feminine' language (despite Lewis's 'star-chamber', p. 475): 'The form masculine. The gender feminine. I see' (p. 505). But although friendship is involved ('my shemblable! My freer!', p. 489), so too is rivalry and the battle of origins: 'Now, are you derevatov of it yourself in any way?' (p. 505). Names, attributions, speak allusively back to the old group: 'Lyons' (p. 475); 'Piercey'[5] (p. 482); 'welsht-breton' (p. 491); 'Tomsky, the enemy' (p. 509). Attendance at the birth of futurity would be 'their quarrel, the way they would see themselves, everybug his bodiment' (p. 475) and their 'souls' groupography' (p. 476) will be 'wombful of mischief and initiumwise' (p. 483), often concerning who 'took the words out of my mouth' (p. 480). If the 'gentle poet' (p. 515 – Pound?) is exempted here, 'Tomsky' is not: 'burial of carcass, fuselage of dump and committal of noisance' in 'Weissduwasland' (p. 479). Nor is the rival proseman exempted: 'tomahawks watching tar elsewhere' (p. 505),[6] 'from Ond's outset till Odd's end'. Contention is always present: 'He feels he ought to be asamed of me as me to be ashunned of him' (p. 489), though, in the end, for all those who speak 'Magis landeguage' (p. 478), it is a matter of 'Fantasy! funtasy on fantasy, amnaes fintasies!' (p. 493).

The book is full of splitting and argumentation – 'Jim-joo Ratner' here as compulsively divided as anything in *Enemy* or *Tarr*. The Shem-Shaun opposition is worked exhaustively to accommodate a whole spectrum of compelling oppositions – not least the rivalries with Lewis, Eliot and, occasionally, Pound. Yet if – in some other dimension – Shem and Shaun are, also, both warring parts of Joyce himself, then the entire book chronicles the tensions in a family group of four: Earwicker as father, Anna Livia as mother, Issey as daughter, and Shem-Shaun the split son. And, in so far as this speaks of the old group, the 'quobus quartet' (p. 513) is far more important as fourway dynamic than any specific assignation of characterisations. The ultimate message is a version of 'quatrain' structuring a dream of quadrille, where the real name of the game is a frantic search within chaos for some meanings of meaning. Hence, granted the power of the number 4 in the whole – whether gospellers, magi, old men in the pub or, indeed, the work's division into four Parts or Books – the dynamics of the Men of 1914 can be extrapolated in a number of interrelated ways. For example, Humphrey Chimpden Earwicker (in whatever variants of his name) is a species of Hugh Selwyn Mauberley – Pound, the tavern-keeper of 'Exile's Letter' – where A. L. P. is Eliot, Pound's 'wife' as in *The Waste Land* fantasy, Lewis Shem-Shaun, as originator of splitting, and Joyce Isabel, the fluid daughter of invention and source of the literary flow. But there are, as in dreams, many other possibilities: where Joyce is Anna Livia, then Eliot is Issy, as derivative stream and Lewis is H.C.E. as founder-builder, while Pound is split like Shem and Shaun between 'E.P.' and Mauberley. Let's try one more: where Joyce is H.C.E., then Pound is Anna Livia as mother of the group, Eliot split, as Shem-Shaun, between rival roles of creator and critic, and Lewis demoted to a minor tributary to the main flow (which is what he eventually became in critical reputation). There are other important dynamics within the group here. Shaun, in the Shem-Shaun dialectic, can be any one of them, including Joyce – and, arguably, Shem too. The male–female, or parent–offspring equation can be worked out variously. In the end, as in *Ulysses*, the author, according to Stephen's version of Shakespeare, is 'all in all';[7] yet the fourway motif is important in terms of his overall offered representation.

As already noted, the main rivalry expressed relates to Eliot and Lewis especially (despite the shared gossip of the three drunken soldiers and the three down-and-outers). In my reading, this continues, from time to time, quite consistently throughout the book as a whole, whatever the main subject, mode and personnel of the chapter involved. The encounter with the Cad is in II; there is a Shem-Shaun argument in V from at least 'Premver a promise of a pril' (p. 110) to 'transhipt from Boston'[8] (p. 111); and in VI is the extended fable of the Fox and Grapes (see above pp. 127–8). The apology and boast in VII contain the occasional thrusts: 'when lovely woman stoops to conk him' (p. 170); 'with limon on, of Lebanon',[9] 'sour grapefruice', 'Fanny Urinia',[10] 'coldblood kodak', 'having buried a hatchet not so long before'[11] (p. 171); 'the tom and the shorty of it is . . . covetous of his neighbour's word' (p. 172); 'your rural troubadouring' (Pound? – p. 173); 'Darkies never done tug that coon out to play non-excretory, anti-sexuous, misoxenetic, gaasy pure, flesh and blood games' (p. 175); '*Wine, Woman and Waterclocks, or How a Guy Finks and Fawkes When He Is Going Batty*'[12] (p. 177). 'Cattlemen's spring meat' on p. 172 is a punning salute to Lewis's story, suppressed in the *Little Review*.[13] Chapter VIII begins with a sideglance at Eliot ('toms will till', p. 196) and continues with a reference to 'antsgrain' and 'the gran Phenician rover'[14] (p. 197) to denounce 'that mormon's thames' ('droming on loft till the sight of the sternes', p. 199), in a chapter whose riverine theme of fair women is a borrow-back from Eliot's Thames maidens in *The Waste Land*.

Chapter IX, first section of Part II, enacts its children's games in 'Feenichts Playhouse', drawing thus upon *Enemy* as well as 'Circe'. The debt seems clear: 'nightly redistribution of parts and players by the puppetry producer'[15] (p. 219). If 'Hump' is one character (p. 220), then later we hear of 'agnols' to be saved from the 'willy wooly woolf' (p. 223). In this 'futurist onehorse balletbattle' (p. 221) there are varieties of allusion: 'chuting rudskin gunerally' refers to Lewis's *Paleface* as 'our national rooster's rag' (p. 220) speaks to Eliot's *Criterion*, while 'card palmer teaput tosspot Madam d'Elta' (p. 221) reminds us of Madame Sosostris, and 'Madame Berthe Delamode' looks back to the heroine of *Tarr*. On p. 222, 'O, Mester Sogermon, ef thes es whot ye deux' perhaps reintroduces Pound in his new role of musician (along with Olga Rudge).[16] The 'lalage of lyonesses, and . . . her knave arrant' (p. 229) refers to Lewis as does 'Mookery mooks, it's a grippe of his gripes' (p. 231). The fun continues throughout the chapter. A few examples: 'may his tarpitch dilute not give him chromitis'; 'Can that sobstuff'[17] (p. 232); 'ebbing wasteward . . . – Xanthos! Xanthos! Xanthos!', 'Percy, the pup' (p. 235); 'frufrocksfull of fun' (p. 236); 'toutes philomelas' (p. 237); 'cockeedoodle aubens Aurore' (p. 244); 'Bing. Bong. Bang-bong. Thunderation!' (p. 245); 'timekiller to his spacemaker' (p. 247); 'you reder!' (p. 249); 'wise ants hoarded' (p. 253); 'Gunnar's gustspells'[18] (p. 257); 'Back-to-Bunk Tom' (p. 258). It is all

quite amusing, if also obsessive. And is it pure accident that this
nursery rendition of the original blasters should end not with a
fathering 'DA' ('the Clearer of the Air from on high has spoken in
tumbuldum tambaldam', p. 258) – but the simple stutter 'Mum-
mum' (p. 259)?

Chapter X keeps up such backchat with the other 'tomthick and
tarry members' (p. 291) of the original group, which reaches a
climax between p. 300 and p. 306 with some notable strikes:
'Chinchin Childaman'[19] (p. 304), 'Thou in scanty shanty!!' or
'republicly royally toobally prussic blue in the shirt after'[20] (p. 305).
In XI most of the allusions occur between p. 322 and p. 341. Here
are the most spectacular: 'his pounds that he pawned from the
burning'[21] (p. 322); 'the rain of Tarar' (p. 329); 'the kilder massed'
(p. 330); 'letting the aandt out of her grosskropper' (p. 331); 'Ala
lala!' (p. 335); 'But da. But dada' (p. 338); 'Mortar martar tartar
wartar!' (p. 341). In XII (mercifully) the obsession loses its grip,
but in XIII, beginning of Section III, it returns. Again some
examples: 'Shaunti and shaunti and shaunti again!' (p. 408); 'Ear!
Ear! Not ay! Eye! Eye!' (p. 409); 'Welsfusel mascoteers'[22] (p. 412);
'the icing-lass of his windhame' (p. 415); 'Rot him!' (p. 422); and
'Taboccoo!' (p. 427). XIV ends with a notable salute to Pound we
shall return to (see below p. 183). In the meantime, there is the
usual mumbling back to 'Temptation Tom' (p. 436) and such
'hippopotamians' (p. 437) (e.g. *'Egg Laid by Former Cock . . .'*,[23]
p. 440) and a specific reference to Lewis's likening of Joyce's
stream-of-consciousness to the speech-habits of Dickens' Alfred
Jingle in *The Art of Being Ruled* and *Time*:

> Could you wheedle a staveling encore out of your imitationer's
> jubalharp, hey, Mr Jinglejoys? Congregational singing. Rota rota
> ran the pagoda . . .   (p. 466)

During this contention *re* 'that worrid expressionism on his megalo-
gue' (p. 467), the heir of the Modernist game is named: 'Sam
knows miles bettern me how to work the miracle' (p. 467) – and
so he would do, but in Lewis's way. XV commences with the
arrival of the Magi, mentioned above, proceeds to a typical work-
out with Lewis – 'a tarrable Turk', 'stairrods', 'Tapley', 'Cad', 'Mrs
Lyons', 'saint ulstar' (p. 520) – but then gets on with the main
business. XVI evokes 'the sycomores, all four of them' (p. 555),
proceeds to an adaptation of Eliot's gendered 'Game of Chess'

(p. 559 ff), a borrowing of 'Mrs Porter' (p. 560), a quip at the 'reverent's nickname ('Has your pussy a pessname?',[24] p. 561), and a variety of variants on 'Cocorico!' (pp. 584–5).

By now, it seems to be clear, that whatever else the *Wake* is about (and it is often claimed it concerns everything), the book clearly expresses a Joycean version of group dynamics and rivalry. Of course, he takes issue with many people, both dead and alive, and all such contentions build up the whole. Yet the preoccupation with dynamics of four is marked, and the obsession with Lewis and Eliot profound and recurrent. If Pound was largely for Joyce a 'crowner' rather than contender (and one who had distanced himself from the wildest 'scout' of the twenties and thirties), nevertheless, the power of the 1914 group remains as insistent rivalry with the other two contenders. Lewis had attacked Joyce and he could not forget it, for all that at times he appears to forgive it. Yet perhaps he understood Lewis's innermost motif – revenge on a usurpation which marginalised him. They had been drinking companions and rival wits – in literary terms, true types of the twins Shem and Shaun. The issue with Eliot seems subtler: he was friend, critic, publisher and stealer of Joyce's thunder. He was also the Possum, and refused to fight, unlike Lewis. Also, the many references to the 'reverent' so-and-so, in proximity to Eliotic allusions, suggests that Tom's move to the Anglican fold disturbed Joyce at even subconscious levels. As writer, the Possum became, in a sense, the priest that Joyce/Stephen had altogether refused to be – and this from the source of 'King Bolo'! It disturbed him, I suggest, at a level far deeper than the aesthetic. Here is an instance, where 'Pease' stands for 'Shantih':

> Skim over *Through Hell with the Papes* (mostly boys) by the divine comic Denti Alligator (exsponging your index) and find a quip in a quire arisus aream from bastardtitle to fatherjohnson. Swear aloud by pious fiction the like of *Lentil Lore* by Carnival Cullen or that *Percy Wynns* of our S. J. Finn's or *Pease in Plenty* by the Curer of Wars, licensed and censered by our most picturesque prelates, Their Graces of Linzen and Petitbois, bishops of Hibernites. . . .   (p. 440)

Joyce brings Lewis ('*Percy Wynns*') in on the act to help reinforce his lifelong choice of art over religion, in opposition to the message he read in *The Waste Land*'s ending – confirmed later in Eliot's conversion. For Eliot, the aesthetic was no longer enough – certainly not the arcane artistry of 'Work in Progress' in a world in need of redemption. He had renounced the role of 'drunken helot'[25] ('heliotrollops!', *Wake*, p. 603) and pure aesthetician. Joyce could play back – and did – to the debt of *The Waste Land* to *Ulysses*, and effect in the *Wake* his own appropriations from Eliot's poem. But he could not retract 'Non serviam' – as Eliot did in *Ash Wednesday*. And that, perhaps, disturbed him most, in the end, with respect to the new 'churchwarden'.

The contentions remain to the end. In the last chapter, voiced through Joyce's own Liffey Maiden ('A lala!', p. 335), is expressed, still, the semiconscious babbling of fraternal tension, whose final need may just be to be heard by members of the old group – among the few who might guess what was afoot in *Finnegans Wake*. Thus the familiar allusive appellation, half ironic wrangling, half a call to be heard: 'Sandhyas! Sandhyas! Sandhyas!' (p. 593): 'Dah!' (p. 594); 'Tom' (p. 597); 'Hyacinssies with heliotrollops', 'Tyro a tora'[26] (p. 603); 'mattinmummur, for dombell dumbs?' (p. 604); 'heliots . . . Taawhaar' (p. 613); 'Cockalooralooraloomenos' (p. 615); 'Morning post as from Boston transcripped' (p. 617); 'No peace at all', 'pearse orations'[27] (p. 620); 'Ming Tung . . . to the Mong Tang',[28] 'traumscrapt from Maston, Boss' (p. 623); 'gopeep where the sterres be' (p. 624); 'laud men of Londub!' (p. 625); 'a sheeny stare to perce me', 'just a lea' (p. 626); 'My leaves have drifted from me. All. But one clings still'[29] (p. 628). As elsewhere, this is a strictly limited list: a book could be written on references in the *Wake* to Lewis, Eliot, Pound and the communal venture. The allusions cry out, resonantly, to a familial dynamic which, in a sense, never was and which has largely ended, just as drunken Earwicker had fantasised the family of his dreamscape. And, under all, persists a voicing of that Messianic ambition which brought the group together to sire a future: 'the child we all love to place our hope in for ever' (p. 621). And such hopes, voiced by one of 'that same four that named them' (p. 625), continue just as Joyce 'lilting on all the time' activates the finally frightening question: 'is there one who understands me?' (p. 627). So finishes the great, arguably monstrous, masterwork as *écriture féminine*. The literary glory, jest and riddle of modern Western man peters out as the poignant voice of a woman, 'moananoaning' (p. 628).

Yet let the last words here concern one of the earliest written and noblest parts of the book. As Pound prepared to leave Paris, for the duration, in the summer of 1924, Joyce penned the following – eventually to form the finale of Chapter XIV:

> . . . crooner born with sweet wail of evoker, healing music . . . friarylayman in the pulpitbarrel. . . . Songster, angler, choreographer! . . . Good by nature and natural by design. . . . My long farewell I send to you, fair dream of sport and game and always something new . . . you who so often consigned your distributory tidings of great joy into our nevertoolatetolove box, mansuetudinous manipulator . . . our rommanychiel!. . . . For you had – may I, in our, your and their names, dare to say it? – the nucleus of a glow of a zeal of soul of service such as rarely, if ever, have I met with single men . . . overlorded by fate and interlarded with accidence . . . from that place where the day begins. . . . Life, it is true, will be a blank without you. . . . *Va faotre*! Eftsoon so too will our own sphoenix spark spirt his spyre and sunward stride the rampante flambe. . . . Brave footsore Haun! Work your progress! Hold to! Now! Win out, ye divil ye! . . . (pp. 471–3)

William York Tindall does not see Pound here – whoever else;[30] but surely someone must have. Only the 'service' and talent of the old group-leader (translator of Anglo-Saxon, Provençale expert) fits. Did Pound brave enough 'circumambient peripherization' to recognise this tribute before in Pisa, after Joyce's death, he evoked 'Jim the comedian singing . . .?'[31] Let us hope so. It is Joyce's most generous homage and salute to the man who launched his career – and it was published in his last book, shortly before he died.

THE FIRE AND THE ROSE

> Time present and time past
> Are both perhaps present in time future
> And time future contained in time past.
> (p. 171)

So begins a verse-sequence of magisterial self-effacement, in which Eliot appears almost wholly beyond the old aesthetic work-group. There is none of the insistent, semiconscious talking back to the other one-time members which characterises parts of *The Apes of God* and *Finnegans Wake*. Most of the time, the new 'Blessed Thomas' seems placed in some mystical time-warp between Krishna and John of the Cross on the one hand, and the 'strained time-ridden faces' of contemporary Londoners on the other. And yet, clearly, the opening of *Four Quartets* represents a major intervention in the Modernist quarrel about space, time and Western man and woman. Eliot places himself, contra Lewis, amongst the connoisseurs and charters of flux. The dynamics of space-time, *sub-specie aeternitatis*, will be his high and elaborated theme. Thus a continuity from *Ulysses*, *The Waste Land*, the first *Cantos* and 'Work in Progress' is apparent, even though some of the scenarios could stand as elements of Lewis's *Human Age*. The Dantesque settings of Limbo, Purgatory and possible Paradise (the rose) are perhaps more pressing here than in any other Modernist text.[32] Yet they are anglicised, and even domesticated, as never before – in a sequence three-quarters written during the ultimate world war (bar global extinction), for the most part while England stood alone. It is a unique and unrepeatable performance – modified Modernism speaking to ultimate personal and geopolitical responsibilities. Since *Four Quartets*, English poetry has been comparatively lightweight.

The style is specifically Eliot's – what Pound would later call 'the true Dantescan voice'.[33] Yet it contrives to combine, in its meditative resonance, the interiorised intellectuality of Stephen Dedalus in 'Proteus' ('*Erhebung* without motion. . . . / Woven in the weakness of the changing body', p. 173), the lyric grace of Ezra Pound ('The black cloud carries the sun away. / Will the sunflower turn to us . . . / tendril and spray / Clutch and cling?', p. 174) and the hellish vacuity of *The Childermass* ('In a dim light . . . / With slow rotation suggesting permanence', p. 173). Yet influence here is so introjected and catalysed into the self-reflexive voice of the whole that it is scarcely visible. The overall rhythm of the verse (however varied – occasionally disastrously) is magnificently restrained, hesitant and careful: a cautious, circuitous tide slowly filling out the estuary of meaning. This is not at all, as *The Waste Land*, a group poem: it is a highly personal poem, with universal implications, made authentic by the draining away, through penance, of most that is normally understood as personality.

And yet the lost group-presence seems inherently relevant to the composition of the whole. In the first place there is the preoccupation (as in Joyce's *Wake*) with the number four. A fourway dynamic is the specific compositional principle of a quartet, which is an aesthetic organisation of four instruments or voices in play together. And, to enforce the point beyond mere synaesthetic imitation of music, there are specifically four of them. This is not to suggest that we are to look, systematically, for four distinct voices within the poem, representing the four Men of 1914 in turn. This would imply a far more conscious (and self-conscious) level of expression than I am suggesting. It is the 'familial' dynamic itself which is important, at a time when the varying projects of Joyce, Pound, Lewis and Eliot had moved in very different directions. The use of four-ness here is a basic structuring principle in a poem that, more than any other of the century, attempts to bring into a cohesive pattern the 'immense panorama of futility and anarchy'[34] that Eliot felt the modern world to be. Where *The Waste Land* is essentially radical collage, haunted by the ghost of a ritual shaping behind the arras of the text, *Four Quartets* foregrounds a four-part patterning as gravitational field into which every fragmentary particle of content can be organised. Thus the five-part sectioning of *The Waste Land* is repeated as the five-part sectioning of each Quartet; but – as the fourway dynamic of the *Wake* structures a family of five persons – the five-pattern is drawn through repetition, into a fourway dynamic and each of the four poems – 'Burnt Norton' (1935), 'East Coker' (1940), 'The Dry Salvages' (1941), and 'Little Gidding' (1942) – is to be construed in terms of instrumentation for four voices. As often noted, the use of the four Elements helps reinforce the fourway dynamic.[35] And here, indeed, there is a temptation to play with identifications which might, just, perform a genuinely interpretative function in probing the less conscious aspects of the dynamic. Thus, where Eliot is predominantly Fire (purgatorial refinement achieving final union with the rose of love in the last line), then Water could be the Joyce of the girl-epiphany in *Portrait*, 'Proteus' (especially) in *Ulysses* – 'full fathom five . . .' – and the 'hither and thithering waters' of the *Wake*; Earth, Lewis (the space-man and linear artist) who founded another 'unreal city' on the plain of *The Human Age*, and in the trenches had endured a mud where 'garlic and sapphires' were scarcely present; while Pound, troubadour-lover of sung lyric, is Air – breath, 'natural cadence', the ear-man who knew, truly, which lines of 'He Do the Police in Different Voices' would sound false on the air-waves of the modern world.[36]

The fourway dynamic in the *Quartets* is as profoundly suggestive
as the four-part extrapolation of the *Wake*'s family of five sketched
out above (see p. 160). Yet the introjected presence of the old
work-group within this masterwork reveals itself, from time to
time, in far less structured ways. For example, the insistent garden
scenarios in the sequence (so different from Eliot's early urban
imagery) often remind us of the earlier Pound – especially in
Cathay. The evocation of river and sea, particularly in 'The Dry
Salvages', invites us to reconsider the profound watery connection
between Eliot and Joyce ('by the waters of babalong'); while an
opening gesture like 'Midwinter spring is its own season' (p. 191)
achieves a peculiar status of consolidation with respect to the
earlier countergesture: 'Midwinter (fruur or kuur?) was in the
offing and Premver a promise of a pril' (*Wake*, p. 110).[37] The
construction of memorable settings in hallucinatory city situations –
the streets, the tube, the hills of London – points back to Lewis's
reappropriation of Eliot's post-Baudelaire vision of the urban in
The Childermass, especially, and there are moments of expressionistic shock (stars heard on the 'sodden floor', p. 172, or the 'wounded
surgeon''s operation, p. 181) which recall an old debt to *Enemy of
the Stars*. At the same time there is enough of the pre-1914 Eliot
here – the metonymic urban details, the 'logopoeia' of philosophical
brooding – to remind us that four separate visions came to the
making of high Modernism, and that this is also Eliot's final poetic
reckoning with his innermost self. In this sense, the poem subsumes
the old group experience and finds its ultimate meaning in a self-
accountability which includes one's own creative emanations as
well as those introjected from others.

Four Quartets is also centred, perhaps obsessionally, on the main
issue within the project of 1914: the relation between the moment
of decisive action ('birthing') and the future and the past. It is a
prolonged meditation on the urge to 'MAKE IT NEW' – in itself,
in terms of the attendant 'Blasting' of the past, and in terms of the
future which is consequent on the new creation. Thus, although
the message of the *Quartets* often appears static and conservative,
the poem insists throughout on the urgency and irrevocability of
present choice and venture: 'any action / Is a step to the block, to
the fire, down the sea's throat' (p. 197). And the shared venture
of the Men of 1914 is implicated in all that is said here about
commitment to art, its consequences and partial failure. So I take
the apparition of the 'familiar compound ghost' (in 'Little Gidding',

II, pp. 193–5) to have a particular poignancy with respect to the old group relations. The word 'compound' is mandatory, and as in *The Apes of God* or *Finnegans Wake*, this is a 'dream' figure where many personalities and influences are condensed.[38] However, I believe Joyce has a significant place among possible dead 'masters'. Joyce had died recently, and Eliot, not long before, had been involved in the publication of his final work, in which the undertones to 'Tom' had varied between ironic play and poignant appeal. Eliot had struggled with Joyce's 'thoughts and theory' since at least his review of *Portrait of the Artist as a Young Man* and his own theorisation of Joyce's method in the review of *Ulysses*. It is scarcely for other main contenders, such as Browning or Dante, that 'both good and bad' would have to be personally forgiven. After the *Wake*'s ambivalent thrusts, however, the lines make specific interrelational sense. Contending to be the main prose and poetic masters of Modernism, both Joyce and Eliot had been at the forefront of the attempt to 'purify the dialect of the tribe' and both would know the possessor of the 'voice' for 'next year's words' – Samuel Beckett, whose *Godot* would be published by Eliot at Faber in 1956. It is fitting that an old drinking-crony should remind Eliot of the trials reserved for old age; and it is apt that Eliot should make Joyce, *post mortem*, a kind of spiritual counsellor – thus restoring to him the religious dimension which he overtly denied (and at whose like in Eliot's Anglicanism he joked in the *Wake*) but which, at deeper levels, animated all his work. Joyce had, of course, 'left [his] body' on the shore of Lake Zurich in a Europe even more 'distant', at the time of writing, by Nazi domination. On this reading, then, the fading of the ghost on 'the blowing of the horn' speaks back to 'the Cock, the Postboy's Horn' (*Wake*, p. 39) which is itself an allusion to the cock-crow and motor-horn in *The Waste Land*. What the ghost has to say is relevant to the 'intolerable wrestle' of artistic creation which is a theme throughout the sequence. He gives his version of experience, even though he is not eager to 'rehearse' the old arguments. Granted the title and whole thematic of *Finnegans Wake*, *re-hearse* is the *mot juste* of an old corpse-saluter (see above p. 126). It is fitting that Eliot's last verse-allusion to Joyce should start with a sly, Possum pun.

As has been observed already, *Four Quartets* is essentially concerned with Time. There is, I believe, a dialogue with Virginia Woolf[39] involved here, as with Lewis, Joyce and Pound. Time, in the poem, is a continuum, or 'pattern',[40] where relations between past, present and future are established on a level beyond the linear, even though chronologial time remains. Love – similar perhaps to what Pound would call 'the quality of the affection' – remains as motive and goal outside the temporal process and yet as, in a sense, the engine of choice. On the spiritual plain, such Love becomes the inspiration for the passion to give birth to the New and so change reality. There is, then, a deeper kind of meaning to the children's voices in the leaves. The children are both present and not present, and their laughter is 'hidden'; they are, we might say, possibilities – the spectres of rebirth which inspire all artistic activity. So the antique matrimonial ceremonies of 'East Coker' figure, in the dance of words, the possibility of a culture renewed, transcending the 'dark' of individuals mown down by the grim reaper – Milton, Yeats, Joyce ('the silent funeral, / Nobody's funeral', p. 180) – even though such renewal can only be temporary: 'a raid on the inarticulate', p. 182. Thus in 'The Dry Salvages' the 'undefeated' (p. 190) are simply those who have 'gone on trying' to give a name and meaning to experience – those who, like the Men of 1914, have taken on and persisted in the task of shaking up the dead patterns of convention and finding a new shape to the flux of experience. In 'Little Gidding' the Poundian 'husk of meaning' is transcended by prayer and com- munication with the worthy dead, who are the grandfathers of any new creation. True achievement is proclaimed where the 'consort' (p. 197) of renewed words dances and, as in *Finnegans Wake*, 'every phrase and every sentence is an end and a beginning'. Time, then, is made meaningful by the right kind of expressive intervention which, for all its partial failure, remains for ever as trace of re-creation. In that sense, the past can never be really past, since its challenge to the future remains operative – just as Modernism, by its very name as well as by the example of its masterworks, remains a gateway to the future long after the term Postmodernism has signalled its demise.

Thus, although its intent is mystical and its concern is with the meaning of all human activity, *Four Quartets* is very much about writing itself, and in this both evokes and continues the 1914 project of making 'a beginning' in new words. The poem places the phenomenon of the 'wholly new start' (p. 182) within the overall Western tradition of *Kerygma*[41] – the perennial Messianic challenge to change the status quo. And if an end is also in that beginning then the major achievements of the Men of 1914 are all embryonic in the *BLAST* era, just as the final 'failure' of their projects is endemic in the urge to make everything new. In this, the four writers have authentically 'kept [their] appointment' – unlike those hollow men, Vladimir and Estragon,[42] who claim to have done so and yet challenge nothing, create nothing. As Pound will say: 'this is not vanity'.[43] Though Eliot's faith is finally in the Word beyond words, it seems clear that only through the struggle with words, the search for a meaning needing *new* words, can he come at last to Logos – and plant a restored garden where once was only waste land.

Of all Eliot's poems, *Four Quartets* ends with the greatest sense of hope and it is, in a way, an endorsement of the whole group project. The Messianic hubris of Modernism created its own bitter self-reckonings – Lewis's self-condemnation or Pound's despairing 'I cannot make it flow thru'.[44] *Four Quartets* sees beyond such disillusionment and sponsors the task to 'purify the dialect', (p. 194) through a longterm view. So 'all shall be well and / All manner of thing shall be well', (p. 198). The efforts of the Men of 1914, which Eliot supported throughout his life, as essayist and editor, will continue to bear witness to the constant need to confront deadness with the promise of renewal. If we 'die with the dying', (p. 197) we are also 'born with the dead'. The yew-tree is flanked by a rose (once Pound's emblem[45]), and it gives place to an apple tree,[46] full of the voices of children. So the 'hint half guessed, the gift half understood, is Incarnation' (p. 190). Rightly assessed, the journey of the Magi leads to a birth which will remain valid in the 'pattern' / Of timeless moments' (p. 197). So the final union of the fire and the rose is achieved in a situation of the same urgency which once animated *BLAST*:

'Quick now, here, now, always.'
(p. 198)

SELF CONDEMNED

Lewis's *Self Condemned*[47] is one of the most powerfully-written, painfully self-honest and incisively relevant English novels of this century, yet it is little known in England at the present time. Its theme is the marginalisation, to the point of total exclusion, of a

visionary man of letters (a historian) who renounces his academic
post, on principle, and goes to Canada as the Second World War
breaks out in Europe. Largely set in an isolated and parochial
Toronto New World (unfair now, but perhaps justified at the time),
the novel demonstrates how the 'Apes' and 'puppets' of modern
society destroy the authentic voices of sanity. It centres on a
hotel (that twentieth-century *locale* of aimless transition which
superseded the old 'Condition-of-England' site, the family house)
and at a key moment the hotel is burnt down and becomes encased
in a fantastic 'iceberg'. It is a superb symbolisation of cultural
paralysis; and yet the issue of individual choice is insisted on, too.
The hero, René Harding (whose name unites French rationalism
with English Puritanism[48]), progressively develops into a species
of personal repression as cold as the hotel's apotheosis – his wife
dead, his past razed, his future empty. *Self Condemned* is a solitary
and terrible work, which Eliot described as 'a book of almost
unbearable spiritual agony'.[49] And its fate, in terms of critical
indifference, fully bears out its sombre message – that mass culture
may destroy its most intelligent writers. *Self Condemned*, a novel of
harrowing reassessment, records the experience of one of the
Modernist Magi as he finally turned his back on the old group-
venture, and England in general, and tried to start again.

The solitary and self-willed nature of this change is made clear
early on. René explains to his mother and sister that: 'I was a
group. . . . The morals of all groups are the same' and so 'I had
to isolate myself' (pp. 22–3). Granted the autobiographical nature
of the book, this is a confession of Lewis's own 'turn' – but it is
written from a position of partial recantation, when the author had
returned to England and a proximity to his own past. The book's
beginning is set in 1939, two years after Lewis had publicly
celebrated the formation of the old work-group in *Blasting and
Bombardiering*. Granted the space given there to discussing both
the group and each of the other contributors to it, it is not surprising
that *Self Condemned* should not talk back to his old cronies in the
manner of *The Apes of God*. Yet one might suggest that the intense
isolation built up in the book is itself predicted against the loss of
these other presences: the old 'family' is negated in the same way
that Harding loses touch with his own sisters and mother ('You
are not by any chance *a fool*, my son?'[50]) and eventually with his
wife, who commits suicide. Seen in relation to *Blasting*, with its
companionable gusto for the old friends, *Self Condemned* bears in

its bleakness the price of finally rejecting those earlier days of sharing. Although neither Lewis nor Harding became converted in the North American Catholic Seminary they took refuge in for a while, this is, in a sense, Lewis's 'Ash Wednesday'. But while it is partly autobiographical, and indeed confessional, it is fully realised in fictional terms. Unlike René Harding, Lewis eventually returned to England with his wife, and continued to create against all the odds (including blindness). The finest fruit of this postwar creation was *Self Condemned* itself, and precisely by expressing, in the figure of René, the negative implications of his own scornful intellectuality, he aesthetically transcends them. Just thus does Lewis 'turn again'.

The experiences which the novel depicts spring essentially from the hero's rejection of his old work-group in Europe. The hero believes it is not possible to 'exist intellectually in London' (p. 342). Involved here is a repudiation of the whole Modernist project since *BLAST*.[51] It is not so much that René transfers a Messianic expectation to the New World (as Lewis might partially have done in seeking out his childhood roots): René sees Canada negatively from the start. What is involved is a major act of renunciation. René gives up his Professorship in History because chronicling mankind's follies (the assumed norm of historical writing) merely serves to normalise and perpetuate them. According to him, history should stress man's productive capacity ('those heroic creators who attempt to build something', p. 86) – in my terms, the urge to birth the New – and marginalise his self-destructive acts. But it does not, and academic history is seen as a collusion with man's aggressive habits. Hence, after the publication of *The Secret History of the Second World War*, which seeks to expose the economic and political forces which generate war, René feels he must resign his post. On the one hand, as 'Rotter' Parkinson points out: 'Men do not turn their lives upside down in response to the summons of a professor of history' (p. 95); on the other, René no longer wants to be implicated in the normal history, which is ideologically allied to the politics of aggression. In the figure of this historian, then, the two functions of Lewis as writer are brought together metaphorically. Both as political and social theorist (*The Art of Being Ruled*, *The Lion and the Fox*, *Time and Western Man*) and as satirist (*Tarr*, *The Childermass*, *The Apes of God*) Lewis feels himself to have failed. Although the philosophy of 'Inferior Religions' remains, in a sense – the creative differ existentially from the puppet-men –

there may also be seen surfacing here an anxiety that satire itself (like history) is complicit with the folly it exposes, by normalising it. Certainly, in René's own terms, a work of irascible caricature like *The Apes of God* is as aggressive and destructive in the small as World War is in the large. So Lewis's 'turn' deeply concerns his own longheld conception of the role of making New. And this is predicated within a context of the breakdown of social values since the *BLAST* project. In this version 'The nineteenth century . . . was no less civilised' than the eighteenth (p. 103): 'There was no sign of *breakdown* there. We fought it on its borders, ['BLAST years 1837–1900', *BLAST* 1, p. 18] but we now realize how wonderful a century it was'. The Great War, and the prelude to the Second World War are, in particular, what has made the difference for René. In terms of the Men of 1914, we might say, their creative efforts have been rendered abortive in terms of any possibility of social redemption. The masculinist self-destructiveness which Lewis had anatomised in *Tarr* has transformed the contemporary geopolitical reality into bloody anarchy which art cannot finally influence.

Unlike Pound, then, Lewis appears to have despaired of the writer's role; and he cannot, though René explores it, accept Eliot's religious solution (the 'springs' of René's life are 'far away from the extremes of mysticism', p. 389). Interestingly, René does contemplate a contrastive strategy which sounds something like a vindication of Joyce's method in the *Wake*. 'Professor René Harding admits as a possibility that history should be written as an Alicean chaos, or even as a violent burlesque' (p. 87) where 'the mad kings, queens, duchesses, hatters and the rest are the more or less dangerous lunatics who surround the baffled hero' (p. 86) – just so do the transmogrified figures of Wellington and Napoleon, Caesar and Brutus, Parnell and the Priests surround the dreaming figure of H. C. E. But it is not an option for the analytical René. He gives up his post and his role for a three-year period of intellectual hibernation in the frozen city of Momaco. And when his imagination and intellect begin working again, in the company of McKenzie the philosopher, he loses his wife and reverts to a conventional form of history, as mindless as it is soulless. So we have the contrast at the end between the man of 'the old days in London . . . buoyant, elastic, inventive and fearless' and the 'present . . . professor of history at the University of Mamaco', the 'Keeper' of a 'freak anti-historical museum . . . containing many

libellous wax-works' (p. 400). Thus, no doubt, in Canada did Lewis see the difference between his past and present situations. When 'it came to one of the acid tests of authenticity, it would be recognized as an imposture'. Lewis himself, however, survived to return to London and write the book – one whose interiorised profundity is in spectacular contrast to the exterior surface-brilliance of *The Apes of God*, that 'libellous wax-works' of the thirties.

It is, as already noted, a solitary book written out of a temporary rejection of the entire Modernist project. Lewis, like René, 'had been deprived of his natural audience' and 'the deep cultural soil in which he has grown . . . that atmosphere and that climate of thought' (p. 401). Yet for all its intense self-preoccupation with the impoverishment of exile it does not, in the writing, lose all contact with what had been renounced. René is aware of the poetry of 'Mr Eliot' (p. 257) and 'the inventions of super-languages, such as that of James Joyce' (p. 315). The final verdict on him is that: 'You cannot kill a man twice, the Gods cannot strike *twice* and the man survive' (p. 406) – which seems to speak back to those early lines in the Pisan cantos: 'but the Twice crucified/where in history will you find it?' (LXXIV, p. 425), at a time when Lewis was again corresponding with Ezra and helping in the campaign to get him released from St Elizabeth's Hospital. Indeed, there is an odd way in which the political convictions and social ostracism of René Harding remind us, in their intensity, of the personal situation of Pound as much as of Lewis. During the three years of isolated incarceration in the Blundell Hotel, René Harding is shown as aware of the suffering of other creative exiles – Stefan Zweig for instance (p. 171). His meditations on the sense of imprisonment are intense – and written at a time when Pound's predicament was much in his mind. As Lewis wrote about Pound to D. D. Paige: 'What has happened to him is terrible, and it does not help to say that it is his own doing'.[52] The words apply equally well to René Harding, who is, after all, *self*-condemned. As the Possum had said, 'any step' may be toward 'the block'.

There is a generally Eliotic flavour to the condition of Harding, which might be summed up as: The fire and the ice are one. Lewis had in mind a Dantesque precedent which holds resonance for his two poet-friends too: in the Lake of Cocytus, as in Momaco, 'Their heads were bowed toward the ice beneath, / Their eyes attest their grief; their mouths proclaim the bitter airs that through the dungeon breathe . . . / at once the fierce frost blocked / The tears between and sealed them shut again'.[53] Harding tells McKenzie 'my brain is burning' and there is enough about intense heat of one kind or another in the book to constitute its own form of 'Fire Sermon'. Further, as Timothy Materer notes: 'The hotel's "icy labyrinth" and its "tunnels ending in mirrors" recall the "contrived corridors" of history and the "wilderness of mirrors" in Eliot's "Gerontion" '.[54] Like Gerontion, René finds that history's 'contrived corridors' lead him to despair. So if Lewis had Pound's current plight, as well as his own past situation, in mind in the writing of *Self Condemned* (and the balance between self-pity, self-condemnation and self-justification here is similar to that in the last cantos), he has also brought to bear a powerful neoDantesque symbolism which the Possum had made his poetic trademark.

Joyce is overtly referred to only once. However, one or two in-jokes inform even this most bleak and self-preoccupied work. Thus René's old London crony (last of the independent belletrists) is given the nickname 'Rotter' (cf. Ratner in *Apes* and the many variants in the *Wake*) and it is a counterthrust that Rotter 'feeds' on René's brain[55] (p. 105). If it is all part of the old game that a quite unpleasant and unreliable homosexual is given the name 'Starr', it is also that René's rescuer in the bar-room brawl speaks back to a lost fellowship:

> 'You were splendid.'
> 'Oh <u>rats</u>,' said <u>Jim</u>, with violent modesty, turning to Hester. 'I wiped the beer off you as it was thrown over you! That's all I did.'
> 'You did more than that. You sided with the limey – <u>you,</u>
> <u>an Irishman!</u>'   (p. 232, underlining mine)

Thus, at the end of a violent incident in which boots are used for kicking as violently as in *Enemy*, does Irish Jim act, like Bloom with an assaulted Stephen, 'in orthodox Samaritan fashion'.[56] The other main connection with Joyce here is on the subject of split-personality. René, 'in order not to be at the mercy of his emotions', has been 'obliged to effect a division of his personality into two parts: he had created a kind of artificial "unconscious" of his own, and thus locked away all acuity of realization' (p. 140). Throughout the book it is Lewis's task, as novelist to mediate between this psychologised Shem-Shaun division and to suggest, with increasing conviction, that in the end it is the suppression of emotion which destroys René and leaves him a 'cemetery of shells'. In the Lewis canon, *Self Condemned* stands out as being the work most appreciative of the feminine. René's mother and sisters, Mrs Harradson, Bess, Affie and above all Hester are given a vigorous life of their own, and while the narration is often ambivalent about female qualities, the whole action of the book ends up as an endorsement of the bond with woman: 'If the personality is emptied of mother-love, emptied of wife-love . . . upon which the will to create depends, then the personality becomes a shell' (p. 400). Lewis's judgement on his hero constitutes a final recognition and acceptance of the emotionally 'feminine' within himself. In terms of the old rivalry with the creator of Molly and Anna Livia Plurabelle, it is ironic that only after Joyce's death could Lewis create a masterpiece which writes out of the fluxive interior of emotionality, and endorses, in the end, the emotional vibrancy of woman – as it condemns the petrified repression of the over-analytic male. Though not Modernist in form, *Self Condemned* finally expresses Lewis's appreciation that Joyce's brand of Modernism – the sponsorship of that fluxive web of feelings which is the individual's lifetime – is more humane and important than the space-man's dedication to the external and coldly satiric eye. Did Joyce have to die, like René's wife, before Lewis could show in print the fate of one who merely despises 'Hesteria'? Certainly, René's pet name for his wife – 'Essie' – is very similar to Joyce's frequent shortening of Isabel, in the *Wake*, to 'Issy'. And 'Essie', as name, is very close to 'Esse' – the state of Being.

Self Condemned stands with *The Apes of God* as a monument to Lewis's contradictory talent. It is a novel of awful self-isolation written out of the impulse to reject the project of the Men of 1914 altogether. But, by birthing the New as exemplum of the folly of denying the springs of creation, it is thereby a strong contribution to the whole group venture. And despite its apparent fearful autonomy, it is also, finally, a group-move in the great game which started in *BLAST* – a concession to Jim, after his death, an appropriation of Tom's Dantesque symbolism, and a self-confession which also spoke to Pound's asylum confinement. It is a work which should be well-known and placed on a par with at least such modern novels as *Sons and Lovers*, *A Passage to India* or *To the Lighthouse*, for it is more honest than the first, more intelligent than the second and more powerful than the third. Though Lewis completed *The Human Age*, and attained thereby a radio success,[57]

he never wrote better than this. *Self Condemned* is a saga of the
spiritual condition – that we are condemned to be free and that
our choices can destroy us and those we love. This destruction is
described in a Nuevo Mundo as cold as it is mindless, but it is
chosen in an England where civilisation appeared to be falling
apart. The portentous transition is embodied on an ocean liner full
of middle-class dining companions, zigzagging across the U-boat
infested waters of early World War Two. As he wrote this passage
(and remembered his own experience to which he was now seeking
meaning) did Lewis, perhaps, have his friend's lines in mind?

> 'Fare forward, you who think that you are voyaging;
> You are not those who saw the harbour
> Receding, or those who will disembark.
>   . . . consider the future
> And the past with an equal mind.'[58]

THE GREAT BALL OF CRYSTAL

Whatever deprivations Lewis had suffered in Toronto during the
war years, they cannot be realistically equated with what Pound
endured, at the end of the war, in the Disciplinary Training Centre
cage near Pisa. His physical and mental agony (however deserved)
must have been unendurable, and the fragmentary, tortuous and
tormented discourse of the 'Pisan' cantos gestures toward a hell
(not now for 'others')[59] which is finally indescribable. The spectre
of a double-crucifixion haunts those lines which cry out the 'magna
NUX animae' (p. 436): here there is, surely, no 'deeper'. The
experience will underlie the rest of Pound's creative work (however,
at times, it returns to dissection and assertion) and re-emerge as
broken desperation in the last 'Drafts and Fragments', before the
final silence. In the 'Pisan' cantos, the old 'scout-master', alone
and rejected as never before, expresses a world where no merit-
badges or troop-loyalties can avail (for all that he randomly evokes
them), and no words – however brilliant – can birth a new world
not dominated by nemesis, confusion and pain. In the cage, Pound
was forced to measure reality by an ant's artistry, a larcenist's
generosity, a murderer-cum-rapist's fantasy, and test on the nerve-
ends of his skin, the breakpoints of his psychic defences, the

limitations of Modernist literary-aesthetic hubris. He, who had recoiled from Eliot's 'love of death',[60] now tasted 'the loneliness of death' (p. 527) and, like his old friend – as imaged in 'Ash Wednesday' – must slowly attempt to rise up 'out of hell, from the labyrinth / the path wide as a hair' (p. 632). Odysseus was now, indeed, sailing through 'dark seas' (p. 5), but he would never, now, really 'return'.

The 'Pisan' cantos, in particular, are littered with references to old literary friends. Those most invoked, I suspect, are not the men Pound had gathered into a group and sponsored – Lewis, Joyce and Eliot – but those 'godfathers' of Modernism who had sponsored him, and to whom he could now psychologically appeal as mentors rather than surrogate pupils – 'Fordie' (Ford Madox Ford) and 'Uncle William' or, simply 'Yeats'. Their names and examples – however bizarre the anecdote – constitute a continuing thread through the cantos from LXXIV onwards. Even when Ezra decides that Yeats (along with 'the Possum' and 'Wyndham') has 'no ground' to stand on (pp. 658 and 728), he continues to memorialise their literary relationship, and Yeats is perhaps the single most evoked presence of all the writers he had personally known in the remaining cantos. For the friendship with Yeats had been sustained, as even that with Ford had not. And in so far as Pound had first come to England to see how 'Yeats did it', had helped pare down the older man's verse, married the daughter of his ex-mistress, and found him an early enthusiast and apologist for the first cantos,[61] the ghost of his now-dead poetic exemplum (in life himself a devotee of communication with spirits) quite naturally materialises, at times, in the continuing 'tale of the tribe'. For example, we have the repeated model: 'Uncle William two months on ten lines of Ronsard' (here p. 686). But the anecdote of the wondrous 'Peeeeacock' is also recurrent, and once vividly in context:

> . . . at Stone Cottage in Sussex by the waste moor
> (or whatever) and the holly bush
>   who would not eat ham for dinner
> because peasants eat ham for dinner
>   despite the excellent quality
> and the pleasure of having it hot.
>
>   (p. 534)

In such ways is a debt to the paternalist inspiration which enabled
Pound to find his own poetic confidence, and set a precedent for
his own fostering of those who could 'Renew' (p. 629), acknowledged and reborrowed. But here it is complicated by the giving
that springs from having taken too: for the last line inscribes a one-
time editorial benevolence for a piece of 'hot gammon' to which
the speaker was invited 'to get the beauty of it hot' (*The Waste
Land*, pp. 166–7). And, of course, in general the Men of 1914 as
well as 'Uncle William', 'Fordie' and others are also luminaries
who go to make up 'the great acorn of light' (p. 795). They are
prominent among the 'good guys in the family' (p. 792) who 'had
thrones' (p. 793), and like the Magi of Eliot, Lewis and Joyce were
'kings' who, in some idealistic realm of imagination, will still 'meet
in their island' (p. 803).

James Joyce comes first – if only because of the Odyssean
precedent, and the starkness of the literary sundering between
them, once 'Work in Progress' was Joyce's final progression.[62]
Despite their differences, Pound never broke with the endeavours
of Eliot and Lewis as he did with Joyce over *Finnegans Wake*. But
Joyce was some years dead already, by the time Pound started
Canto LXXIV, and his presence is attractively invoked out of the
broken 'ant-hill / from the wreckage of Europe' (p. 458):

> . . . and Jim the comedian singing:
>   'Blarrney castle me darlin'
>   you're nothing now but a StOWne'.   (p. 433)

There are other references in the remaining cantos: 'recalling the
arrival of Joyce et fils / at the haunt of Catullus / with Jim's veneration
of thunder . . .' (p. 456); 'Mr Joyce also preoccupied with
Gibraltar / and the Pillars of Hercules / not with my *patio* . . .'
(pp. 447–8); 'But Mr Joyce requested sample menus from the
leading hotels' (p. 473). There are further passages where an
influence from the early parts of *Ulysses*, which Pound most
admired, seems pertinent: for instance, in LXXXIII:

>   The eyes, this time my world,
>   But pass and look *from* mine
>   between my lids
>   sea, sky and pool.   (p. 535)

Compare 'Ineluctable modality of the visible . . . thought through my eyes . . . seaspawn and seawrack . . . Snotgreen, bluesilver, rust' (*Ulysses*, p. 42). 'Sea-wrack' is also a phrase in the *Cantos* (e.g. p. 612). In general, whenever the *Odyssey*, sea-description or thunder ('Confucians observe the weather, / hear thunder', p. 702) are involved, it seems likely that Ezra had Jim partially in mind.

Wyndham, too, remains as exemplum – and finally as emblem of intellectual courage. Some examples: 'Gaudier's word not blacked out / nor old Hulme's, nor Wyndham's' (p. 479); 'Mr Lewis had been to Spain' (p. 506); 'So it is to Mr Binyon that I owe, initially, / Mr Lewis, Mr P. Wyndham Lewis' (p. 507); ' "Constantinople" said Wyndham "our star" ' (p. 661); 'and Wyndham' (p. 685); 'old Wyndham' (p. 728). The phrasal gestures that Lewis had pioneered in *Enemy* remain here, as they had figured in the earliest cantos:

Butterflies, mint and Lesbia's sparrows. . . .   (p. 428)

the wind mad as Cassandra. . . .   (p. 475)

grey wing, black wing, black wing shot with crimson.   (p. 608)

Gems sunned as mirrors, alternate.   (p. 792)

Yet Lewis's presence is more important than such imitations of his early Vorticist prose-experimentation. With Hulme, Gaudier and young Epstein ('Rock-Drill'), he stands as a model of incisiveness, accuracy, integrity and order. In this he serves as an introjected compound of Malatesta, Pisanello, 'Muss' and Confucius, for Pound. Despite his 'asperities',[63] Lewis had painted a major portrait of Pound, and his *Self-Condemned* had spoken to Pound's own dire experience. According to Hugh Kenner, when visited in old age Pound had finally laughed at an anecdote about Wyndham on Tom, which deployed his own old simile: 'he doesn't come *in here* [Lewis's flat] disguised as Westminster Abbey'.[64] And the late fragment of Canto CXV honours Lewis's example (as well as memorialising a relationship) in the context of nuclear 'terror' and the breakdown of 'the mind of Europe':

Wyndham Lewis chose blindness
rather than have his mind stop.
          (p. 794)

Contention with the Possum also remains virtually to the end. CXV itself peters out as an endorsement of Eliot's vision of unredeemed man from (at least) *The Waste Land* onwards:

> where the dead walked
>   and the living were made of cardboard.
>   (p. 794)

In earlier cantos we find a quite continuous talking back to Pound's old friend and rival: 'with a bang not with a whimper' (p. 425); 'the Possum/pouvrette et ancienne' (p. 436); 'until I end my song' (p. 437); 'things have ends and beginnings'[65] (p. 462); 'Mr Eliot may have/missed something, after all' (p. 466); 'there is/no end to the journey' (p. 477 – least of all for Magi?); 'a literary program 1920'[66] (p. 481); 'Mr Eliot's version' (p. 497); 'tradition' and 'talent' (p. 506); 'Possum observed . . .' (p. 518); 'Terreus! Terreus!'[67] (p. 525); 'and have speech with Tiresias, Thebae' (p. 533); 'waste lands' (p. 590); 'Yeats, Possum, Old Wyndham' (p. 728); 'these fragments shored against ruin/. . . Mr Rock . . ./his fragments sunk (20 years)' (p. 781); 'Here from the beginning, we have been here/from the beginning' (p. 784); 'No man can see his own end' (p. 787). To the close, Pound, like Eliot, will continue to play off Dante; though his hell is more conflictual, his purgatory less purposeful, his Paradise more fragmentary than that of his rival. In a sense, the whole *Cantos* is a continuation of *The Waste Land* by other means – a fulfilment of Pound's sense that the 'Uranian Muse' had birthed Modernist verse as Open Field heterogeneity where anything goes. Thus its ending, in brilliant fits and starts which come to no closure, replicates the 'shored' fragments of *The Waste Land* and serves as implicit disclaimer of the end-directed conclusions of 'Ash Wednesday' and 'Four Quartets'. Pound, too, contends about 'ends' and 'beginnings' but leaves us merely a hopeful 'rushlight', where the fire is not the rose, to stand as a beacon for 'splendour' (p. 797). And even this is not quite the conclusion: that honour goes to the 'Courage' of Olga (p. 815), as discourse subsumes in the feeling that fired it. Unlike the Possum, Pound, to the end, refused to conform to the formalised dance.

Yet formal order had been his dream: order within, making order without. Confucius, Ming, Malatesta, Adams, Jefferson,

Gaudier, Mussolini; carved stone or jade, the rose in 'steel-dust', Venice, Torcello, Ravenna, swansdown, 'ply over ply' – the ideal of pattern made real, of a world as a 'great ball of crystal' or Ecbatan with its star-coloured terraces, lies at the heart of the fifty-year long project – the 'palimpsest'[68] of cantos. Yet what, in both structure and content, the cantos express is a world of confusion and flux. So the poem implicitly embodies the torsions of conflict between Lewis and Joyce, the 'space'-connoisseur in Pound (ideo-gramme, 'Poet as Sculptor'[69]) undone by the time-flux of modern Western man. 'I cannot make it cohere' (p. 796), he confesses – yet the confession is true witness to realities beyond him, that no one could shape. So we might reverse Confucius here: if a man have not order about him, he can not spread order within him. Just so with Ezra: 'That I lost my center / fighting the world' (p. 802). He tried the impossible – to bring synthetic vision to bear on a world whose economy and politics ensured that the Modern would mean mass-conflict and mess. The effort, I suggest, almost drove him mad; perhaps did so:

> in short / the descent
> has not been of advantage either . . .
>   The States have passed thru a
>   dam'd supercilious era
> Down, Derry-down /
>   Oh let an old man rest.
>
>   (p. 536)

The Modernist Lear is nearly in pieces: thoughts of a fractured brain in a fractured season.

The Cantos resolves as flotsam and jetsam thrown from the onetime shared Vortex of 1914, the gathered power now drained away into ripples that 'cannot . . . flow thru' (p. 797). It had started as a birthing, astride the land of the dead; the Muse ('Venerandam . . . Aphrodite', p. 5) presiding where new life starts as genetic linkage ('Sordello, and my Sordello?', p. 6). And if, from the first, the features and shape of the new text-child were always in question, the forward pulse of poetic life was not: 'So that: . . .' (p. 5); 'And . . .' (p. 10); ' "Nec Spe Nec Metu" ' (p. 12). Neither hopes nor fears could stem the flood as it flowed from the East to the West, the past to the present – energy, breadth, virtū in search of a shape to contain them (the carpet's weave, the fugal variations, the fountain to balance the ball) which never emerged. This formless sprawl, playing at patterns, is a family child born from a tension where Lewis's aggression, Joyce's fluidity, Eliot's precision and Pound's own technique and gusto had finally nowhere to go – except on and on till the life drained away. Yet in this it is characteristic and faithful to modern flux: Lewis's contra-history of *Self Condemned*, his 'Woddle ah doo?'; Bloomsday, with the Odyssean scaffold removed, or the *Wake* without Vico's outdated theory; a waste land where the 'rose' is a gleam not a pattern; or 'Hugh Selwyn Mauberley' where the twice-dead man retires to no island, 'an hedonist', but strives, to the end, to keep the blossoms from falling – where 'leaves blow' (p. 628) and 'Gestalt seed' (p. 635) is sown again as the lines pant away to the ultimate stillness.

Yet though formally formless, *The Cantos* is still an egregious and powerful species of life, a poetic birthing that lives to the end, however tormented. Its insistent life continues beyond the demise of the one-time 'godfathers', Yeats and Ford, flows into new intensity, through acute suffering, beyond Anna's circular closure of the *Wake* and onwards (dogmatic often still, yet still at times breathtaking) until just after Wyndham Lewis died in 1957. Noel Stock writes that 'fragments of cantos, all written before 1960, were published in various magazines'[70] and, of course, were later published in *The Cantos* as 'Drafts and Fragments of Cantos CX–CXVIII'. Those fragments constitute the last ebb of the group that gathered under the puce banner of *BLAST* in 1914, and shared and fought and interacted as witnessed in the pages above. The presence of all of them remains, one way or another, in that last heave of Poundian endeavour: say – 'dolphin on sea-brink' (p. 777); 'a wind of darkness hurls against forest' (p. 781); 'if love be not in the house there is nothing' (p. 796). The 'scouts' died in the order of that registration of influence, but the 'scout-master' lived on until 1972. Beyond the Olga tribute, he wrote no addition to the *Cantos* after the death of Eliot in 1965. He had already stopped writing verse, to all intents and purposes: after the 'Dantescan' tribute to Eliot (below, p. 188), he added words, immeasurably moving to those who feel words still matter, the right words still matter, in the age of critical politics and mass television: 'I can only repeat, but with the urgence of 50 years ago: READ HIM'.[71] The

Cantos deserve to be read too – none more so than the 'Pisan' and 'Drafts and Fragments'. For Pound's ending-gesture, final legacy of the Men of 1914, looks – like so much of Modernism – not to its own self-confident closure, but to those who come after ('You in the dinghy (piccioletta) astern there!', p. 774). CXVI, the effective last canto asks: 'I have brought the great ball of crystal; / who can lift it? / Can you enter the great acorn of light?' (p. 795). Nothing in English creative writing or criticism since those words were written in the late 1950s really seems an adequate response, except perhaps the *via negativa* words of the male heir of Modernism, Samuel Beckett, and the myriad murmurings of Modernism's literary daughters.

TO EARTH O'ERGIVEN

James Joyce died on 13 January 1941, in the small hours of the morning, alone in hospital. He was in Zurich where most of *Ulysses* had been written more than 20 years before – and, again, the chief reason for his presence there was world war, the shuddering of an historical nightmare which his last book, the *Wake*, could elaborately mock and transmogrify, but not truly interpret or control. Yet for the last two years, however exiled and stricken with illness, Joyce had the inner consolation that he had written and had published two of the most extraordinary, massive and inventive novels in the entire history of fiction writing. In terms of the original group-project, he had succeeded in becoming the most spectacular literary innovator of the century. In this, the presence of the group and, above all, the futuristic insistence of its leader, Ezra Pound, had played a major role. As Joyce had acknowledged in the early thirties, 'it is probable that but for him, I should still be the unknown drudge that he discovered'.[72] In the final event, however Joyce's death and funeral were marginalised in war-ravaged Europe, he maintains his reputation in the Postmodernist world as chief penman of international Modernism, and Richard Ellmann's great biography of him is a fitting tribute to his achievement. However, Joyce's literary career is not explained simply as the development of an Irish exile of genius; it is also to be understood as a species of group activity in which a brilliant, but once unregarded, writer was shorn of his poetic and dramatic pretensions and pitted against a novelist and poet of coequal talent (and initially of greater forward-looking impetus) – all presided over by another highly-talented poet, whose concern for literature at first overrode his own desire for personal literary glory. The two major works which Joyce created were forged out of the frictional coalescence within this group. So, when he died, a communal project partly died with him – even though both he and the project would be fruitfully remembered and invoked in the later works of the surviving group-members. The grave in Zurich is a permanent epiphany of what the Men of 1914 were all about: above all, the mutual desire to create new literary life in a world determined, by finally unknowable forces, to effect mass-death by the terrible means of war.

Granted the times, the other three group-members could scarcely respond fittingly to Joyce's demise. They were scattered anyway: Lewis in Canada, Eliot in London and Pound in Axis Italy. For none of them could the old literary ideals be paramount any longer, and even the death of so important a friend must find its place within the larger geopolitical turmoil which affected them all. Joyce's great prose rival, Lewis, remained isolated and depressed in Canada for the duration of the Second World War – living the bleak experiences out of which *Self Condemned* would be written. But unlike his fictional hero, René Harding, Lewis returned to London in 1945 and, for the second time, attempted to rebuild a postwar artistic career. Like Joyce, the older Lewis suffered from eye-trouble and by the early 1950s he was virtually blind – a continuous 'sea-mist' finally preventing him from either painting or reviewing new artistic works.[73] His pugnacity and proclivity for public quarrels continued, if in less passionate vein, but a more affectionate side of him was now in evidence – as in his loyalty to Pound at St Elizabeth's Hospital and his offers to campaign on his behalf. He also maintained a prickly but basically warm bond with Eliot, whose Nobel Prize apotheosis now enabled him to help Lewis financially as well as critically[74] – even though for some years Eliot's life seemed as calcified as that of Harding at the end of Lewis's novel.[75] In 1951 Lewis published some seedily evocative stories about contemporary London life under the Poundian[76] title of *Rotting Hill*, and in the mid-1950s he completed *The Human Age* with the visionary, Dantesque fictions *Monstre Gai* and *Malign Fiesta* (themselves in somewhat Eliotic vein, with the once-Joycean Bailiff now falling foul of the Devil). He achieved considerable success when the trilogy and other novels were adapted for radio by the

BBC. In 1955 the Tate Gallery mounted a retrospective exhibition called 'Wyndham Lewis and Vorticism' (to which the ageing William Roberts – one of the original *BLAST* contributors – took public exception). However, Lewis retained some of his old admirers and gained new ones – even though his public reputation has never, to this day, matched either his early promise or his mature achievements. Despite a radical change of political opinion after World War II (which included support for the Labour Party in 1945[77]), Lewis remains tarred as an aggressive Fascist and has never attained the cultural acceptance that he always wanted. In the 1980s it is still hard to obtain some of the books which most justify a Lewis 'revival' – and, by the same token, his work is rarely seen as the natural 'shadow' to the triumphal phenomenon of Joycean Modernism. Yet whatever critical opinion says, or ignores, about his work, Lewis was indisputably one of the most courageous writers of the century – persisting with pen, pad and a hand-guiding device long after the onset of blindness and, in fits and starts, to the day of his death. That day was 7 March 1957, and the day after, London County Council wreckers began breaking up his Notting Hill flat – as thoroughly and uncaringly as any of the Bailiff's henchmen in *The Childermass*. T. S. Eliot, the next of the Men of 1914 to die, wrote simply: 'a great intellect is gone, a great modern writer is dead'.[78]

By this time Eliot had become, in Lewis's phrase, the 'super-Tennyson'[79] of Modernism. The shy, awkward young man whom Pound had introduced to the literary world in 1915 lived on into the 1960s as an international aesthetic monument – prosperous, powerful in the world of letters, and highly respected – even idolised. As editor, critic and friend he remained loyal to all the old group members, and – even more so than Lewis – he was influential in pressing for Pound's final release from St Elizabeth's. As he had published Joyce's last great work at Faber, so he republished Lewis's *One Way Song* as well as offering suggestions on drafts of *Monstre Gai* and *Malign Fiesta*, and he also brought out the developing sections of Pound's *Cantos*. After *Four Quartets*, Eliot had virtually discontinued writing poetry and contented himself with writing verse-plays which attained a degree of West End success. His second marriage in 1957 finally brought him the personal happiness which had hitherto always eluded him – an experiential enactment of the end of 'Little Gidding' where the 'fire and the rose are one'. It was, perhaps, touchingly appropriate that the wedding breakfast, quite by accident, took place at Pound's old Kensington address[80] – the one-time 'exile' and fellow-magus a 'familiar . . . ghost' at Tom's unlikely rendezvous with contentment. So the least self-confident and optimistic of the Men of 1914 ended up laden with honours and emotionally fulfilled. The poem that Pound had helped bring into the world, *The Waste Land*, was now canonical literary reading and the chief aesthetic ideals the two poets had agreed on were now established in the New Criticism – the Modernist movement had prevailed and Eliot lived on to enjoy the official honours attendent on its success. Not so Pound, who was now in a torment of self-doubt about the worth of his career. In 1959 Eliot wrote at length to reassure him about his literary contribution – the old roles now almost entirely reversed. However, Pound's desolation would last longer than Eliot's lately-come contentment. Eliot died on 4 January 1965; where Lewis's last words had been 'mind your own business' Eliot's consisted of the utterance of his wife's name.[81] He was cremated and the ashes were taken to St Michael's Church in East Coker – but his name (and a quotation from *Four Quartets*) remains permanently honoured in Poets' Corner at Westminster Abbey.

When Eliot died Pound wrote self-effacingly: 'His was the true Dantescan voice', and added, poignantly, 'who is there now for me to share a joke with?'[82] Pound himself was to live on for twenty-seven years after the ending of the Second World War. Many of these were spent at the American Mental Hospital he was sent to as a solution to the problem of his Axis war-propaganda. His initial self-justification and opinionated belligerence did not help the cause of his release at all, as both Eliot and Lewis came to realise. Yet he was able to rely on the goodwill of the other two surviving group-members – a goodwill perhaps most movingly expressed in a letter Lewis wrote:

> Pound is one of my oldest friends and one whose welfare I have most at heart. His literary influence has been very great and *very good*: immeasurably outweighing of course any nonsense he may have talked about economics or about politics or any harm he could possibly do in that direction. What has happened to him is terrible. . . .[83]

Lewis wrote to Pound likening his plight to that of Villon[84] – which must have pleased Ezra: Eliot, who after the war visited America frequently, went to see him at St Elizabeth's on an almost yearly basis.[85] Eventually, the combined influence of Anglo-American writers contrived his release and he returned to Italy.

As we have seen, the *Cantos* continued on into the late fifties – with frequent references to Joyce, Lewis and Eliot. But then Pound's amazing, and at times appalling, self-confidence broke. Ford and Yeats, the old literary god-fathers were long-since dead; so too, by the mid-sixties were Joyce, Lewis and Eliot, as well as other old friends such as 'Hem', Cocteau and Antheil. Solitary, notoriously silent now, Pound lived on another seven or so years, embodying the reality of his own early translation:

> Grey-haired he groaneth, knows gone companions,
> Lordly men are to earth o'ergiven.[86]

Finally his own turn came. On the night of his eighty-seventh birthday, 30 October 1972, the last of the Men of 1914 died in Venice, where his poetic career had started sixty-four years earlier.[87] The founder of the core Modernist group, and the last spokesman of literary Modernist ideals, was buried on the island of San Michele, on the Venetian Day of the Dead. In Paris, at that time, the true heir of the Men of 1914 and a future Nobel Prize winner, Samuel Beckett, was then at the height of his fame. Yet this was the conclusion of Modernism proper – if it had not already died.[88] That year I ended an obituary of Pound in a Canadian student newspaper: 'Pound is now dead and no poet remains of his stature. But poetry is "NEWS that stays NEWS". READ him: Read HIM'. Yet Pound's real achievement is far greater than his own poetical works – enormously significant though these are. Without the work-group that he set up and fostered, so selflessly, the Modernism we know could not have existed – as this book has laboured to emphasise and detail. And that remains his glory in a career of flawed brilliance. So it is fitting that this study should conclude with endnotes of all four of the Men of 1914:

> Finn, again! Take. Bussoftlhee, mememormee! Till thousendsthee. Lps. The keys to. Given![89]

> At that moment he knew he should never have assisted at the humanisation of the Divine – because he was now in the divine element.[90]

. . . to arrive where we started
And know the place for the first time.[91]

Do not move
Let the wind speak
that is paradise.[92]

Notes

1. INTRODUCTION

1. See, for instance, Maud Ellmann, *The Poetics of Impersonality: Ezra Pound and T. S. Eliot* (Harvester Press, 1987) for a recent example of the former, and Grover Smith, *The Waste Land* (Allen & Unwin, 1983) for an example of the latter.
2. See Wyndham Lewis, *Blasting and Bombardiering: An Autobiography (1914–1926)*, first published in 1937 (John Calder, 1982), p. 252.
3. Anthony Burgess, *Joysprick: An Introduction to the Language of James Joyce* (André Deutsch, 1973); Jeffrey Meyers, *The Enemy: A Biography of Wyndham Lewis* (Routledge & Kegan Paul, 1980); John Tytell, *Ezra Pound: The Solitary Volcano* (Bloomsbury, 1987); Hugh Kenner, *The Invisible Poet: T. S. Eliot* (Methuen, 1959).
4. James D. Watson, *The Double Helix: being a personal account of the discovery of the structure of DNA* (Weidenfeld & Nicolson, 1968).
5. I have been particularly struck by the ideas about 'influence' in Harold Bloom, *The Anxiety of Influence: a Theory of Poetry* (New York: Oxford University Press, 1973). However (in authentically Bloomian terms?), I have appropriated his ideas for my own ends: I construe 'influence' not in the sense of Bloom's neo-Freudian narrative of confrontation between individual literary sons and forefathers, but in terms of post-Freudian psychoanalytic interpretation of group activity between coequal rivals. At the same time, I am aware that my use of the terms 'monovocal' and 'polyvocal' is close to 'monology' and 'dialogy' in Mikhail Bakhtin, *Problems of Dostoevsky's Poetics*, edited and translated by Caryl Emerson (Manchester University Press, 1984) and *The Dialogic Imagination*, edited by Michael Holquist and translated by Caryl Emerson and Michael Holquist (Austin: University of Texas Press, 1981). However, I have not read Bakhtin in any detail

and I prefer my own somewhat gestural metaphors to what I take to be Bakhtin's theoreticist methodology.

6. See, for instance, W. R. Bion, *Experiences in Groups and Other Papers* (Tavistock, 1972) and S. H. Foulkes and E. J. Anthony, *Group Psychotherapy: The Psychoanalytic Approach* (Pelican, 1967). See also *Bion and Group Psychotherapy*, edited by Malcolm Pines (Routledge & Kegan Paul, 1985) and W. R. Bion, *Attention and Interpretation* (Maresfield Reprints, 1984).

7. 'The basic assumption of pairing (ba P) is, in narrative terms, the collective and unconscious belief that whatever the present problems and needs of the group, something in the future or somebody still unborn, will solve it: in other words that there exists a hope of a messianic type . . . . In this emotional state what matters is the idea of the future, rather than the solution of present problems. In religious terms it is the hope of the birth of the messiah'. From *Introduction to the Work of Bion: Groups, Knowledge, Psychosis, Thought, Transformations, Psychoanalytic Practice*, edited by Leon Grinberg, Dario Sor and Elizabeth Tabak de Bianchedi, translated by Alberto Hahn (Roland Harris Educational Trust, 1975), p. 15.

8. A word most associated with Ezra Pound. E.g. 'Tching prayed on the mountain and / wrote MAKE IT NEW / on his bath tub', Canto LIII, Ezra Pound, *The Cantos* (Faber and Faber, 1986), p. 265.

9. 'The map of the souls' groupography rose in relief within their quarterings', James Joyce, *Finnegans Wake*, first published in 1939, (Faber and Faber, 1982), p. 476. Cf. also: 'the big four' (p. 384); 'senators four' (p. 474); 'four claymen' (p. 475); 'Three kings of three suites and a crowner' (p. 475) and 'the quobus quartet' (p. 513). See also above, pp. 159–60.

10. Joyce, Pound and Eliot quite literally so: Lewis, who was born off the coast of Canada, was educated in England; his father deserted him and his mother. Before 1914 he spent some years travelling in Europe and during the Second World War he lived, isolated, in Canada. Emotionally, all four men had the temperaments of exiles. I also had in mind Terry Eagleton's book *Exiles and Emigrés: Studies in Modern Literature* (Schocken, 1970).

11. Within six months of a full, term-time teaching year, with the research as well as the writing completed during this period.

12. Such prestige (and hubris) is now invested more in theoretical

critics rather than imaginative writers – a power-shift worthy of note in the Postmodernist era. Even critics who denounce the 'canon' frequently set up one of their own – of the kind, Louis Althusser, Pierre Macherey, Jacques Derrida, Jacques Lacan, Michel Foucault, Jean-Francois Lyotard, Jürgen Habermas, Julia Kristeva, etc.

13. Not always strictly so; thus, I have treated *The Childermass* before 'Work in Progress' because the latter was spread over a long period of time.

14. I have particularly relied upon Richard Ellmann, *James Joyce*, New and Revised Edition (Oxford University Press, 1983); Jeffrey Meyers, *The Enemy* (see note 3, above); Noel Stock, *The Life of Ezra Pound* (Penguin, 1985), and John Tytell, *Ezra Pound, The Solitary Volcano* (Bloomsbury, 1987); Peter Ackroyd, *T. S. Eliot* (Hamish Hamilton, 1984).

15. I have been most influenced by the following, more general, books: Stephen Spender, *The Struggle of the Modern* (Berkeley: University of California Press, 1965); Hugh Kenner, *The Pound Era* (University of California Press, 1973); Julian Symons, *Makers of the New: The Revolution in Literature*, 1912–39 (André Deutsch, 1987).

16. Dennis Brown, *The Modernist Self in Twentieth-Century English Literature: A Study in Self-Fragmentation* (Macmillan, 1989).

2. TO ANNOUNCE A NEW AGE

1. For such information I have relied mainly on the biographies listed under note 14 to the Introduction, and Julian Symons' *Makers of the New*.

2. See Jeffrey Meyers, *The Enemy*, p. 9.

3. Quoted by Noel Stock, *The Life*, p. 16.

4. See Jeffrey Meyers, *The Enemy*, p. 10.

5. See Robert Wohl, *The Generation of 1914* (Weidenfeld & Nicolson, 1980). See also Roland N. Stromberg, *Redemption By War: The Intellectuals and 1914* (Lawrence: Regents Press of Kansas, 1982).

6. Wyndham Lewis, *Blasting and Bombardiering*, p. 252. Ford was then called Ford Madox Hueffer; I have used the better-known name throughout.

7. T. E. Hulme, *Speculations: Essays on Humanism and the Philosophy*

of Art, edited by Herbert Read (Routledge & Kegan Paul, 1965), p. 122.

8. To Harriet Monroe, 18 August 1912, in Ezra Pound, *Selected Letters 1907–1941*, edited by D. D. Paige (Faber and Faber, 1982), p. 10. Pound is here writing about a specifically American 'Risorgimento' to the Chicago editor. However, the same spirit animates his enthusiasm for new art on an international basis.

9. Quoted by Peter Ackroyd, *T. S. Eliot*, p. 55.

10. *BLAST* 1, 1914 (reissued by Black Sparrow Press, Santa Barbara, 1981), p. 7.

11. In a letter to Grant Richards, quoted by Richard Ellmann, *James Joyce*, p. 221.

12. These are all terms used by Pound in his early criticism. See Ezra Pound, *Literary Essays*, edited by T. S. Eliot (Faber and Faber, 1968) and *Selected Prose 1909–1965*, edited by William Cookson (Faber and Faber, 1973), *passim*.

13. See James Joyce, *A Portrait of the Artist as a Young Man* (Penguin, 1968), p. 253.

14. See Ezra Pound, *Antheil and The Treatise on Harmony* (Chicago: William Bird, 1927).

15. In 'Tradition and the Individual Talent', T. S. Eliot, *Selected Essays* (Faber and Faber, 1958), p. 16.

16. See James Joyce, *Portrait*, pp. 212–13.

17. A tendency continued by the *Scrutiny* circle and F. R. Leavis of Cambridge, in particular: Leavis was considerably influenced by the critical thinking of early Pound and Eliot.

18. In this work, of course, Conrad compares and contrasts the writer's work with that of the 'man of science'.

19. In his review of *Ulysses*. See above, pp. 93–4.

20. See Jeffrey Meyers, *The Enemy*, p. 55, and Julian Symons, *Makers of the New*, p. 46.

21. Ezra Pound, *Literary Essays*, p. 58.

22. See, for instance, Marshall McLuhan, *The Gutenberg Galaxy: the making of typographic man* (Routledge & Kegan Paul, 1962).

23. Shelley's belief in the importance of the poet was inherited by the Modernists, but the twentieth-century emphasis was on presentation rather than explicit 'legislation'. Cf. note 25 below.

24. See T. S. Eliot, *Selected Essays*, p. 289.

25. 'Clear presentation is of the noblest traditions of our craft . . . . It means constatation of fact. It presents. It does not comment'. Ezra Pound, 'The Approach to Paris' – V, *New Age*, XIII, 23

(2 October 1913), p. 662. 'Permanent literature is always a presentation', T. S. Eliot, *The Sacred Wood: Essays on Poetry and Criticism* (University Paperbacks, 1969), pp. 64–5. See, too, Joyce's comparison of the artist to an 'indifferent' god, *Portrait*, p. 215.

26. See the poems 'Alba' and 'In a Station of the Metro', Ezra Pound, *Selected Poems* (Faber and Faber, 1981), p. 53.
27. T. S. Eliot, *Selected Essays*, p. 14.
28. See *Self Condemned*, above, pp. 171–8.
29. Most particularly, *Ulysses*, *The Waste Land*, *The Childermass*, *The Cantos*, *Four Quartets* and *Self Condemned*.
30. See Anne Wright, *The Literature of Crisis* (Macmillan, 1984). She sees the uncertainties about the outcome of the war as crucial to the 'end-anxiety' expressed in such texts as Shaw's *Heartbreak House*, Lawrence's *Women in Love* and *The Waste Land*.
31. By association with *BLAST*. See above, pp. 46–8.
32. See Henry Adams, *The Education of Henry Adams* (1907), especially chapter 25, 'The Dynamo and the Virgin', reprinted in *The American Tradition in Literature*, edited by Sculley Bradley, Richard Croom Beatty and E. Hudson Long (New York: Norton, 1967), pp. 867–76.
33. The phrase of Harold Rosenberg – *The Tradition of the New* (New York: Horizon, 1959).
34. See Hugh Kenner, *The Pound Era* and Paul Johnson, *A History of the Modern World: From 1917 to the 1980s* (Weidenfeld & Nicolson, 1984), pp. 1–48.
35. See C. G. Jung's letter to Joyce quoted in Richard Ellmann, *James Joyce*, p. 629.
36. See Wyndham Lewis, *Time and Western Man*, *passim*.
37. That is, in terms of his 'creative' translations and insistence on the visually-representative nature of the Chinese ideogramme, his somewhat exclusivist sponsorship of the anthropological writings of Leo Frobenius, his championship of Sigismundo Malatesta *contra* Burkhardt and other historians and his egregious propaganda for the economic theories of C. H. Douglas in particular.
38. Harold Bloom, *The Anxiety of Influence*, *passim*.
39. See Maud Ellmann, *The Poetics of Impersonality*, pp. 23–34.
40. See Steven Foster, 'Relativity and *The Waste Land*: A Postulate', *Texas Studies in Literature and Language*, VII, 1 (Spring, 1965), p. 87.

41. Quoted by Richard Ellmann, *James Joyce*, pp. 86–7.
42. To William Carlos Williams, 21 October 1908, Ezra Pound, *Selected Letters*, p. 4. Williams was, of course, a medical man.
43. *BLAST* 1, p. 9.
44. Wyndham Lewis, *The Complete Wild Body*, edited by Bernard Lafourcade (Santa Barbara: Black Sparrow Press, 1982), p. 315. The essay 'Inferior Religions' was originally published in September 1917 in *The Little Review*. See above, p. 75.
45. T. S. Eliot, *Selected Essays*, pp. 17–22.
46. James Joyce, *Finnegans Wake* (Faber and Faber, 1982), pp. 4–5.
47. Nikolaus Pevsner, *Pioneers of Modern Design from William Morris to Walter Gropius* (Penguin, 1966).
48. Aaron Scharf, *Art and Photography* (Allen Lane, 1968).
49. Luigi Russolo, 'The Art of Noises' (1913), translated by 'C.T.' in *Futurist Manifestos*, edited by Umbro Apollonio (Thames & Hudson, 1973), p. 85.
50. Ford's term especially: it was, perhaps, scarcely more than metaphoric.
51. Ford's original title for *The Good Soldier* (1915). Part of that novel appeared in *BLAST* 1 under the original title. See *BLAST* 1, pp. 87–97.
52. T. E. Hulme, *Further Speculations*, edited by Sam Hynes (Minneapolis University Press, 1955), p. 73. For earlier quotations, see also *ibid.*, p. 79 and T. E. Hulme, *Speculations: Essays on Humanism and the Philosophy of Art*, edited by Herbert Read (Routledge & Kegan Paul, 1965), pp. 135 and 149.
53. For an account of their meeting see above, p. 46.
54. These were later collected together in Wyndham Lewis, *The Wild Body*. See note 44 above.
55. According to Ford, Lewis first brought him the manuscript while he was in the bath and proceeded to read it to him there. According to Lewis, he merely left the manuscript. See Jeffrey Meyers, *The Enemy*, pp. 27–8.
56. Quoted by Jeffrey Meyers, *ibid.*, p. 29.
57. Frank Rutter's description, quoted by Jeffrey Meyers, *ibid.*, p. 35.
58. This is definitively described by Richard Ellmann, *James Joyce*, pp. 349–56.
59. It is possible that Pound feared a poetic rival – yet not very likely granted his generous encouragement of Eliot's verse.
60. For an account of Joyce's complicated family set-up at this

time, see Richard Ellmann, *James Joyce*, from, say, 1912 to 1922.

61. Quoted by Richard Ellmann, *ibid.*, p. 406.
62. See Richard Ellmann, *ibid.*, pp. 219–22.
63. See above, pp. 127–32, 140.
64. See Wyndham Lewis, *Time and Western Man*, chapter XVI 'An Analysis of the Mind of James Joyce', pp. 91–130. See also above, pp. 95–7.
65. See especially the story 'Grace'. All references to passages from Dubliners will be from *The Essential James Joyce*, edited by Harry Levin (Penguin, 1963). 'Grace' is from pp. 458–77.
66. See above, p. 10.
67. James Joyce, *Portrait*, p. 253.
68. E.g. 'Ireland is the old sow that eats her farrow', *Portrait*, p. 203.
69. In *The Wild Body* he is, in fact, as interested in Slavs and itinerants as native Bretons.
70. Lewis's usage of the term 'Pole' as bizarre parasite tolerated by the Bretons is explained in his story 'The Pole', *Complete Wild Body*, p. 209.
71. See above, pp. 61, 68.
72. See above, pp. 60–7.
73. See above, pp. 75–6.
74. See Ezra Pound, *Selected Poems*, pp. 15–34 for a selection from the poems in *Personae*.
75. On reading Pound's early poems, Ford rolled about on the floor in merriment. Pound would claim that the roll saved him 'two years'. See Noel Stock, *The Life*, p. 130.
76. Dorothy Pound was the daughter of Olivia Shakespeare. Pound met her through Olivia's friendship with Yeats.
77. Pound's cult of the feminine was not the same as Robert Graves's later formulation: nevertheless, both are recognisably in the same tradition.
78. Ezra Pound, *Gaudier-Brzeska: A Memoir* (Bodley Head, 1916), p. 98.
79. See Roland Stromberg, *Redemption by War, passim*.
80. Ezra Pound, *Literary Essays*, p. 4.
81. 'The artist seeks out the luminous detail and presents it. He does not comment. His work is the permanent basis of psychology and metaphysics', Ezra Pound, *Selected Prose: 1909–1965*, edited with an introduction by William Cookson (Faber and Faber, 1973), p. 23. The Introduction to 'I gather the Limbs

of Osiris' from which the quotation comes was first published in *The New Age*, December 1911. It should be read in its entirety to understand the notion of 'luminous detail' out of which Pound later developed his idea of the ideogramme. See also 'Ernest Fenollosa, *The Chinese Written Character as a Medium for Poetry*', edited by Ezra Pound (republished by Black Mountain Press, San Francisco, 1969).

82. Quoted by John Tytell, *Ezra Pound*, p. 80.
83. Quoted by John Tytell, *ibid.*, p. 103.
84. See above, pp. 46–7.
85. Noel Stock, *The Life*, pp. 185–219.
86. See John Tytell, *Ezra Pound*, pp. 102–11, in particular the chapter 'Vortex Lewis' in Hugh Kenner, *The Pound Era*, pp. 232–47.
87. Lewis's phrase to describe Pound, Wyndham Lewis, *Time and Western Man*, p. 54.
88. See 'A Pact', Ezra Pound, *Selected Poems*, p. 45.
89. Ezra Pound, *Selected Letters*, p. 40. To Harriet Monroe, 30 September 1914.
90. In Boston Massachusetts. However, he had written parts during his stay in Paris in 1910–11.
91. See Peter Ackroyd, *T. S. Eliot*, p. 34.
92. See T. S. Eliot, *The Complete Poems and Plays* (Faber and Faber, 1969), pp. 587–606.
93. See Peter Ackroyd, *T. S. Eliot*, p. 55.
94. This has been acknowledged since at least the publication of Herbert Howarth's *Notes on Some Figures Behind T. S. Eliot* (Chatto & Windus, 1965). See too: Peter Ackroyd, *T. S. Eliot*, pp. 40–1 and Maud Ellmann, *The Poetics of Impersonality*, pp. 23–51 in particular.
95. See Eric Trudgill, *Madonnas and Magdalenes: the Origin and Development of Victorian Sexual Attitudes* (Heinemann, 1976).
96. Lewis quoted these 'especially fine lines' in *Blasting and Bombardiering*, p. 285.
97. However, Eliot had no contact with English Imagism at this time. He developed the technique from the same source that helped influence T. E. Hulme and F. S. Flint – French Symbolism.
98. See Peter Ackroyd, *T. S. Eliot*, pp. 253–4.
99. See my section on this poem in *The Modernist Self*, pp. 30–6.
100. Wyndham Lewis certainly thought so. See above, p. 95.

101. See especially the chapter 'Ezra Pound Etc.' in Wyndham Lewis, *Time and Western Man*, pp. 54–64.
102. Ezra Pound, *The Cantos*, p. 507.
103. Wyndham Lewis, *Blasting and Bombardiering*, p. 271.
104. Quoted by Jeffrey Meyers, *The Enemy*, p. 32.
105. Wyndham Lewis, *Blasting and Bombardiering*, p. 274.
106. Wyndham Lewis, *ibid.*, p. 272.
107. See Richard Ellmann, *James Joyce*, pp. 349–55.
108. Richard Ellmann, *ibid.*, p. 350.
109. See *Finnegans Wake*, pp. 471–3.
110. See Richard Ellmann, *James Joyce*, p. 353.
111. Quoted in Peter Ackroyd, *T. S. Eliot*, p. 56.
112. Ackroyd, *ibid.*, p. 60. Eliot later wrote: 'in 1914 . . . my meeting with Ezra Pound changed my life'. See *The Letters of T. S. Eliot*, vol. I, 1898–1922, edited by Valerie Eliot (Faber and Faber, 1988), p. xvii.
113. Wyndham Lewis, *Blasting and Bombardiering*, p. 252.
114. Wyndham Lewis, *ibid.*, pp. 265–70, 271–81, 282–9.
115. To the best of my knowledge. That was largely, of course, because Joyce lived on the Continent.
116. See above, pp. 138, 152, 187–8.
117. Ezra Pound, *Selected Letters*, pp. 106–7, 143 and 259.
118. *Ibid.*, p. 222.
119. *Ibid.*, p. 219.
120. *Ibid.*, p. 239.
121. *Ibid.*, p. 234.
122. See Peter Ackroyd, *T. S. Eliot*, p. 56.
123. Eliot later compared their critical efforts in terms of Pound making a commotion at the 'front door' while he stole round the back to make off with the family silver.
124. These included such normally anti-establishment writers as G. B. Shaw, G. K. Chesterton and H. G. Wells.
125. Pound somewhat hijacked Dora Marsden's *New Freewoman*, persuading her and Harriet Shaw Weaver to change the title to the *Egoist*. H.D. was, of course, the first of Pound's Imagists, and Pound encouraged a variety of women writers throughout his life. For the picture from women writers' point of view see Gillian Hanscome and Virginia L. Smyers, *Writing For Their Lives: The Modernist Women, 1910–1940* (The Women's Press, 1987).
126. One of the main Basic Assumptions (BA) of group-dynamics

worked out initially by W. R. Bion. The other two are Dependence and Pairing. Group-leaders cannot maintain their authority if they fail the group in organising BA Fight/Flight activity, and the group then casts about for a new leader. Pound certainly held leadership authority until he left his London base.

127. In its advance notice. See Jeffrey Meyers, *The Enemy*, p. 64.
128. Ezra Pound, *Selected Essays*, p. 410.
129. *Ibid.*, p. 425.
130. *Ibid.*, p. 418.
131. See above, pp. 133–5, 148, 159, 180.

3.   THE FIRST HEAVE

1. This was Joyce's working title for his autobiographical novel. A version of the early writing has been published as James Joyce, *Stephen Hero*, edited with an introduction by Theodore Spencer. A revised edition has been published, with additional material and a Foreword by John J. Slocum and Herbert Cahoon (Jonathan Cape, 1956).
2. First published in book form by the Egoist Press in 1916. All references are to the easily-accessible James Joyce, *A Portrait of the Artist as a Young Man* (Penguin, 1976, etc.), hereafter referred to as *Portrait*.
3. See Richard Ellmann, *James Joyce*, pp. 354–5.
4. See the account, for instance, in Colin MacCabe, *James Joyce and the Revolution of the Word* (Macmillan, 1979).
5. See Richard Ellmann, *James Joyce*, p. 147.
6. *Ibid.*, p. 147.
7. *Ibid.*, p. 296.
8. *Ibid.*, p. 297.
9. Quoted by Richard Ellmann, *ibid.*, p. 355.
10. Ezra Pound, *Literary Essays*, p. 412. Pound's review first appeared in *The Future*, May 1918.
11. For a description of the novel's structure, see the section 'The Smithy of My Soul' in Dennis Brown, *The Modernist Self*, pp. 36–42.
12. First published in *BLAST* 1, 1914 and reproduced in the Black Sparrow edition of 1981. Two versions of the play have also been published in Wyndham Lewis, *Collected Poems and Plays*,

edited by Alan Munton, with an introduction by C. H. Sisson (Manchester: Carcenet, 1979). All quotations are from the earlier version printed in *Collected Poems and Plays*, pp. 93–119.

13. See Jeffrey Meyers, *The Enemy*, pp. 60–2.

14. 'If you want a picture of the future, imagine a boot stamping on a human face – for ever', George Orwell, *Nineteen Eighty-Four* (Penguin, 1971), p. 215.

15. See especially Ernest Jones, *The Life and Work of Sigmund Freud*, edited and abridged by Lionel Trilling and Steven Marcus (Penguin, 1977), 'The War Years', pp. 424–47.

16. 'When Eliot was living in Russell's flat during the second year of the war, Russell confided strange observations which later found their way into *The Waste Land*. After watching the troop trains – full of patriotic Englishmen – depart from Waterloo, he would see London's bridges collapse and sink, and the whole great city vanish like morning mist . . . . He would wonder whether the world in which he thought he lived was not merely a product of his own nightmares'. See Lyndall Gordon, *Eliot's Early Years* (Oxford University Press, 1977), p. 81.

17. See Paul Delaney, *D. H. Lawrence's Nightmare: The Writer and his Circle in the Years of the Great War* (Harvester Press, 1979) and Stanley Weintraub, *Bernard Shaw 1914–1918: Journey to Heartbreak* (Routledge & Kegan Paul, 1973).

18. Quoted by Hugh Kenner, *The Pound Era*, p. 550.

19. Hugh Kenner, *ibid.*, p. 240.

20. Fredric Jameson, *Fables of Aggression: Wyndham Lewis the Modernist as Fascist* (University of California Press, 1979), p. 2.

21. Hugh Kenner, *The Pound Era*, p. 240.

22. See Harold Bloom, *The Anxiety of Influence*, *passim*.

23. Ezra Pound, *The Cantos*, pp. 13, 17 and 61.

24. 'Salutation The Third', *BLAST* 1, p. 45.

25. James Joyce, *Ulysses, The Corrected Text*, with a preface by Richard Ellmann (Penguin, 1984).

26. *Ibid.*, p. 356.

27. Perhaps unfair to the 'Breton' stories. See above, pp. 31–6.

28. T. S. Eliot, *Selected Essays*, p. 18.

29. See Ezra Pound, *Gaudier-Brzeska*, p. 86.

30. See T. S. Eliot, *'The Waste Land': A Facsimile and Transcript of the Original Drafts, Including the Annotations of Ezra Pound*, edited by Valerie Eliot (Faber and Faber, 1971), p. 22.

31. T. S. Eliot, *Complete Poems and Plays*, p. 63.
32. 'Journey of the Magi', *Complete Poems and Plays*, p. 103.
33. Jeffrey Meyers, *The Enemy*, p. 331.
34. I have borrowed this term from group-psychoanalysis and use it here somewhat metaphorically. The 'container', as I understand it, is the group-structuring which allows a new idea (the 'contained') to struggle into being through oppositionality. (See Grinberg et al., *Introduction to the Work of Bion*, p. 20). Lewis and the *BLAST* project, we can say, provided the structure within which, and against which, Joyce's experimentalism in *Ulysses* (most particularly) could realise itself. Yet in the larger social order, contemporary literary convention was the 'container' and *BLAST* the 'contained'.
35. I am trying to have it both ways. Lewis's *BLAST* project, by becoming notorious, represented a new group 'container' out of which new ideas and experiments could emerge. Yet Lewis thought of himself (as Pound thought of Lewis at first) as the chief 'mystic' creating new ideas and forms (the 'contained'). Certainly when Lewis went to war, Pound was the leader who organised the 'container' and Joyce now became the 'mystic' of the new idea (*Ulysses* – the 'contained'). By the time Lewis had returned from the war Joyce had consolidated his group-role as 'mystic'. Cf. 'The mystic or genius, bearer of a new idea, is always disruptive for the group . . . . The mystic needs the *Establishment* and vice versa; the institutionalised group (work group) is as important to the development of the individual as is the individual to the work group'. Grinsberg et al., *ibid.*, pp. 20–1. See also 'The Mystic and the Group', chapter 6 of W. R. Bion, *Attention and Interpretation*, pp. 62 ff.
36. During 1914 and 1915.
37. In 1916. It was first published in book form in 1918. Lewis revised it in 1928 and that edition is now the standard one. All references to Wyndham Lewis, *Tarr* (Penguin, 1982).
38. Ezra Pound, *Literary Essays*, p. 424.
39. In fact, he does little painting, simply aspiring to be the artistic type.
40. 'His face, wearing, it is true, like a uniform the frowning fixity of the Prussian warrior . . . . The true bismarckian Prussian . . . .', *Tarr*, p. 76.
41. Along with *The Rainbow*, it began as *The Two Sisters*. The first chapter shows Ursula and Gudrun rejecting the idea

of marriage because 'the man' makes it 'Impossible'. D. H. Lawrence, *Women in Love* (Penguin, 1985), p. 9. Thereafter, arguably, male issues (and prejudices) take over the book. However, I think Kate Millett's reading in *Sexual Politics* (Virago, 1977) is naive and reductionist.

42. *Tarr* (1982), 'Preface'.
43. Canto LXXIV, *The Cantos*, p. 425. This is an overt response, of course, to Eliot's celebrated ending to 'The Hollow Men'.
44. See Ezra Pound, 'Harold Monro', *Criterion* (July 1932), p. 590.
45. Most of the Imagists contributed to Amy Lowell's anthologies. Pound did not and severed his connections with Imagism.
46. See Peter Ackroyd, *T. S. Eliot*, p. 56.
47. 'Ezra Pound: His Metric and Poetry', see John Tytell, *Ezra Pound*, p. 138.
48. The Beckett trilogy of novels and *Waiting For Godot* and other plays were originally written in French.
49. It was the subject of a spate of rival interpretations in *Essays in Criticism* in the fifties. See C. S. Lewis, *They Asked For A Paper* (Geoffrey Bles, 1962), pp. 18–9.
50. See Noel Stock, *The Life*, p. 203.
51. It included the words: 'The most fascinating personality of our time . . . . In the work of Mr. Lewis we recognise the thought of the modern and the energy of the cave man.' Quoted by Jeffrey Meyers, *The Enemy*, p. 76.
52. Reprinted in Wyndham Lewis, *The Complete Wild Body*, pp. 315–19.
53. T. S. Eliot, 'Tarr', *Egoist*, September 1918. Quoted by Bernard Lafourcade, *ibid.*, p. 148. Since writing this book I have read the account of Eliot's interest in Lewis's essay in Erik Svarny, *The Men of 1914: T. S. Eliot and Early Modernism* (Open University Press, 1988). See pp. 130–6.
54. Pound in his Editor's Note, The Little Review, September 1917. Quoted by Lafourcade, *The Complete Wild Body*, p. 314.
55. Originally published, in revised form, in 1927.
56. *The Complete Wild Body*, p. 318.
57. *Ibid.*, p. 317.
58. *Ibid.*, p. 315.
59. *Ibid.*, p. 319, note 1.
60. Samuel Beckett, *Molloy* in *The Beckett Trilogy: Molloy, Malone Dies, The Unnamable* (Picador, 1979).
61. Stephen Spender, *T. S. Eliot* (Fontana/Collins, 1975), p. 57.

62. From 'Whispers of Immortality' and 'Mr. Eliot's Sunday Morning Service', T. S. Eliot, *Complete Poems and Plays*, pp. 52 and 54.

63. See, for instance, the rather doggerel effect of 'One Way Song', Wyndham Lewis, *Collected Poems and Plays*, pp. 19–91.

64. From 'Sweeney Erect', and 'Mr. Eliot's Sunday Morning Service', *Complete Poems and Plays*, pp. 42 and 54.

65. From 'Burbank with a Baedeker: Bleistein with a Cigar', 'Sweeney Erect' and 'Mr. Eliot's Sunday Morning Service', *Complete Poems and Plays*, pp. 41, 42 and 55.

66. From 'Burbank . . .', 'Sweeney Erect', 'Whispers of Immortality' and 'Sweeney Among the Nightingales', *ibid.*, p. 40, 42, 52 and 56.

67. 'Say . . . / . . . the modern world / Needs such a rag-bag to stuff all its thoughts in'. From an early draft of Canto I, quoted in Michael Alexander, *The Poetic Achievement of Ezra Pound* (Faber and Faber, 1975), p. 135.

68. T. S. Eliot, *Selected Essays*, p. 15.

69. See his essay 'Ezra Pound Etc.' in *Time and Western Man*, pp. 54–64.

70. Ezra Pound, *Selected Poems*, p. 99.

71. See above, p. 104.

72. 'He has done what Flaubert set out to do in *Bouvard and Pécuchet*, done it better, more succinct. An epitome', Ezra Pound, *Literary Essays*, p. 416.

73. Cf. 'Too much of *Hugh Selwyn Mauberley* is *attitudinizing*. The poem is the elaborate culmination of Pound's attempts to be urbane; but urbanity did not come naturally to him, on the contrary he rather often adopted the wrong stratagems in social situations'. Donald Davie, *Pound* (Fontana/Collins, 1975) pp. 54–5.

74. To Felix Schelling, June 1915, Ezra Pound, *Selected Letters*, p. 61.

75. To John Quinn, 10 March 1916, *ibid.*, p. 83.

76. To Wyndham Lewis, 24 June 1916, *ibid.*, p. 83.

77. To Margaret C. Anderson, ? January 1917, *ibid.*, p. 107.

78. To Wyndham Lewis, 27 April 1921, *ibid.*, p. 166.

79. Joyce's phrase, see above, p. 192, note 9.

80. To Kate Buss, 9 March 1916, *Selected Letters*, pp. 71–3.

81. To John Quinn, 10 March 1916, *ibid.*, p. 74.

82. To Harriet Shaw Weaver, 17 March 1916, *ibid.*, p. 75.

83. To John Quinn, 3 April 1918, *ibid.*, p. 134.
84. See Peter Ackroyd, *T. S. Eliot*, p. 64.
85. Wyndham Lewis, *Blasting and Bombardiering*, p. 282.
86. Quoted in Richard Ellmann, *James Joyce*, p. 476.
87. See above, pp. 126 and 180.
88. See above, pp. 134 and 142.
89. Wyndham Lewis, *Blasting and Bombardiering*, pp. 269–70.
90. Wyndham Lewis, *ibid.*, pp. 292–3.
91. See *T. S. Eliot: 'The Waste Land': A Facsimile*, p. 4.
92. 'Ezra performed the Caesarean Operation'; see Pound's poem 'Sage Homme', To T. S. Eliot, 24 December 1921, *Selected Letters*, p. 170.
93. But he did not mean it, saying it would be 'madness', Richard Ellmann, *James Joyce*, p. 474.
94. Richard Ellmann, *ibid.*, p. 476.
95. Jeffrey Meyers, *The Enemy*, p. 102.
96. Quoted by Jeffrey Meyers, *ibid.*, p. 102.
97. Published by the *Egoist* in 1919. It has been reissued as Wyndham Lewis, *The Caliph's Design*, edited by Paul Edwards (Santa Barbara: Black Sparrow Press, 1986).
98. Wyndham Lewis, *Blasting and Bombardiering*, p. 266.
99. Wyndham Lewis, *ibid.*, p. 297.

4.   THE GREAT DECADE

1. All references will be to James Joyce, *Ulysses, The Corrected Text*, with a preface by Richard Ellmann (Faber and Faber, 1986).
2. First published in the *Little Review* (New York) from March 1918 onwards.
3. See Richard Ellmann, *James Joyce*, p. 421.
4. See above, pp. 127, 159, 161.
5. See the insistent play on the title as evidenced on, for instance, pp. 127, 162, above.
6. See Richard Ellmann, *James Joyce*, p. 409.
7. Lewis accused him of imitating Stein too, a charge he denied, indirectly in *Finnegans Wake*. See above, pp. 127–8.
8. Quoted by Richard Ellmann, *James Joyce*, p. 360.
9. Joyce wrote to Harriet Shaw Weaver: 'You may . . . prefer the initial style much as the wanderer did who longed for the rock

of Ithaca.' Quoted by Richard Ellmann, *ibid.*, p. 462.
10. Quoted by Richard Ellmann, *ibid.*, p. 459.
11. Quoted by Richard Ellmann, *ibid.*, p. 430.
12. See Stephen's meditations on genre in *Portrait*, p. 214.
13. *Ulysses*, p. 100.
14. For a further discussion of the characterisation of Bloom, see Dennis Brown, *The Modernist Self*, pp. 83–6 and 36–40. For Joyce's view of Odysseus see Richard Ellmann, *James Joyce*, pp. 416–7.
15. See the last footnote in Richard Ellmann, *ibid.*, p. 51.
16. T. S. Eliot, 'James Joyce's *Ulysses*', *Dial* (November 1923).
17. Cf. 'the immense panorama of futility and anarchy' with 'history would not be a long chronicle of folly and crime . . .' J. G. Frazer, *The Golden Bough: A Study in Magic and Religion*, abridged version (Macmillan, 1978), p. 427.
18. It seems to me that Joyce rejected Eliot's construction of the mythic 'method' in *Finnegans Wake*. See above, p. 126.
19. First printed in the *Dial* in 1922. See Ezra Pound, *Literary Essays*, pp. 403–9.
20. 'Wall, Mr Joice, I recon your a damn fine writer . . .' Quoted by Richard Ellmann, *James Joyce*, p. 421.
21. Ezra Pound, *Literary Essays*, p. 425.
22. See 'An Analysis of the Mind of James Joyce', *Time and Western Man*, pp. 91–130.
23. See Richard Ellmann, *James Joyce*, p. 596.
24. See above, pp. 181–2.
25. See above, pp. 129–30.
26. See above, pp. 113–14.
27. See above, pp. 117–18.
28. It seems likely, however, that *Finnegans Wake* will receive far more attention in the Poststructuralist era than it has achieved in the past among most academic critics.
29. Peter Ackroyd, *T. S. Eliot*, p. 112.
30. The working title. See above, p. 201, note 30.
31. Eliot later recalled seeing his friend Verdenal coming toward him in the Tuileries with flowers in his arms. Cf. the 'hyacinth girl', *The Waste Land*, lines 35–41.
32. Cf. 'Tarr stopped at a dairy. He bought saladed potatoes, a Petit Suisse' (*Tarr*, p. 45); 'He halted before Dlugacz's window, staring at the hanks of sausages, polonies, black and white' (*Ulysses*, p. 48).

33. The book was begun well before the war but not finished until 1915.
34. See T. S. Eliot, *Selected Essays*, p. 15.
35. I do not mean to imply that Eliot was an alcoholic; but according to Peter Ackroyd's biography he drank regularly. In addition to his other problems, Eliot's father had died in 1919. He was under great strain while writing *The Waste Land*.
36. In this, of course, it is similar to 'Hugh Selwyn Mauberley'. See above pp. 78–80.
37. For my views about the role of Tiresias in the poem see *The Modernist Self*, p. 93.
38. See To T. S. Eliot, 24 December 1921, Ezra Pound, *Selected Letters*, pp. 170–1.
39. See 'Sage Homme', *ibid.*, p. 170.
40. The first line of the original manuscript. See T. S. Eliot: *'The Waste Land': A Facsimile*, p. 5.
41. This figure may owe to Aldous Huxley. See Grover Smith, *The Waste Land*, p. 47.
42. After the rape by Kreisler, Bertha feels 'as though nothing had happened. It was nothing actually, nothing in fact had happened: what did it matter what became of her? The body was of little importance', *Tarr*, p. 194. Cf. too Eliot's Thames maiden: 'I made no comment. What should I resent? . . . I can connect / Nothing with nothing', *The Waste Land*, lines 299–302.
43. Wyndham Lewis, *Collected Poems and Plays*, p. 98.
44. See Grover Smith, *The Waste Land*, pp. 55–61.
45. He wrote a paper on 'The Interpretation of Primitive Ritual' at Harvard. See Peter Ackroyd, *T. S. Eliot*, p. 48.
46. See Tennyson's remark that 'if a man were endowed with such faculties as Shakespeare's, they would be more freely and effectively exercised in prose fiction with the wider capabilities than when "cribbed, cabined and confined in the trammels of verse".' *Tennyson and His Friends*, Hallam Tennyson (Macmillan, 1911), p. 53.
47. As in, for instance, children's dancing-chants; e.g. 'London Bridge is falling down'; cf. *'Here we go round the prickly pair'* in 'The Hollow Men', *Complete Poems and Plays*, p. 85.
48. The epigraph to *The Waste Land* is from Petronius; Nerval is quoted in line 429.
49. See above, p. 125.
50. See above, p. 125–32, 158–65.

51. Eliot later called *The Waste Land* 'private rhythmical grumbling'.
52. See Paul Fussell, *The Great War and Modern Memory* (Oxford University Press, 1975).
53. To Felix E. Scelling, 8 July 1922, Ezra Pound, *Selected Letters*, p. 180.
54. 'Lewis's work impressed Joyce, but he was still dubious of Eliot's verse', Richard Ellmann, *James Joyce*, p. 492. Nevertheless, *Finnegans Wake* frequently addresses itself to Eliotic lines.
55. Ezra Pound, *Selected Letters*, p. 170.
56. *Ibid.*, p. 169.
57. Ezra Pound, 'Harold Monro', *Criterion* (July 1932) p. 590.
58. See above, pp. 141 and 181.
59. See Samuel Beckett, *Poems in English* (Calder & Boyars, 1961), pp. 9–12.
60. Printed in *Poetry* (Chicago) in 1917.
61. 'As regarding rhythm: to compose in the sequence of the musical phrase, not in sequence of a metronome', Ezra Pound, *Literary Essays*, p. 3.
62. Ezra Pound, *The Cantos*, p. 795.
63. Quoted by Timothy Materer, *Wyndham Lewis The Novelist*, p. 51.
64. Ezra Pound, *The Cantos*, pp. 24 and 10.
65. Wyndham Lewis, *The Childermass* (John Calder, 1965), p. 9.
66. That is cantos XIV–XVI.
67. 'OY TI . . . "I am noman, my name is noman"', *The Cantos*, p. 426. The idea that the name Odysseus was cognate with 'nobody' was Joyce's notion first.
68. See W. B. Yeats, *A Vision* (Macmillan, 1956), p. 4.
69. Ezra Pound, *The Cantos*, p. 56.
70. E.g. see Michael Alexander, *The Poetic Achievement*, p. 132.
71. 'to arrive where we started / And know the place for the first time', T. S. Eliot, *Complete Poems and Plays*, p. 197.
72. Tiresias' prophecy in Canto I is that 'Odysseus / 'Shalt return through spiteful Neptune, over dark seas, / 'Lose all companions', *The Cantos*, p. 4–5.
73. Ezra Pound, *Selected Prose*, p. 236.
74. *The Cantos*, p. 60.
75. This, of course, had been announced in the *BLAST* prospectus. But after the publication of *Ulysses* he began to date his letters in relation to that event: later he would date them from Mussolini's march on Rome.

76. Keats's phrase about poetic didacticism.
77. *The Cantos*, p. 766 – the first words of Canto XVII.
78. According to Hugh Kenner. See *The Pound Era*, p. 556. For the earlier anecdote see p. 396.
79. *Our Exagmination Round His Factification for Incamination of Work in Progress*. The book had twelve writers. Beckett wrote about Joyce's Viconian schema. See Richard Ellmann, *James Joyce*, p. 613.
80. See 'T. S. Eliot, The Pseudo-Believer' and its appendix in Wyndham Lewis, *Men Without Art*, edited with afterword and notes by Seamus Cooney (Santa Rosa: Black Sparrow Press, 1987) pp. 55–82. The book was first published in 1934.
81. *Ibid.*, p. 55.
82. 'Lewis would have read the fable of the Gracehoper and the Ondt in *Transition* for March 1928', Timothy Materer, *Wyndham Lewis The Novelist*, p. 176, note 22.
83. Ezra Pound, *Selected Poems*, p. 110. This was Mauberley's fate.
84. 'We understand the term "semiotic" in its Greek sense . . . distinctive mark, trace, index, precursory sign, proof, engraved or written sign, imprint, trace, figuration . . . . a *chora*: a non-expressive totality formed by the drives and their stages in a motility that is as full of movement as it is regulated', Julia Kristeva, *The Kristeva Reader*, edited by Toril Moi (Basil Blackwell, 1986) p. 93.
85. See note 75 above. Pound also wrote 'It is after all a grrrreat littttttterary period'. Quoted by John Tytell, *Ezra Pound*, p. 176.
86. See Richard Ellmann, *James Joyce*, p. 523.
87. In *The Apes of God* most particularly. See above, pp. 145–51.
88. 'Paris is the laboratory of ideas', Ezra Pound, *Selected Prose*, p. 385.
89. 'Sophomoric exultation in the latest thing'. Quoted by John Tytell, *Ezra Pound*, p. 158.
90. Quoted by John Tytell, *Ezra Pound*, p. 167.
91. 'I doubt if Conrad is weighty enough to stand the citation', To T. S. Eliot, 14 December, Ezra Pound, *Selected Letters*, p. 169.
92. See Peter Ackroyd, *T. S. Eliot*, chapters 4–6.
93. This was Pound's generous, but quixotic, attempt to raise enough money by individual conscriptions to 'save' Eliot from the bank and for full-time poetry writing. See Peter Ackroyd, *ibid.*, pp. 122, 126, 128 and 129–30.
94. See Wyndham Lewis, *Blasting and Bombardiering*, p. 277.

95. For instance, Eliot published an early part of the future *Apes of God* in his *Criterion*.
96. See Richard Ellmann, *James Joyce*, p. 515.
97. James Joyce, *Finnegans Wake*, p. 3; the second to the fifth words in the completed book.
98. 'When someone asked about a prostitute, Pound, who had heard Lewis was an unconventional rebel, stared at him and said: "This young man could probably tell you"'. Jeffrey Meyers, *The Enemy*, p. 33.
99. See Richard Ellmann, *James Joyce*, p. 501.
100. Eliot had collaborated closely with his wife Vivien in the early stages of the writing and some of the original lines were written by her, while she helped sharpen up the cockney speech in 'A Game of Chess'. Pound deleted some of her contributions. My erstwhile student Marilyn Miller-Pietroni examined the psychoanalytic and gender implications of the Eliot–Pound collusion in her dissertation 'The Signifying Practice in the Epigraphs and the Sanskrit Voice of the Thunder in T. S. Eliot's *The Waste Land*', Hatfield Polytechnic, MA in English, 1987.
101. Peter Ackroyd, *T. S. Eliot*, p. 52. Parts of this have now been published in *The Letters*, edited by Valerie Eliot. To read these see 'Eliot . . . King Bolo' in the Index.
102. Quoted by Jeffrey Meyers, *The Enemy*, p. 76.
103. To T. S. Eliot, ? January 1922, Ezra Pound, *Selected Letters*, p. 171.
104. See Richard Ellmann, *James Joyce*, p. 489.
105. Quoted by Noel Stock, *The Life*, p. 323.
106. See John Tytell, *Ezra Pound*, p. 193.
107. The completed work to be published in 1939 as *Finnegans Wake*. Pound called it 'circumambient peripherization'. Quoted by Noel Stock, *The Life*, p. 320.
108. Quoted by John Tytell, *Ezra Pound*, p. 193.
109. See Richard Ellmann, *James Joyce*, p. 796.
110. Ezra Pound, *Selected Poems*, introduction by T. S. Eliot (Faber and Faber, 1959).

5. LOST IN THE LABYRINTH

1. Joyce began writing his last work in March 1923. Ford Madox Ford coigned the title 'Work in Progress' when he published an early draft in his *transatlantic review* (February 1924). Joyce liked the name and kept it until the whole work was published in 1939. See Richard Ellmann, *James Joyce*, pp. 563 and 794.

2. The final name, *Finnegans Wake*, was kept an elaborate secret and a guessing-game for such as Harriet Shaw Weaver. See Richard Ellmann, *ibid.*, p. 597.

3. A clear reference to Eliot's 'Gerontion'.

4. William York Tindall, *A Reader's Guide to 'Finnegans Wake'* (Thames & Hudson, 1969).

5. Cf. 'What the Thunder Said', Part V of *The Waste Land*.

6. A reference to the 'Thames Maidens' in 'The Fire Sermon', Part III of *The Waste Land*.

7. There is much about the 'heart' and rocks and stones within the musical mosaic of Eliot's poem. Pound once later called Eliot 'Mr Rock': see above, p. 182.

8. See footnote to line 433 of *The Waste Land* (*The Complete Poems and Plays*, p. 80).

9. *The Waste Land*, lines 182 and 320. 'Windward' is, of course, the contrast to 'Leeward'.

10. 'The eyes are not here' ('The Hollow Men', *ibid.*, p. 84): 'The air . . . now thoroughly small and dry' ('Ash Wednesday', *ibid.*, p. 90).

11. Cf. Eliot's poem called 'The Hippopotamus' (*ibid.*, p. 49). In a notebook Joyce called Eliot 'Bishop of Hippo', and he once said to Eliot, during the famous meeting in Paris, 'I was at the Jardin des Plantes today and paid my respects to your friend the hippopotamus'. Richard Ellmann, *James Joyce*, p. 459.

12. T. S. Eliot, *The Collected Poems and Plays*, p. 63.

13. 'Only a cock stood on the rooftree / Co co rico co co rico', *The Waste Land*, *ibid.*, p. 74; 'The sound of horns and motors', *ibid.*, p. 67.

14. There may be a reference to Lewis too. In 1922 he wrote to Harriet Shaw Weaver that 'Mr Lewis told me he was told that I was a crazy fellow who always carried four watches and rarely spoke except to ask my neighbour what o'clock it was'. Richard Ellmann, *James Joyce*, p. 510.

15. Yeats's version of the conclusion of their first meeting has

Joyce saying: 'I have met you too late. You are too old'. Richard Ellmann, *ibid.*, p. 103.

16. The original name of the *Egoist* was the *New Freewoman*.

17. Joyce missed his first appointment with Pound through a train delay. He went shortly afterwards to meet him at Sirmione. See Richard Ellmann, *ibid.*, pp. 476–9.

18. Cf. Lewis's 'Enemy of the Stars'.

19. See above, p. 140.

20. I do not mean to imply that Joyce is always to be equated with Shem.

21. I.e. Lewis's *Time and Western Man*.

22. A play on Eliot's triple 'Shantih' again.

23. Joyce met her at a party at Eugene Jolas's: it seems they had nothing to say to each other. See Richard Ellmann, *James Joyce*, p. 529.

24. I.e. Proust's *À la Recherche du Temps Perdu*.

25. Pages 126–68 were composed in the summer of 1927 (Ellmann, *ibid.*, p. 795). Lewis's 'Analysis of the Mind of James Joyce' appeared in *Enemy* 1 and then in *Time and Western Man* (September 1927). It is possible that A. Walton Litz, whose chart Ellmann uses, set the date too early. However, he says pp. 152–9 were revised in 1929.

26. William York Tindall, *Reader's Guide*, pp. 117–18.

27. William York Tindall, *ibid.*, p. 121.

28. These may well be the result of later insertions. *The Childermass* was published in 1928.

29. See Wyndham Lewis, *Time and Western Man*, ' "Time"-children. Miss Gertrude Stein and Miss Anita Loos' and 'The prose-song of Gertrude Stein' pp. 71–82.

30. Nicholas Breakspear was the only English pope.

31. Wyndham Lewis, *Time and Western Man*, p. 79.

32. I.e. the Ant and the Grasshopper. The fable runs pp. 414–19.

33. *Finnegans Wake*, p. 419.

34. That of Stephen Dedalus, *Portrait*, p. 247.

35. For Lewis, as we have seen, *Ulysses* had already effected the end of the project.

36. E.g. *Bagdad* (1927), *Snooty Baronet* (1932), *The Roaring Queen* (1936 – but withdrawn), *The Revenge For Love* (1937).

37. W. B. Yeats, from 'Nineteen Hundred and Nineteen', *Collected Poems*, p. 235.

38. 'The demand that I make of my reader is that he should devote

his whole life to reading my works.' Quoted by Richard Ellmann, *James Joyce*, p. 703.

39. The King Roderick O'Connor fragment, pp. 380–2. See Richard Ellmann, *ibid.*, p. 794.

40. Quoted by Richard Ellmann, *ibid.*, p. 697.

41. By the same token, it constitutes an implicit rhetorical critique of the Demythologisation Theology of such as Rudolf Bultmann.

42. 'The blossoms of the apricot/blow from the east to the west, / And I have tried to keep them from falling', Ezra Pound, *The Cantos*, p. 60; 'Ecbatan/City of patterned streets', *ibid.*, p. 17; 'as to who will copy this palimpsest?', *ibid.*, p. 797.

43. Its critical apotheosis in England has only occurred over the last twenty years or so. This may have been partly to do with its reputation for obscenity, which kept it off academic syllabuses.

44. I. A. Richards even invited Eliot to teach at Cambridge on the basis of his earlier poems. See Peter Ackroyd, *T. S. Eliot*, pp. 99–100.

45. E.g. 'Portrait of a Lady', 'Prufrock' and 'Gerontion'.

46. 'A Girl', *Ezra Pound, Selected Poems*, with an introduction by T. S. Eliot (Faber and Faber, 1959), p. 75. The poem does not appear in Faber's later *Selected Poems* (which includes some cantos) which I have normally referred to in this book. It appears Eliot had a particular fondness for this poem, which he singled out for comment in his introduction (p. 14). And he there calls attention to this last line with the comment that it 'is one which I . . . might have written'. The introduction is dated 1928 – one year after 'Journey of the Magi'. With respect to flowers in Pound and Eliot, Ezra sent a short verse to his friend in 1935 beginning: 'Ez Po and Possum/Have picked all the blossom'. To T. S. Eliot, 28 March 1935, Ezra Pound, *Selected Letters*, p. 272.

47. 'Now I remember that you built me a special tavern', *Selected Poems*, p. 70.

48. 'The proper and perfect symbol is the natural object', Ezra Pound, *Literary Essays*, p. 9.

49. See, for instance, Joyce's Olympian statement about coming war and the publication of *Finnegans Wake*, quoted above, p. 158.

50. Cantos LXXIV, *The Cantos*, p. 425.

51. Ezra Pound, *Selected Prose*, p. 434.

52. Peter Ackroyd writes: 'Apart from specific correspondences of imagery and language, Eliot had originally given Dantesque titles to five of the six poems in the sequence', *T. S. Eliot*, p. 179. The first line is, of course, Eliot's version of Dante's 'Perch'io non spera'.

53. T. S. Eliot, *Complete Poems and Plays*, p. 148.

54. By I. A. Richards. See Wyndham Lewis's comments on the exchange between Richards and Eliot in 'The Pseudo-Believer', *Men Without Art*, pp. 55–82.

55. They are traditionally played by the same actors. According to Peter Ackroyd, Rupert Doone conceived the idea of the Four Tempters (*T. S. Eliot*, p. 226). However, Eliot clearly found the idea one his imagination could work with.

56. Except, of course, for satiric purposes – as in Pope or (sometimes) Wyndham Lewis.

57. See Stephen Spender, *Eliot*, pp. 129–30.

58. See Jeffrey Meyers, *The Enemy*, p. 237.

59. Lewis picked up the joke himself. When Hugh Kenner visited Pound in his 80th year, the broken old poet finally laughed when he heard Wyndham's remark about Tom: 'Oh, never mind *him*. He's like that with everybody. But he doesn't come *in here* disguised as Westminster Abbey'. Hugh Kenner, *The Pound Era*, p. 444.

60. T. S. Eliot, *Complete Poems and Plays*, p. 262.

61. E.g. with such as Louis Zukofsky, Basil Bunting and James Vogel.

62. See Peter Ackroyd, *T. S. Eliot*, pp. 220–1.

63. Quoted by Noel Stock, *The Life*, p. 349.

64. The theorist of Social Credit was Major C. H. Douglas; Pound's old editor A. R. Orage helped circulate Douglas's ideas.

65. See Ezra Pound, *Selected Poems*, pp. 100–1 and *The Cantos*, pp. 61–75.

66. Harriet Shaw Weaver's phrase, see Richard Ellmann, *James Joyce*, p. 590.

67. To James Joyce, 15 November 1926, *Selected Letters*, p. 202.

68. Cf. his manifesto of 1936: 'WE ASSERT that the direction of the will is the dominant factor: and not the inertia of chaos'. Quoted by Noel Stock, *The Life*, p. 434.

69. Quoted by Noel Stock, *The Life*, pp. 326–7.

70. Wyndham Lewis, *Men Without Art*, p. 56.

71. See Noel Stock, *The Life*, p. 395.

72. See Hugh Kenner, *The Pound Era*, p. 505.
73. 'The Waste Land', *Completed Poems and Plays*, p. 74.
74. T. S. Eliot, *ibid.*, p. 66.
75. See Hugh Kenner, *The Pound Era*, pp. 336–8.
76. The vacation was in 1919.
77. Ezra Pound, *Literary Essays*, p. 46.
78. Ezra Pound, 'Affirmations – 1', *New Age*, XVI, 10 (7 January 1915).
79. Ezra Pound, *Impact: Essays on Ignorance and the Decline of American Civilisation*, edited by Noel Stock (Chicago: Henry Regnery, 1960), p. 227.
80. Quoted by Noel Stock, *The Life*, p. 460.
81. Eliot gave him his 'Memorial' edition of Thomas Jefferson's works. See Noel Stock, *The Life*, p. 312.
82. 'The ideogrammic method consists of presenting one facet and then another until at some point one gets off the dead and desensitized surface of the reader's mind, onto a part that will register'. Ezra Pound, *Guide To Kulchur* (Peter Owen, 1966), p. 51.
83. Ezra Pound, 'The Approach To Paris – V', *New Age*, XIII, 23 (2 October 1913), p. 662.
84. William Carlos Williams, *Paterson* (New York: New Directions, 1963), p. 18. Cf. 'To make a start, / out of particulars / and make them general', *ibid.*, p. 11 – the first words of Williams's major poem.
85. Of course he was also actively badgering thinkers, writers, and United States Congressmen – as well as feuding with economists.
86. Like his own 'E.P.' in 'Hugh Selwyn Mauberley', *Selected Poems*, p. 98.
87. 'An epic is a poem including history', Ezra Pound, *Literary Essays*, p. 86.
88. An ironical phrase in 'Hugh Selwyn Mauberley', *Selected Poems*, p. 98.
89. See Canto LXXIV, *The Cantos*, p. 431.
90. From Eliot's 'Journey of the Magi', *Complete Poems and Plays*, p. 104.
91. All references to Wyndham Lewis, *The Apes of God* (Penguin, 1965).
92. See Jeffrey Meyers, *The Enemy*, pp. 181–3.
93. From Pound's 'Papyrus', quoted by Hugh Kenner, *The Pound Era*, p. 62.

94. From 'Hugh Selwyn Mauberley', Ezra Pound, *Selected Poems*, p. 103.
95. From Canto II, Ezra Pound, *The Cantos*, p. 6.
96. James Joyce, *Ulysses*, p. 45.
97. *Ibid.*, p. 22.
98. *Ibid.*, p. 392.
99. Cf. chapters XII (pp. 71–81) and XVI (pp. 91–130) in *Time and Western Man*.
100. Wyndham Lewis, *The Roaring Queen* (Secker & Warburg, 1973). It was not published in the thirties for fear of libel action. See Jeffrey Meyers, *The Enemy*, p. 224.
101. See, for instance, Timothy Materer, *Wyndham Lewis the Novelist*, pp. 83–97.
102. In 'Four Quartets', *Complete Poems and Plays*, p. 182.
103. According to Peter Ackroyd, *T. S. Eliot*, p. 222.
104. Peter Ackroyd, *ibid.*, p. 220.
105. *Ibid.*, p. 235.
106. *Ibid.*, p. 251.
107. Wyndham Lewis, *Collected Poems and Plays*, p. 58.
108. E.g. 'For that matter explain to me how the pages of *Cathay*/Came out of the time-bound Ezra into the light of common day' and 'the light in Boston' (p. 25); 'publicly polyglot . . . my witch's vortex' and 'hippical treatises' (p. 29); 'No hollow man, a tin pulse in his wrist' and 'a time to spar and not to spar' (p. 40); 'You must know who your enemy is my god' (p. 46); 'A pubic hair to me, with the old british whiff!' (p. 76); 'The Wave Men' (p. 59); 'a new order to the Dead/who yet exist' (p. 51); 'Make towers of wells' (p. 77 – cf. *The Waste Land*, lines 383–4); 'four-dimensional quartette' (p. 82); 'drunk with the New' (p. 87).
109. Jeffrey Meyers, *The Enemy*, p. 148.
110. To T. S. Eliot, 26 April 1936, Ezra Pound, *Selected Letters*, p. 281.
111. To James Joyce, 8 December 1937, *ibid.*, p. 300.
112. To Wyndham Lewis, 3 August 1939, *ibid.*, p. 323.
113. *Ibid.*, p. 300.
114. To T. S. Eliot, 16 April 1938, *ibid.*, p. 306.
115. *Ibid.*, p. 323.
116. Quoted in John Tytell, *Ezra Pound*, p. 234.
117. Quoted by Richard Ellmann, *James Joyce*, p. 675.
118. From Notes for CXII et seq., *The Cantos*, p. 802.

119. See Richard Ellmann, *James Joyce*, pp. 547 and 549.
120. *Ibid.*, p. 586.
121. Quoted *ibid.*, p. 609.
122. Quoted *ibid.*, p. 572.
123. Quoted *ibid.*, p. 606.
124. *Ibid.*, p. 626.
125. *Ibid.*, p. 607.
126. *Ibid.*, p. 628n.
127. *Ibid.*, p. 661n.
128. *Ibid.*, p. 643.
129. Jeffrey Meyers, *The Enemy*, p. 141.
130. See below, p. 180.
131. 'In the nightmare of the dark / All the dogs of Europe bark', from 'In Memory of W. B. Yeats, W. H. Auden', *Collected Poems 1930–1944* (Faber & Faber, 1958), p. 66.
132. Quoted in Richard Ellmann, *James Joyce*, p. 729.
133. Quoted *ibid.*, p. 730.
134. *Ibid.*, p. 739.
135. W. H. Auden, *Collected Poems*, p. 66.
136. From 'The Magi', W. B. Yeats, *Collected Poems*, p. 141. The poem was (aptly) published in Yeats's 1914 collection 'Responsibilities'. I take it that Eliot's 'Journey of the Magi' partly speaks back to this poem by the 'godfather' of the Men of 1914.

6. THESE THE COMPANIONS

1. Quoted by Richard Ellmann, *James Joyce*, p. 733.
2. From 'The Second Coming', W. B. Yeats, *Collected Poems*, pp. 210–11.
3. C. G. Jung, who treated Joyce's disturbed daughter Lucia, insisted that Joyce was a 'latent schizoid' (Ellmann, *James Joyce*, p. 680): if so, he used his condition to amazingly creative effect.
4. I am not, of course, suggesting that Matthew, Mark, Luke and John in the *Wake* refer only to the Men of 1914; however, I believe they are included in the allusive resonance as chief 'gospellers' of the Modern.
5. It is interesting that the young Lewis sometimes wrote to his

mother as 'Pierce-Eye the Lewis'. See Jeffrey Meyers, *The Enemy*, p. 15.

6. There is a reference to Lewis's *Paleface* (1929) as well as to Tom (Eliot) and *Tarr* here.

7. James Joyce, *Ulysses*, p. 174.

8. A reference to Eliot's poem 'The "Boston Evening Transcript"' (*Complete Poems and Plays*, p. 28): one of several references in the *Wake*.

9. See above p. 211, note 9. Phoenicians, like Phlebas, lived in what became modern Lebanon. Joyce adhered to the view of Victor Bérard that the *Odyssey* was based on actual Phoenician maritime adventures.

10. Cf. 'By the Uranian muse begot' – Pound's fantasy about the engendering of *The Waste Land*. See above p. 100.

11. Another reference to Lewis's *Paleface* – as well as, perhaps, to Eliot's 'Burial of the Dead', Part I of *The Waste Land*.

12. References to *Time and Western Man* and the Guy Fawkes allusions in Eliot's 'The Hollow Men'.

13. Lewis's 'Cantleman's Spring-Mate' was published in the *Little Review* in 1917, but the edition was suppressed by the United States Post Office for alleged obscenity. This forged another bond between Lewis and Joyce whose 'Nausicaa' chapter of *Ulysses* (*Little Review*, 1920) was confiscated by the same body. Later again, *Ulysses*, in book-form, would be successfully defended against an American obscenity charge.

14. Another reference to Eliot's Phlebas.

15. Lewis's theory of comedy was essentially a matter of satiric puppetry. See above, pp. 75–6.

16. During his musical phase of the early 1920s Pound developed a relationship with the violinist Olga Rudge who became his mistress and thereafter a contender with Dorothy for Pound's affections for the rest of his life. See above, p. 182 for Pound's tribute to Olga.

17. Cf. Lewis's 'seabird-girl sob-slobber' quoted above, p. 114.

18. Lewis was a gunner in an RMA battery during the war, and wrote of his experiences of both gunnery and the Men of 1914 in *Blasting and Bombardiering* – itself a 'gustspell' of a kind.

19. Cf. 'Childermass' and Pound's Orientalism; Joyce particularly admired Pound's *Cathay*.

20. I take this to be a reference to Eliot's notorious declaration that he was 'classicist in literature, royalist in politics, and anglo-

catholic in religion'. Quoted by Peter Ackroyd, *T. S. Eliot*, p. 174.

21. A reference to Eliot's reliance on Pound's editorial skills for the final form of *The Waste Land* – whose third section, 'The Fire Sermon', had much about 'burning'.

22. Because of his Welsh name, Lewis is here made a Welsh Fusilier. *Blasting and Bombardiering* is very much a tale of four 'mascoteers' at the end.

23. A reference to Eliot's poem 'A Cooking Egg' and the cockcrow in *The Waste Land*.

24. I.e. the Possum – and his book on Practical Cats; perhaps there is also another reference to 'peace' ('Shantih').

25. Arthur Waugh had called Eliot and Pound 'drunken helots' in a famous early review. See Peter Ackroyd, *T. S. Eliot*, p. 290.

26. Lewis edited his own magazine *Tyro* in 1921–2; the *Tarr* allusion is obvious.

27. Cf. 'Piercey', p. 159 and note 5 above.

28. Again probably a reference to Pound's Orientalism.

29. Cf. Pound's 'Liu Ch'e': 'and the leaves / Scurry into heaps and lie still, / And she the rejoicer of the heart is beneath them: / A wet leaf that clings to the threshold', *Selected Poems*, p. 49.

30. See William York Tindall, *A Reader's Guide*, pp. 247–8. Cf. 'mansuetudinous manipulator' with Pound's comment on 'Circe': 'megascruptious-mastodonic' – see above, p. 120.

31. In Canto LXXIV, *The Cantos*, p. 433.

32. However, Lewis proposed a kind of 'Paradiso' to complete *The Human Age*, but it was never written – partly because he was then too old and ill after completing *Malign Fiesta* (1955). A rejected synopsis called 'The Trial of Man' remains and is published as an appendix to the Jupiter edition of *Malign Fiesta* (Calder & Boyars, 1966) pp. 215–28.

33. See 'For T.S.E.', Ezra Pound, *Selected Prose*, p. 434 and above p. 188.

34. See above p. 93.

35. The four seasons are also relevant. Although 'Burnt Norton' was originally written as a single piece, the four-way dynamic is present from the start, and the end of 'Four Quartets' is immanent in Eliot's beginning.

36. It is very much a work of the 'auditory imagination' and was successfully broadcast on the radio. It should never, I believe, be read by a single voice (not even the poet's) but by a variety of speakers in different accents.

37. There seems to me another contribution to the dialogue (initiated in Lewis's spring-evocation in *Tarr*) in the opening of *The Family Reunion*: 'Will the spring never come?'; 'She should go south in the winter', etc. See T. S. Eliot, *Complete Poems and Plays*, p. 285. In the light of my reading of *Murder in the Cathedral* (see above pp. 137–8), the title of the later play takes on a particular interest as an Eliotic fantasy of reparation. It is Amy's wish 'to keep the family alive, to keep them together' (p. 287), but Arthur and John never appear and Harry's guilt drives him off to some 'mission' accompanied only by the faithful Downing – himself perhaps a version of the once-indispensable Ezra.

38. Eliot himself suggested Yeats, Mallarmé, Swift and Poe (Peter Ackroyd, *T. S. Eliot*, p. 271). This may be Possumish play (Swift?) – or evasion. Yet there may be a clue in the citing of Yeats (who also fits) and who was paired with Eliot in the Cad section of *Finnegans Wake* (see above p. 126).

39. The relationship to *The Waves* (1931) seems especially pertinent; both works are obsessed with the problem of time.

40. For a consideration of the theme of time in 'Four Quartets', see the section 'Falls the Shadow' in Dennis Brown, *The Modernist Self*, pp. 149–58.

41. I.e. the 'Proclamation' of the Gospel.

42. In Samuel Beckett, *Waiting For Godot* (Faber and Faber, 1956), p. 80.

43. *The Cantos*, p. 522.

44. *Ibid.*, p. 797.

45. See 'Envoi', Ezra Pound, *Selected Poems*, pp. 105–6.

46. Cf. Canto III: 'Bright gods and Tuscan . . . / And from the apple, maelid, / Through all the wood, and the leaves are full of voices / A-whisper', Ezra Pound, *The Cantos*, p. 11.

47. First published by Methuen in 1954; all references to Wyndham Lewis, *Self Condemned* (Santa Barbara: Black Sparrow Press, 1983).

48. René – as in René Descartes; Harding – as in hard (cf. Bunyan's Mr. Great-heart).

49. Quoted by Jeffrey Meyers, *The Enemy*, p. 312.

50. The title of the second chapter, and what René's mother says to him on p. 26.

51. It had been, in some ways, Pound's repudiation for many years too.
52. Quoted by Jeffrey Meyers, *The Enemy*, p. 298.
53. Quoted by Jeffrey Meyers, *ibid.*, p. 317.
54. Timothy Materer, *Wyndham Lewis the Novelist*, p. 149.
55. Although this also refers to Lewis's relationship to Hugh Gordon Porteus; see Jeffrey Meyers, *The Enemy*, p. 314.
56. 'Mr Bloom brushed off the greater bulk of the shavings . . . and bucked [Stephen] up in orthodox Samaritan fashion.' James Joyce, *Ulysses*, p. 501.
57. See Jeffrey Meyers, *The Enemy*, pp. 324–5.
58. From T. S. Eliot, 'Four Quartets', *Complete Poems and Plays*, p. 188.
59. In *After Strange Gods*, Eliot had suggested that in Cantos XIV–XVL Pound's hell was essentially one for other people: in my view a fair charge – yet perhaps Dante's was too. Unlike Sartre, Eliot seems always to have felt that hell was oneself.
60. See above, p. 142.
61. See above, p. 208, note 68.
62. Pound never retracted his negative view of Joyce's final style. His sense of certainty, at times, worried Joyce himself: in 1927 he wrote to Harriet Shaw Weaver: 'It is possible Pound is right, but I cannot go back'. Quoted by Noel Stock, *The Life*, p. 336.
63. In Canto CXV the tribute to Lewis's courage leads to lines that seem to evoke Lewis's combativeness: 'When one's friends hate each other / how can there be peace in the world? / Their asperities diverted me in my green time'. See Ezra Pound, *The Cantos*, p. 794.
64. Quoted by Hugh Kenner, *The Pound Era*, p. 44.
65. Cf. 'In my beginning is my end . . .' T. S. Eliot, *Complete Poems and Plays*, p. 177.
66. Eliot and Pound discussed a 'program' for the *Criterion* in 1920. Pound later complained that Eliot had not followed up his suggestions. See Hugh Kenner, *The Pound Era*, p. 337.
67. Cf. 'Tereu', *The Waste Land*, l. 206.
68. 'And as to who will copy this palimpsest?', Canto CXVI, *The Cantos*, p. 797.
69. Davie's excellent title: see Donald Davie, Ezra Pound: *The Poet as Sculptor* (Routledge & Kegan Paul, 1964).
70. See Noel Stock, *The Life*, pp. 584–5.

71. Ezra Pound, *Selected Prose*, p. 434.
72. Quoted by Richard Ellmann, *James Joyce*, pp. 661–2.
73. See Jeffrey Meyers, *The Enemy*, pp. 304–5.
74. Jeffrey Meyers, *ibid.*, pp. 303, 308 and 323.
75. 'Ever since the Twenties . . . Eliot had manifested so many signs of melancholy and weariness that "poor Tom" had become the constant refrain of his friends', Peter Ackroyd, *T. S. Eliot*, p. 306.
76. See Jeffrey Meyers, *The Enemy*, p. 286.
77. Jeffrey Meyers, *ibid.*, p. 295.
78. Quoted by Jeffrey Meyers, *ibid.*, p. 330.
79. In a letter to Pound Lewis wrote; 'You might almost have contrived this climax to your respective careers: yours so Villonesque and Eliot's super-Tennyson.' Quoted by Jeffrey Meyers, *ibid.*, p. 291.
80. See Peter Ackroyd, *T. S. Eliot*, p. 320.
81. See Jeffrey Meyers, *The Enemy*, p. 329 and Peter Ackroyd, *T. S. Eliot*, p. 334.
82. Ezra Pound, *Selected Prose*, p. 434.
83. Quoted by Jeffrey Meyers, *The Enemy*, p. 298.
84. See note 79 above.
85. See Peter Ackroyd, *T. S. Eliot*, p. 282.
86. From 'The Seafarer', Ezra Pound, *Selected Poems*, p. 38.
87. Of course he had written and even published poems before 1908. But he arranged and published his first book of poems, *A Lume Spento*, in Venice that year.
88. Although in some ways the thirties marked the end of Modernism as such, one cannot, I think, exclude either 'Four Quartets' or the later cantos from the overall Modernist project. However it seems sensible to regard Beckett's postwar work as a species of neo-Modernism or even Postmodernism.
89. James Joyce, *Finnegans Wake*, p. 210.
90. Wyndham Lewis, *Malign Fiesta*, p. 211.
91. T. S. Eliot, *Complete Poems and Plays*, p. 197.
92. Ezra Pound, *The Cantos*, p. 802.

Index